TEACHING EARLY LITERACY

teaching EARLY LITERACY

DEVELOPMENT, ASSESSMENT, AND INSTRUCTION

Diane M. Barone | Marla H. Mallette | Shelley Hong Xu

THE GUILFORD PRESS

New York   London

© 2005 The Guilford Press
A Division of Guilford Publications, Inc.
72 Spring Street, New York, NY 10012
www.guilford.com

Printed in the United States of America

This book is printed on acid-free paper.

Last digit is print number: 9 8 7 6 5 4 3 2 1

Library of Congress Cataloging-in-Publication Data

Barone, Diane M.
    Teaching early literacy: development, assessment, and instruction / Diane M. Barone,
Marla H. Mallette, Shelley Hong Xu.
        p.   cm.
    Includes bibliographical references and index.
    ISBN 1-59385-106-5 (pbk.) — ISBN 1-59385-107-3 (hard)
    1. Reading (Early childhood)   2. Language arts (Early childhood)
  I. Mallette, Marla H.   II. Xu, Shelley Hong.   III. Title.
    LB1139.5.R43B36 2005
    372.4—dc22
                                                           2004017181

ABOUT THE AUTHORS

Diane M. Barone, EdD, is Professor of Educational Specialties at the University of Nevada, Reno. Her research has centered around longitudinal case studies of young children's literacy development. The first one of these studies investigated the literacy development of children prenatally exposed to crack cocaine. The second longitudinal study is nearing completion, as the students she selected to follow in kindergarten are now completing their elementary school experience as sixth graders. This work has centered on the children's literacy development as well as the instruction provided to them in their school. Dr. Barone's work has appeared in *Journal of Literacy Research*, *The Reading Teacher*, *Gifted Childhood Quarterly*, and *Research in the Teaching of English*. She has also written or edited several books, including *Literacy and Young Children*, *Resilient Children*, *Developing Literacy*, and *The National Board Certification Handbook*.

Marla H. Mallette, PhD, is Assistant Professor of Literacy Education at Southern Illinois University, Carbondale. Her research interests include literacy teacher education, literacy instruction and learning with students of culturally and linguistically diverse backgrounds, and the convergence of early literacy and technology. She is very interested in research methodologies and has used various methodologies in her own work. Dr. Mallette has also published and presented on literacy research methodologies and the preparation of literacy researchers.

Shelley Hong Xu, EdD, is Associate Professor of Teacher Education at California State University–Long Beach, where she teaches graduate and undergraduate literacy courses. Her research interests include early literacy development of English language learners, preparing preservice and inservice teachers for diversity, and integrating children's experiences with multimedia texts in outside-school settings into a school literacy curriculum. Dr. Xu's work has appeared in literacy journals and edited books, including *Journal of Literacy Research*, *Language Arts*, *Young Children*, *Journal of Teacher Education*, and the *Yearbook of the National Reading Conference*. She is the incoming essay book review editor for *Reading Research Quarterly*.

PREFACE

Teaching Early Literacy: Development, Assessment, and Instruction provides a comprehensive exploration of young children's (preschool to grade 3) literacy development, assessment, and resulting instruction. The book is grounded in three dominant beliefs: (1) Teachers are critical to student learning; (2) student learning happens best in conversation-rich classrooms; and (3) instruction is most productive when it is matched to student literacy development. These three beliefs set the foundation for each chapter. This book also seriously considers the development and instruction that are most appropriate for young students who are learning English as a new language (English language learners, or ELLs) as they simultaneously learn to read and write in English. This work is not just embedded throughout the text; two chapters are focused totally on the needs of ELLs. The book is also enriched with descriptions of how to integrate technology, involve parents, understand and provide early interventions, and contemplate the use of popular culture in the classroom.

We believe that this book is important to teachers because it is grounded in the current scientifically based research centered on early literacy. We have provided this theoretical background to support the learning strategies and assessment that are identified in this book. To extend the practical nature of this book, several chapters end with an in-class visit. In these visits, real teachers explain how they have organized for instruction and describe some of the dilemmas they face. The vignettes allow teachers to reflect on their own practices. The final chapter extends this practical focus by providing numerous web resources to support the work of teachers. It also includes a guide to all of the assessment and informational materials presented throughout the book. Teachers can easily copy the masters for in-class use.

We hope that this book will be used by teachers as they consider how best to teach reading, writing, and word study to their young students. It can be a text adopted for a graduate class in literacy, or it can serve as a reading for a professional development community within a school. The many practical activities and assessments included in the book will serve to help teachers in their daily work. We also think that teachers-to-be will find this text beneficial. It will provide them with a synthesis of research-based practices that they can bring to their classrooms. They can also use it as a guide during their internship experience.

CONTENTS

Chapter 1. THE INTERSECTION OF LITERACY LEARNING AND INSTRUCTION   1

Chapter 2. EXPLORING DEVELOPING LITERACY   14

Chapter 3. DEVELOPING LITERACY AND ENGLISH LANGUAGE LEARNERS   46

Chapter 4. BEGINNING LITERACY   80

Chapter 5. EARLY LITERACY AND TECHNOLOGY   101

Chapter 6. TRANSITIONAL LITERACY   112

Chapter 7. TRANSITIONAL LITERACY AND ENGLISH LANGUAGE LEARNERS   139

Chapter 8. ENGAGING FAMILIES   170

Chapter 9. ISSUES IN EARLY LITERACY   196

Chapter 10. GETTING PRACTICAL   211

CHILDREN'S BOOKS CITED   223

REFERENCES   227

INDEX   241

Chapter 1

THE INTERSECTION OF LITERACY LEARNING AND INSTRUCTION

With one big paw, he knocked a book off the pile, to land face down in the dirt. . . . Finally, one of his claws caught the cover, and the book flipped open. . . . There on the page were row after row of marks, tiny marks, like those on the piece of paper in his cave. He stared at them, while his nose filled with the scents of paper, glue, ink. . . . The bear gazed up at her as she said the words and turned the pages. He couldn't understand any of what she was saying. But as he listened to the sound of her voice, happiness washed over him like waves.

—HASELEY (2002), *A Story for Bear*

This quote about discovering books and the power of a reader comes from a fanciful book where a bear learns to read. Although bears (outside of books) don't read, this description provides a sense of the mystery of all those squiggles in books and the power of the storyteller's voice, which young children experience as they become familiar with books and the words contained inside.

After Bear experiences a summer of listening to this reader, she leaves her books behind so that Bear can enjoy them on his own during winter. In a sense, parents and teachers play a role similar to that of the storybook reader in this book. They are close to a young reader as he or she begins to understand how books are organized and why text is important. They help a child by carefully identifying words or illustrations as they chat about the meaning of a story or informational text. As the child develops some understandings about reading, the parents and teachers move away a bit and let the neophyte reader explore alone, always allowing for return visits to the adults for support or clarification. Soon these needed visits diminish in number as the child develops competence in independently engaging with text.

Although this description of learning to read sounds simple enough, children, parents, and teachers all recognize the complexity of the process on a moment-to-moment basis. In a home setting, it is much easier to react and respond to a child's need for support with reading or writing activities. However, when this same child becomes a member of a classroom, a single teacher (in most cases) is expected to respond to this need for support, and to respond in a similar manner to all of the children in his or her classroom. This becomes one of the many challenges to teachers in providing exemplary literacy instruction to their students.

Because we recognize the complexity of the teaching/learning process of reading and writing, our book is guided by three core concepts. First, teachers—not programs—are critical to the literacy development of students. Second, instruction that is grounded in a social-constructivist philosophy provides the best environment for children to learn. And, third, teachers who carefully link informal assessment to instruction and understand children's literacy development provide students with a curriculum that is built on individual strengths and needs, and results in student achievement. Each of these core concepts is further discussed in this chapter, and they are evident in the discussions in later chapters of this book.

The Importance of the Teacher

In the 1960s, the Cooperative Research Branch of the U.S. Office of Education undertook the First Grade Studies (Bond & Dykstra, 1967). In this research, 27 individual projects focused on beginning reading were studied. The studies were guided by three questions:

1. To what extent are pupil, teacher, class, school, and community characteristics related to pupil achievement?
2. Which approach is superior for student achievement?
3. Is any program better for students of high or low readiness for reading?

Among the methods studied were the Initial Teaching Alphabet, phonic methods, linguistic methods, individualized methods, and language experience methods. While some minor differences were found from program to program, the major finding of this work was the clear importance of the teacher for student achievement. Dykstra (1968), one of the researchers, wrote: "Reading instruction is more likely to improve as a result of improved selection and training of teachers, improved in-service training programs, and improved school learning climates, rather than from minor changes in instructional materials" (p. 66).

Although the First Grade Studies were done quite a while ago, the importance of teachers was firmly established in the 1960s and remains true today. In 2000, the International Reading Association (IRA) stated: "Every child deserves excellent reading teachers because teachers make a difference in children's reading achievement and motivation to read" (p. 1). Here, as in the earlier statement, the focus is on the power of the teacher—not the power of a program used by a teacher. Programs can help or hinder a teacher's instruction, but exemplary teachers know how to tailor the available programs to the unique strengths and needs of their students.

Being an exemplary teacher of literacy is no easy task. Various authors have talked about the essential qualities of such a teacher. Following are some of these expectations, although many more have been identified:

1. Exemplary teachers have strong knowledge of reading research and theory. They understand how reading research and theory connect to instructional practice (Farstrup, 2002).
2. Exemplary teachers provide personalized and small-group instruction, contextualized skills teaching, many reading and writing opportunities, and interactive lessons (Allington, 2002b).
3. Exemplary teachers believe that all students can be successful academically, and they provide the support that students need to be successful (Ladson-Billings, 1994).
4. Exemplary teachers create a caring environment in their classrooms. Their practice is grounded in the relationships that they forge with their students, their students' parents, and other teachers (Dillon, 2000).
5. Exemplary teachers are thoughtful about their teaching, and constantly reflect upon their practice and change it as needed (Schon, 1987).
6. Exemplary teachers realize how important each minute of each day is in helping students learn to read and write. They also reflect on their practice, as noted above, and learn from mistakes (Block & Mangieri, 2003).

Importantly, exemplary literacy teachers are always learning more about their practice and their students. They constantly strive for more current knowledge and better ways to teach the students entrusted to their care.

Teachers may worry that being exemplary literacy teachers is something for just a few—that "either you are exemplary or you aren't." This misconception hurts teachers, for if they believe that they are not one of the "chosen," they may lose hope that their individual teaching practices can improve. Day (2001), in describing her own development into an exemplary teacher, says, "It [exemplary teaching] develops as teachers become expert observers of students and learning, as they seek continually to learn and grow, and as they reflect on their own teaching and experiences in learning" (p. 216).

Exemplary literacy teachers, in addition to providing appropriate literacy instruction to students, must also balance the numerous challenges prevalent in the 2000s. Some of these current challenges are centered on keeping abreast of the latest research on reading and writing, and applying these discoveries to teaching in the classroom. Other challenges are centered on technology and its use as a tool to foster literacy knowledge and understanding. A third group of challenges relates to the expectations for teachers and schools that come from the No Child Left Behind legislation, which includes more assessment and accountability requirements.

The instructional expectations of exemplary teachers are closely connected to classrooms that are grounded in social-constructivist teaching theory and the practices connected to this theory. The following section describes this theory, a major tenet of which is the belief that the teacher is key to the learning accomplished by students.

Social-Constructivist Teaching

The examples for literacy instruction and the views inside classrooms that are evident throughout this book are all grounded in a social-constructivist theory of learning (Vygotsky, 1978). This theory acknowledges that learning is more than just a cognitive process. Learning is much more complex, for it involves constructions of meaning that are dependent on other individuals and the learning environment. According to Dillon (2000), "this perspective helps us understand that literacy learning is embedded in culture" (p. 108). From Dillon's observations, it is obvious that teachers' and students' constructions of meaning are influenced by their cultural practices and beliefs.

In social-constructivist teaching and learning, a classroom is filled with conversations among students and among students and teachers as they are engaged in instruction. An observer will note multiple academic conversations occurring throughout instructional activities. In addition, a careful observer will see how understandings are shaped as students and teachers engage in these conversations. For example, a simple understanding may be deepened through dialogue, or a misconception may be clarified. In addition, students and teachers recognize that multiple perspectives can be brought to discussions centered on interpretation of text.

Dyson (1997) provides a vivid example of a classroom grounded in social-constructivist theory. She carefully shows how young children's stories are composed and revised through interactions with classroom peers and ideas gleaned from popular culture. She shares many conversations as her students negotiated the words and ideas they represented in stories that would be publicly shared in the classroom. For example, in the following dialogue, Tina, Kristin, and Victor discussed the roles of girls and boys in the stories they were writing:

> TINA: It should be more about the girls winning instead of the boys.
> KRISTIN: So should every story have the girls winning instead of the boys?
> TINA: No, not all, just some, just some of 'em, not all of 'em. Because in every story the boys always have to win. And that's not really fair to the girls.
> VICTOR: Not fair to the girls? Not fair to the boys? (Dyson, 1997, p. 99)

This snippet from a longer conversation shows the issues that these children were exploring in their writing. They were doing much more than just getting words on paper; they were pondering the roles of girls and boys in stories and in television shows they watched. This discussion was part of a bigger classroom conversation where the children wondered about the roles of girls in popular culture. By having such conversations in the classroom, students considered serious issues as they connected characters in popular culture with their own experiences shared through their stories. Dyson observed that when different children composed stories together, the stories took different shapes. So if students other than Kristin and Victor responded to Tina's first statement, the resulting story could be very different, thus demonstrating the power of the social context of the classroom.

Paley (1990) describes her own kindergarten classroom, which was also grounded in this theory. Throughout her book, she shares conversations and her thought-provoking questions that encouraged her kindergarten students to consider multiple perspectives or to think deeper. Following is a short excerpt from one of the verbal interactions that happened routinely in her classroom:

PALEY: We're not using the time-out chair anymore.

WILLIAM: Why not?

PALEY: Because it doesn't do any good. I've been watching carefully. No one behaves any better after being in the chair.

WILLIAM: I do.

PALEY: But the next day you're in the chair again.

WILLIAM: Then I get good again.

PALEY: No, I made up my mind. You'll have to learn to act properly without the chair.

JILLY: How will William be good? (Paley, 1990, p. 89)

The conversation continued as the children problem-solved how they would be good without the time-out chair. By "listening in" to these conversations, readers can witness how children's thoughts and questions were respected. Paley nudged her students continually through her questions to think in other ways and value other people's perspectives. Both Paley and Dyson bring their social-constructivist classrooms to life and make visible the learning in these classrooms.

Embedded within this theory is a student-centered approach to teaching. Children's ideas and interests are valued as learning is constructed. However, this child-centered approach does not mean that teachers are not important and cannot make curricular decisions (Dillon, 2000). Rather, teachers are mindful of how to use the interests of students—for instance, as they create their curriculums and learning experiences. Teachers creatively find ways to teach to the expected standards by including their students in their thinking, as they design instructional sessions and activities.

In many cases, teachers allow individual students to respond to reading or to engage in writing in ways that are personally meaningful to the students. They encourage students to write about reading or to create visual representations of informational text to use in conversations they will have with other students. These written comments or drawings provide for deeper understanding of reading and serve as an entry to the academic conversation (Barone & Lovell, 1990). For example, Barone had students write daily about their reading. Within her first- through third-grade classroom, one book club group was reading *The Egypt Game* (Snyder, 1967). Following is one entry written by Michael at the conclusion of the book. His entry demonstrated his ability to reflect on the book and to synthesize the overall structure of the book:

I like the first chapter where they all met and the last chapter when the professor gave them the key to his yard. And I didn't like when the girl got kidnapped. They found her

in a lake and that was sad. I remember in the beginning when they were having a cere-
mony for a bird. (Barone & Lovell, 1990, p. 143) [spelling corrected]

Michael used this written entry as a means to enter into the academic conversation
about this book in his group. When his group met, he asked, "What chapter did you
like best? I liked the first chapter." Other students picked up on his question and
extended the conversation by talking about their favorite chapters and the reasons
for their choices.

An example of writing where the teacher provides students with choices might
be an assignment to write a report. The teacher connects this report-writing assignment with the current content in science (animal groups of mammals, reptiles, and
birds) and has each child select an animal to write a report about. Then the teacher
explains to the students the critical parts of the report and suggests where students
might find information. The teacher has thus constrained the assignment through
the topic and format for the completed report. However, the teacher has also
allowed each student to pick an animal that he or she wants to research, thus supporting individual choices and interests. The teacher also groups students by the
types of animals that they have selected, so that they can work together and collaborate on the research portion of their reports. In a classroom where the teacher con-
structs this assignment in this way, students may be working together as they craft
their reports. They will also be observed reading an Internet selection that provides
information on their selected animals, or looking through a book or encyclopedia
together. These academic conversations provide opportunities for them to share
new information and to clarify misconceptions as they create their individual
reports.

A final consideration for social-constructivist teaching is that the teacher must
be aware of individual students' strengths and needs, so that each student can be
moved from current understandings to more sophisticated ones. Vygotsky (1978)
has described the *zone of proximal development* (ZPD) as the most efficient place to
provide instruction to students. This zone is defined as the distance between a
child's current level of development and the level he or she has the potential to
reach with the support of more knowledgeable peers and/or the teacher. Once this
learning occurs on a social plane, the child is able to internalize it and make it his or
her own, thus moving to a higher developmental level.

The ZPD is coupled with the idea of *scaffolded instruction*. Pearson and
Gallagher (1983) have described this process as involving a gradual release of
responsibility. In this process, the teacher provides close supervision and interaction
as a student begins to learn a new concept. The teacher carefully models the learning for the student. Then the teacher works with the student through guided practice, where the teacher is next to the child to provide support when necessary. As
the child becomes increasingly successful, the teacher moves away, and the child
can demonstrate this learning independently. Although this process may seem quite
linear, there is continual adjustment as the teacher provides and withdraws learning
support.

Implicit within social-constructivist teaching is the teacher's constant awareness of each student's development in literacy. The following section describes a developmental model of literacy that facilitates the teacher's matching of instruction to each student's current level of knowledge.

A Developmental Model of Literacy

Embedded throughout this book is an emphasis on the need to match instruction to each student's current knowledge of literacy. This type of instruction implies more than a teacher's administering informal or formal assessments to students and then developing instruction. It requires moment-to-moment, day-to-day observation of students as they talk, read, and write in the classroom. From these ongoing observations, the teacher crafts lessons or conversations with students that nudge them toward more complex understandings in literacy.

Children's literacy typically develops with close relationships among reading, writing, and word knowledge (Bear & Barone, 1998; Henderson & Templeton, 1986). For example, a young child who scribbles when he or she writes a message will probably pretend to read when given a book, and will use scribbling or random letters or numerals to record a word. By recognizing benchmarks of literacy development, a teacher can provide instructional support that is appropriate to the literacy level of the child. Table 1.1 provides an overview of these benchmark behaviors. Because the focus of this book is on young students, the benchmarks do not include more sophisticated readers' or writers' development.

Often teachers want to determine appropriate grade levels that match these benchmarks. Most often, students in preschool to early first grade are considered *developing literacy learners*. Students in kindergarten though second grade are typically *beginning readers and writers*. Children in first to fourth grades can be considered *transitional readers and writers*. There is no single grade level for these benchmarks, as there is so much variability in literacy development evident within a grade. For example, a student who has just arrived from a country where another language is spoken may be placed in second grade based on age, but his or her literacy development in English may be more like that of developing literacy learner. Or a child entering kindergarten may have experienced multiple reading and writing activities at home, and may display characteristics of a beginning reader and writer.

Importantly, there are no fixed boundaries between one level and another. As children move from one developmental level to another, they carry with them some of the less sophisticated behaviors from a previous level. Also, a student may revert to less sophisticated ways of responding when the text he or she encounters is at a more difficult level. For instance, a student may retell what has been read when he or she is struggling with the content or more complex vocabulary of a book, rather than providing connections between this text and others with similar content that have been read previously.

TABLE 1.1
Benchmarks of Literacy Development

Level	Reading	Writing	Word knowledge
Developing literacy	Does not have concept of word. Pretends to read. May memorize predictable text. When asked about reading, shares pieces, but does not give a cohesive description.	Pretends to write. Recognizes the difference between drawing and writing.	Scribbling. Uses random letters or numerals (*red* spelled as), or uses initial consonants (*red* spelled as R).
Beginning literacy	Has concept of word. Reads word by word. Even when asked to read silently, child vocalizes. When asked about reading, most often retells.	Writes letter by letter. Slow process, but another person can read what has been written. Does not produce much text.	Moves from using the initial and final consonants, to including a vowel in representing single-syllable words (*red* spelled RAD, *pig* spelled PEG, or *rope* spelled ROP).
Transitional literacy	Reads silently. Approaching fluency; reads in phrases, rather than word by word. When asked about reading, may retell, summarize, or provide personal connections to text.	Can write word by word and in phrases. Faster process, and produces significant amount of text. Can focus on meaning during the process of writing, not just on representing words.	Able to represent most single-syllable words. May struggle with long-vowel patterns. Recognizes that some sounds are represented by two letters (s<u>h</u>ip), and some letters without sounds must be represented (rop<u>e</u>) (spelled as ROAP or ROEP).

Dyson (2003b) describes this process as one of "complex variation" (p. 107). She describes children as holding on to "familiar forms of reference and well-known materials to help them enter into new possibilities" (p. 107). Her view, which we share in this book, is not a narrow perspective of development that fragments reading and writing knowledge. Rather, this developmental view values children's knowledge, and the instruction that teachers provide must match development and nudge it toward more complex reading and writing practices.

For the remainder of this chapter, the glosses of literacy behaviors presented in Table 1.1 are extended through broader descriptions. In later chapters, each of these developmental levels is explored in much more detail, with a focus on assessment and instruction that are relevant to students' strengths and needs at the various levels.

Developing Literacy Readers and Writers

Children who are considered to be developing literacy readers and writers most often *pretend* to read and write. They are learning about literacy in more global ways. For instance, a young child may pick up a book and look at the illustrations. When observing this child, an adult may notice that the book is upside down and the child has begun this exploration at the end of the book, rather than the beginning. If this same child later picks up paper and markers, he or she may carry on a full dialogue about what is being represented. However, without the child there, an adult would just note a picture composed of scribbling.

Reading

In reading, young children learn about books, print, and illustrations. In learning about books, they become aware of the covers of books, the pages, and the way the pages are turned, among other concepts (Clay, 1972). And as Lenhart and Roskos (2003) note, they also learn that books aren't to be torn or colored in.

Once children understand the general conventions of a book, they observe the illustrations and text on each page. Eventually, they realize that the story goes across all the pages in a book, and that each page is not a separate story. They also learn that the text carries the storyline and is what is read by a parent or older sibling, and that the illustrations most often embellish or extend the text.

Even though young children can memorize simple, predictable text, they are unable to point to individual words as they read; they do not have *concept of word* in print. They may run a finger under a line of text, but that is as close as they come to the individual words. And if an adult asks the child to point to a specific word, he or she may select a word at random, or may again run a finger under a line of text (Morris, 1983).

As they engage with print, early literacy learners often identify the pictures on each page. They move from this discrete way of approaching a book to connecting the illustrations from page to page (Sulzby, 1985). If adults ask children at this level to read a book, they often tell the story, like an oral story. When they do this, most adults will be unable to decipher the story unless they have the book in front of them. As young children develop, they begin to read a book by using book language. That is, at this point children begin to include words such as "Once upon a time" and "They lived happily ever after." A listener to children using book language may be convinced that the actual words on each page are being read. However, children are reading using the gist of the story and borrowed language from it (Sulzby, 1985).

Writing

Developing literacy learners enjoy writing and often complete numerous stories and letters to relatives and friends. Because they are not aware of the correspondence of sounds with letters of the alphabet, they freely put marks down on a paper. The difficulty with their writing is that they are the only ones who can read it. The random marks and letters, while they convey a message to a child, are indecipherable to others.

As children mature in this level, they may copy words from a board or their friends' names from cubbies. This copying is difficult, and young children will often leave out letters or write letters backward. This is not because there is something inherently wrong with the children; rather, they do not have a full understanding of the specifics of making a letter, do not understand directionality of print, and find it difficult to find their place when copying from one location to another.

Word Knowledge

Certainly word knowledge is similar to writing. Young learners use scribbles or random letters or numerals to represent words. At first a child may see a letter or word as an object like a table or car (Martens, 1996). The child may draw a series of circles, with each circle representing a word, or may even use wave-like shapes to represent the cursive writing of adults. Eventually, the child leaves these types of word representations and moves to using the initial consonant in a word to represent a word. However, during early literacy development, children never completely represent all of the phonemes in words. They may become consistent with beginning consonants and final consonants, but the vowels in the middle are missing (Bear & Barone, 1998).

Beginning Readers and Writers

Chall (1983) has described beginning readers and writers as children who have "cracked the code" of the English language system. They understand the alphabetic principle and are able to map letters and sounds. They rely heavily on the letters of the alphabet to facilitate reading and writing activities. Their reading is more often focused on decoding the words—cracking the code—than on exploring meaning.

Reading

Three dominant reading behaviors are exhibited by beginning readers. First, they read aloud even when they are reading silently. They need to hear the words as they read, to facilitate decoding and comprehension. Second, they often use their fingers to point to the words they are reading. And, third, they read word by word and are not expressive during a first reading of text. They spend most of their energy just deciphering the words. Beginning readers are thus not particularly fluent in reading. In order for them to read text smoothly and rapidly, beginning readers require multiple opportunities to reread a text (Kuhn, 2003).

Unlike early literacy learners, beginning readers have concept of word in print. They can point to the individual words they are reading, and they can find specific words in text (Morris, 1983). Because beginning readers have developed concept of word, they are able to read text and do not have to rely on memorization.

When beginning readers are asked to chat or write about what they have read, they most often focus on the literal events of stories. They generally retell the story or provide a summary (Barone, 1992).

Writing

There are two major differences between beginning readers' and writers' writing production and that of developing literacy students. First, they are aware of the match between letters in words, so their writing tends to be shorter (even if they have many ideas to convey). It is more cognitively challenging to represent the phonemes in words accurately than it is just to put random marks on paper. The cognitive energy required for writing using the alphabetic principle limits the amount of text that a child produces. The second difference is that others can read their writing. Even though these children do not represent each phoneme in a word, their representations are sufficient to carry a message. For example, a beginning reader and writer might write, "I can drw ad rit." It is not difficult to read this message as "I can draw and write."

Word Knowledge

The major difference in the way beginning readers and writers represent words is that they include vowels and thus have more complete phonemic representations of words. However, they don't always use the correct short-vowel or long-vowel pattern representations. In short-vowel consonant–vowel–consonant (CVC) words, they often use the vowel that precedes the correct vowel in the alphabet. For example, they often spell *pet* as PAT, *pit* as PET, *pot* as PIT, and *putt* as POT. The difficulty with short vowels is that the alphabet is confusing. Although there is an *a* in the alphabet, there is no letter that represents the /a/ sound in *pat*. Children have to rely tacitly on how they make the sound in their mouths. They choose the long vowel that is closest in point of articulation to the short vowel they want to write (Read,

1975). Read (1975) discovered that the errors children made in representing short vowels were predictable and followed this substitution pattern.

In addition to the issue of representing short vowels, beginning readers and writers exhibit interesting ways of representing long vowels. They use a one-to-one correspondence strategy when writing words. This means that they record one letter for each sound they hear. Most long vowels are represented through the use of two letters or more (e.g., *eigh*, *ae*, or *ou*); however, these children simplify these more complex spellings. They may spell *nose* as NOS or *mean* as MEN. They choose the letter of the alphabet that has the sound they need: a for long *a*, o for long *o*, and so on. They utilize a direct mapping of the letter to the long-vowel pattern.

Transitional Readers and Writers

Transitional readers and writers tend to be more fluent in reading and writing than beginning readers and writers. Although these children exhibit many characteristics, three are most dominant: (1) the ability to read silently (they do not vocalize orally as they read); (2) the ability to read fluently without having to decode each word; and (3) an increased focus on meaning.

Reading

Because these children have an increased sight word bank, they read more fluently (Carver, 1990). They process text in chunks, rather than word by word. These children also read more widely, as more text is at their instructional level. They may choose narrative or informational text with much illustrative support. Or they may elect to read books organized by chapters with little illustrative support. They often discover favorite authors or genres and read multiple books in a series. This type of reading builds their reading skills so that they are ready for more complex text.

When writing or discussing what they have read, these students may elect to focus on the literal elements. However, they are also able to move beyond this more narrow focus and share personal connections to the text, or to be critical of their reading or the author's craft. Although younger readers can participate in similar inferential understandings, they typically must experience the text on more than one occasion. Transitional students can decode the text and consider these higher-level understandings simultaneously.

Writing

Transitional readers and writers explore more complex ideas in writing. They are no longer limited to writing letter by letter, and they include writing conventions such as punctuation in their first-draft writing. They are able to write whole ideas or phrases at one time. Their writing is longer and includes more ideas. They are also able to seriously revise their work, including adding to and deleting from text (Calkins, 1986). They recognize that others are reading their writing, and they want these readers to understand what they have written. They also begin to explore writing in multiple genres; they move beyond writing about themselves to writing reports, plays, and poems.

Word Knowledge

Transitional readers and writers are able to represent short-vowel words correctly most of the time. They are exploring the multiple ways there are to write long-vowel patterns. They refine their knowledge of when to represent single-syllable, long-vowel words with a consonant–vowel–consonant–final *e* (CVCe) pattern (*hope*), a consonant–vowel–vowel–consonant (CVVC) pattern (*nail*), or a consonant–vowel–vowel (CVV) pattern (*hey*). They also have mastery of many sight words and do not have to think about each letter in these words when they write them. They are more fluent in putting words on a page.

Final Thoughts

Throughout this book, all instruction and assessment are grounded in the three core principles shared in this chapter. First, teachers are critical to student learning. Second, students learn best in classroom contexts that are social-constructivist in theory. And, third, students learn about literacy developmentally; it is critical for teachers to understand this development, so that they can plan instruction appropriately.

In addition to these fundamental principles, this book is guided by the joint position statement issued by the IRA and the National Association for the Education of Young Children (NAEYC) (see IRA & NAEYC, 1998). Throughout the statement, these two groups have presented a continuum of literacy development, together with instruction and activities that teachers and parents might provide children at various locations along the continuum. We have utilized the same type of organization throughout this book, so that the reader has a clear picture of a child's development, appropriate assessment, and instructional suggestions that are relevant to a level of development. The advantage of this organization is that each major point along the continuum of literacy development is clearly described. However, the disadvantage is that the reader might not recognize the connections and similarities across practices and assessments that are described at various levels. We encourage readers to read this book in multiple ways. Perhaps on a first reading, a focus on the developmental levels of students might be most relevant. Then, on a second reading, the developmental progression across reading and writing might be explored. Each successive reading provides a different lens through which to consider the reading and writing of young children.

Chapter 2

EXPLORING DEVELOPING LITERACY

> When Pa was taking Jim to school for the first time, Jim said, "Will I have a friend at school?" "I think you will," said Pa. And Pa smiled down at him.
> —COHEN (1967), *Will I Have a Friend?*

Jim is like other children who enter preschool (typically their first school experience): They are more worried about making friends and meeting their new teacher than about what they might learn. Teachers, on the other hand, have a broader agenda. They are concerned about coming to know their new students and bringing them to an understanding of classroom expectations, but they are also thoughtful about the curriculum that will help their students learn.

Importantly, both teachers and students are interested in how this new classroom community will become familiar. For children, this community is very different from the ones they have experienced within their home and family environments. They leave what is familiar and enter into a classroom filled with a multitude of children and (in most situations) only one teacher. Unlike students, teachers are familiar with classroom structures; they are just not sure about the uniqueness of each new class, or about their new students' strengths and needs. They also realize that it is important to include their students' backgrounds in classroom learning and to make connections between children's homes and the school, to assure that all students are successful.

Simultaneously, as early childhood teachers create a classroom community, they engage their students in literacy assessment and instruction that will build a strong base for the more complex literacy understandings to be nurtured later. One key area is vocabulary and language development. Dickinson and Tabors (2001) have identified several practices in this area that they see as essential for early childhood teachers to engage in if children are to be successful as literacy learners. Among these practices are opportunities for children to hear unusual words spoken by their teachers to extend their vocabularies, engagement in extended conversations with their teachers, hearing books read, and being encouraged to discuss the books that are read. Beyond these language experiences, Snow, Burns, and Griffin (1998) have documented the importance for future literacy achievement of developing phonological awareness, knowledge of letter names and their corresponding sound associations, and the alphabetic principle where children learn the connections between sounds and letters and knowledge of their representation in words.

The challenges of developing a classroom community where most children have had no previous school experiences, and discovering children's literacy strengths as well, are considerable. Clearly, effective early childhood teachers must be masters at doing both simultaneously. With the current emphasis on the importance of early literacy learning (Snow et al., 1998), early childhood educators have huge pressure and responsibility to facilitate the literacy development of each student in their classrooms. In recognizing these responsibilities and expectations, this chapter highlights the way a teacher can help a child make the transition from home to the classroom. It then focuses on literacy assessment and instruction targeted to young children who are discovering reading and writing.

Creating the Classroom Community

In the quote that begins this chapter, Jim wants to know whether he will have friends in preschool. Importantly, children need to feel comfortable in their new surroundings before they can experiment with reading, writing, and other learning activities. Although this getting comfortable with new surroundings is particularly important in preschool, it never loses its significance as children enter a new classroom each year. There are many ways that teachers can organize their rooms to enhance positive, language-rich interaction among children, as well as to support students in forming friendships. And certainly, after the children arrive and are settled in the new environment, teachers can engage in a curriculum that enhances communication among students as they engage in learning.

Transitions into the Classroom

Because teaching and learning are the central activities in any classroom, teachers most often start out by considering their classroom space and how they can organize it to facilitate these activities. The first area to be pondered is the entrance to the classroom. How parents and children enter the classroom is an important consideration when teachers are thinking about transitions between home and school (Roskos & Neuman, 2001). In most homes, there is a place to greet guests near the door and to bring them into the new environment. A teacher might replicate this greeting area by creating a welcoming space outside the classroom. This might include a bulletin board for parents to learn about upcoming events and to share news about their children. Following are a few other suggestions for this transition space (and time) in classrooms:

Welcome Sign

A sign that welcomes children in a variety of languages can be placed near or on the door. It is important for children and their families to see that their home languages have value in the classroom. Figure 2.1 is an example of a welcoming sign.

Family Literacy Activities Bulletin Board

In addition to the bulletin board for classroom and family news described above, a family bulletin board can be provided where parents can place literacy activities that were done at home. Parents can bring their children's drawings, letters, writing, or stories and post them on this board. Then, if possible, the parents and children can talk about these during a sharing time within the day. This type of display builds connections between the literacy activities that happen at home and those in the classroom. It also provides an opportunity for the teacher to better understand and appreciate the activities that are occurring in each child's home.

Children's Sign-In Chart

A poster or chart paper can be provided where children write their names each day as they enter the room. For young children, their names are the most meaningful words in print; name writing is thus an important first step in literacy, and an accomplishment that is tied to a child's literate identity (Bloodgood, 1999; Clay, 1975; Lieberman, 1985). Bloodgood (1999) observed young children as they engaged in writing their names over time. Three-year-olds who used mock letters or scribbles in the fall were able to represent their first names correctly by spring. In addition, these children recognized the letters in their names and could read their classmates' names as well. Moreover, as children became competent in writing their names, they began to grasp knowledge of letter names and the alphabet. Figures 2.2 through 2.4 include samples of Briunna's work as she learned to write her name from the ages of 3 to 4. It is clear in Figure 2.2 that she was using scribbles for her name, and the scribbles were large, not different from her drawings. In Figure 2.3, she was making symbols that were more like letters and closely resembled the letters in her name. And in Figure 2.4, she was able to represent her name with letters, although it was a laborious and slow process for her to do so.

Our class says hello!

FIGURE 2.1. A welcoming sign.

FIGURE 2.2. Briunna's scribbling.

FIGURE 2.3. Briunna's writing with letter shapes.

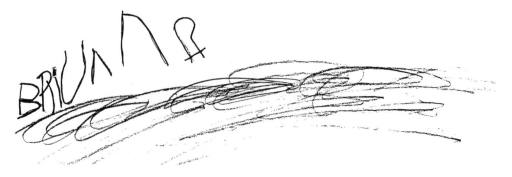

FIGURE 2.4. Briunna's name.

Name writing can be used as an assessment of literacy for young children (see Figure 2.5). Children who are still scribbling are not able to represent letters yet. Children who are starting to use symbols and perhaps their first initials are aware of letters, although they are probably not able to identify the majority of them. And children who are able to represent their names correctly are able to recognize many letters of the alphabet and are probably ready to explore sound–symbol relationships, beginning with the first letters of their names (Bloodgood, 1999).

A teacher can use a child's name knowledge to help this child and others with the same sounds used in other words. For example, a child named Marie might be asked to help with the first sound in *man*, as she is already familiar with this sound–symbol relationship.

Teachers might also want to read the book *Froggy Goes to School* (London, 1996) to show children the importance of their names. In this book, Froggy heads to school for the very first time. When he gets there he notices his name on his desk. Following is the text surrounding his discovery:

> At school, Froggy found his name tag on his table. He liked his name. It was the first word he knew how to read. It was the only word he knew how to read. FROGGY. He read it louder and louder. (n.p.)

After hearing this book, teachers and children might engage in a discussion of when they learned to read and write their own names, thus supporting the importance of name recognition and its connections to reading and writing.

Literacy Instruction and Assessment

This section of the chapter is organized discretely around areas of literacy teaching and learning. However, in classrooms, these areas are taught synergistically; teaching about writing also includes instruction in letters and conveying meaning, for example. Moreover, teachers develop oral language throughout all instruction, and reading to children will enhance their phonological awareness and increase their

FIGURE 2.5
Assessment of Name Writing

Name _____   Date _____

____ Does not differentiate between drawing and writing, and
uses large scribbles for both.

____ Uses a tight scribble for writing and broad scribbles for
drawing.

____ Uses letter-like forms to represent name.

____ Uses initial consonant for name.

____ Represents most letters in name.

____ Represents name.

Observations as child writes name:

comprehension. This section's organizational structure is just a way of sharing this information. The section is divided into four parts: oral language, reading, writing, and word study.

Oral Language

Children enter school with great variability in vocabulary knowledge (Hart & Risley, 1995). Some of this variability is the result of different book-reading and other literacy experiences at home. Cunningham and Stanovich (1998) discovered that primary-level books often have vocabulary that is more sophisticated than the daily conversation provided by college-educated parents. And Whitehurst and Lonigan (1998) indicated that children from high-poverty backgrounds typically had even less experience with books, writing, hearing stories, learning and reciting rhymes, and other literacy experiences when they entered school than their middle-class counteparts. Although there is always great variability within groups identified by income level, children from lower-income situations often begin school with fewer literacy experiences and less literacy knowledge—or, at least, less knowledge about literacy that is *valued in school*. Importantly, these children have had some literacy experiences in their homes, such as storytelling, but these experiences tend not to be valued as picture-book-reading experiences in school settings. This makes the role of the early childhood teacher critical, as low-income children rely more heavily on school to facilitate their literacy learning than do middle-class children. However, the good news is that teachers can make a difference. Socioeconomic levels demonstrate only modest effects on children's later achievement, and effective instruction allows children to progress at rates equivalent to those of children from homes with more financial resources (Goldenberg, 2001); these findings indicate the importance of the teacher to children's academic lives.

The following are activities that support the development of oral language for early literacy learners.

Reading Books Aloud

One of the most traditional activities that early childhood teachers engage in is reading aloud to children. The recommendation to read to children continues to be important, especially for developing communication and vocabulary. Now, with the wide availability of *big-book* versions of stories and informational text, students can see the illustrations as well as hear the text. Mautte (1990) found that through repeated big-book-reading sessions, children made significant advances in language development. Importantly, teachers need to reread a book several times, for children's comments and questions increase after hearing a text on multiple occasions (Pappas, 1991). Valdez-Menchaca and Whitehurst (1992) noted that Spanish-speaking young children developed language competence when the books were read interactively with the children—that is, when parents or teachers carried on conversations about the text as they read. In connecting these research discoveries, it makes sense that young children benefit from the repeated reading of books with much discussion before, during, and after reading, so that they gain an understanding of the vocabulary within a story or informational text as well as the meaning conveyed in it.

Beck, McKeown, and Kucan (2000) offer an additional strategy to build vocabulary learning for children during reading aloud. They ask teachers to highlight important words in stories to help children acquire academic language. For example, if a teacher reads the book *Swimmy* (Lionni, 1963), he or she can highlight words such as *fierce* and *swift*. Children can offer suggestions of what they mean. They can also act them out, and then, throughout the day and week, the teacher can use these words in the daily conversation. In a play activity, a teacher may overhear a student say, "That lion is fierce. I can hear it roar." During a second reading, other words can be selected—for instance, *lobster*, *anemone*, or *eel*. The goal in choosing such words is to develop content vocabulary for young children. Teachers can spend considerable time describing the sea creatures in this book, and then move to informational books to expand on the knowledge found here. There are also rich descriptions in this book that can serve for yet another reading: "a lobster who walked about like a water-moving machine," "strange fish pulled by an invisible thread," or "sea anemones who looked like pink palm trees swaying in the wind." In all of these conversations, the teacher is moving from the text to focus on interesting words and phrases that are outside most young children's speaking vocabularies. The goal is to make these less familiar words familiar, so that students will understand them in their reading and use them in writing.

Teachers can include informational text in their reading-aloud sessions as well. For example, if a teacher reads a book like *Nests, Nests, Nests* (Canizares & Reid, 1998), children should have no difficulty understanding the words in text: "This is a nest. A nest can be in a tree. . . . " However, the teacher can engage young children in conversation about the various birds that live in each nest. In this way, the familiar (nests) is used to ground a discussion of things that are less familiar (the various birds and their characteristics). Furthermore, when narrative text and informational text are mixed, children become familiar with the different text structures through their listening and talking experiences.

Play Events Related to Reading

McGee (2003) and Pellegrini and Galda (1982) have noted that when children act out stories that have been read to them, they develop more elaborate vocabularies, use more complex language, and have better story comprehension. Children can simply act out a story after the teacher has read it several times and after the children have engaged in discussion about it. For example, after children have heard *Henny Penny* (Galdone, 1968), they can take turns being Henny Penny, Ducky Lucky, and so on. A teacher can even make simple paper collars or hats so that the children are clear about their characters' identities. If these simple props and the book are left at a center, children can independently recreate this story numerous times. Through this play, children can practice vocabulary that is in the book, but that is unlike the conversational speech they routinely engage in with peers or family members.

Play Centers

Previously, teachers of young children created centers where children could experiment with being moms, dads, or store clerks, for example. Most of the time, these centers did not include objects related to literacy. Now teachers embellish these centers with literacy-related materials. So if an area is set up as a restaurant, children have menus, order pads, and so on. In this way, children practice the literacy events related to each context. This literacy play allows them to see the uses of literacy outside school, and to make connections to in-school literacy practices.

Parents as Language Teachers

Teachers can invite parents to their classrooms to share stories or to engage in activities related to learning, such as a cooking experience. This is a subtle way for children to see that their teachers value the experiences of their parents, and that they are connected to in-school learning.

In addition, parents can read to students in the classroom. Neuman (1996) and Delgado-Gaitan (1994) interacted with small groups of parents in discussions of children's books, and they practiced reading them together. Parents then read these books to their own children at home, and read to students in the classroom. These researchers found that this practice resulted in parents reading more frequently to their children. Moreover, children saw that their parents valued schooling and were a part of it.

Assessment of Oral Language

Assessment of oral language takes careful observation on the part of teachers. They need to observe students during play, during small-group work, and at other times during the instructional day. Figure 2.6 is a chart for recording the oral language used by individual students.

Reading

This section focuses on comprehension of text and learning about the concepts of print, such as what print is, top-to-bottom orientation on a page, and so on. Although phonological awareness is certainly essential to children's development as readers and writers (International Reading Association [IRA] & National Association for the Education of Young Children [NAEYC], 1998), this discussion is placed in the section of this chapter on word study.

Assessment of Oral Language

Name _____

HOME LANGUAGE

Child relies on home language and is unaware that the teacher and other students do not have the background to understand what he or she is communicating.

Whole-class conversations _____

_____

Small-group conversations _____

_____

TELEGRAPHIC LANGUAGE

Child names objects and people. He or she uses greetings and responses. However, these responses are brief (one word often represents a whole sentence).

Whole-class conversations _____

_____

Small-group conversations _____

_____

CONVERSATIONAL LANGUAGE

Child uses phrases or sentences to communicate. Enough background is provided that the listener can understand, based on this conversation.

Whole-class conversations _____

_____

Small-group conversations _____

_____

ACADEMIC LANGUAGE

Child uses academic language in conversations.

Whole-class conversations _____

_____

Small-group conversations _____

_____

Note. Teachers should record specific language they hear a child using. Teachers may want to include more conversational contexts (play centers, library, etc.). They may also want to include a language category that reflects the new words that children use in various activities. For example, when does a child use the word *fierce* after he or she has explored it on several occasions?

Comprehension

The most important activity for young children's later reading success is reading aloud to them (Bus, van IJzendoorn, & Pellegrini, 1995; Wells, 1986). This reading is not a solitary activity in which only a teacher's or a parent's voice is heard. It is interactive, in that children, teachers, and parents ask questions and discuss the book before, after, and during reading. As noted in the joint position statement about early literacy (IRA & NAEYC, 1998), "It is the talk that surrounds the story-book reading that gives it power, helping children to bridge what is in the story and their own lives" (p. 199). Moreover, as discussed in the previous section, children engage in more complex talk when a book has been shared multiple times.

Following is an example of Briunna, almost 3 years old, sharing a story with her grandmother. This example demonstrates the meaningful dialogue that occurred between them, and it shows how Briunna picked up the language used by her grand-mother. They were reading an alphabet book, although Briunna was not yet aware of the alphabet. She constructed the reading activity almost as a guessing game— "What's this, Granny?"—and then Granny responded.

GRANNY: Let's read this book (*turning to a page*).

BRIUNNA: Fish.

GRANNY: It's a *K*.

BRIUNNA: What's this, Granny? What here?

GRANNY: That's a monkey. Mouse.

BRIUNNA: What's this, Granny?

GRANNY: Mouse. M (*Granny traces the M with her finger*).

BRIUNNA: (*Traces the M after Granny*) I've got to turn the page. What's this? Fish.

GRANNY: That's not a fish. That's a bird.

BRIUNNA: That's a fish? I see glass.

GRANNY: That's not a glass. It is something else. What is this that is all deco-rated?

BRIUNNA: All decorated. A cake. Birthday.

GRANNY: Where are the fish?

The conversation continued as the two of them moved back and forth throughout the book, with Briunna and Granny taking turns asking questions. In this one inter-action, Granny was helping Briunna identify illustrations that began with the cor-rect alphabet letter. This was evident when Briunna guessed "Fish" and Granny said, "It's a *k*." Granny was teaching Briunna the letter names and shapes when the two of them traced an M. And finally, Briunna was picking up the language used by Granny when she repeated, "decorated," a word new to her. It is easy to see how repeated book-reading events like this help a child become familiar with books, their structure, new vocabulary, and the meaning within.

Teachers engage students in whole-class, small-group, and one-on-one reading. In whole-group situations, some children remain quiet and do not get a chance to interact with a book. They often move to the back of the group, and sometimes never even look at the book. In smaller settings, and especially one-on-one sessions, children have more opportunity to talk about a book, as seen in Briunna's example.

Beyond books, teachers also want to make sure that children become familiar with more functional print, such as signs and labels (McGee, Lomax, & Head, 1988). Teachers can easily do this by labeling with children the important parts of the room, such as bookcases, tables, and chairs. Young children can also help in labeling their cubbies with their names. Through this activity, they realize that their names represent them, and they can find the names of their friends as well. A child also learns (sometimes sadly) that some other children's names begin with *my* letter—the first letter in the child's name.

Following are other ways to support children as they learn about print in and out of books.

Environmental Print. Even though most preschool children have not developed the ability to read independently, many have learned to read signs that are embedded in logos (logos for fast-food restaurants and breakfast cereals, for instance). So teachers might prepare small blank books where children paste pictures of items that they can read without adult help. This is an activity that parents can easily help with at home, especially if the blank book is put in a plastic bag with scissors and glue. Children can cut up cereal boxes, pictures from catalogues, newspapers, clean fast-food wrappings, and so on to build their own books.

Christie and Enz (2003) share how they use environmental print to move children into reading. They identify four levels of working with environmental print. The first level has children identify the environmental print as it is—the name on a cereal box, for example. Once children are comfortable with this level, they move to exploring color—that is, identifying a replica of the logo with text. The next level is identifying a black-and-white copy of the text without the logo. At this level, the children no longer have the visual aid of the logo to help with identification. The last level has children identifying the text written in generic print. In addition to identifying these levels, Christie and Enz have developed activities that can be used at any level. Children might create puzzles or flip books with the text at whatever level they are exploring. They also encourage students to sort their text by initial-consonant sound. For instance, a child might place a logo for McDonald's under M. As the support of the logo dissipates, the child's attention is drawn closer and closer to the initial-consonant sound.

These activities also serve as a way to bring materials from home into the class. Xu and Rutledge (2003) share many ways to use environmental print that connect home and school as well. They highlight the use of environmental print brought from home during show and tell. During this sharing, each child has a concrete item with text that he or she can chat about.

Class Books. There are all kinds of ways to make *class books*—books to which each child in the classroom contributes a page. A beginning-of-the-year class book might be focused on the children in the class. Each child draws a self-portrait and then writes about him- or herself. The teacher then encourages each child to talk about his or her drawing and writing. Children read this book with the help of their classmates. Each classmate becomes the expert for his or her page.

Family Books. Each child is given a small book with blank pages, and the child builds a book with a family member on each page. Parents help with these books. In most cases each page will just have a person's name, but some families may choose to record a whole sentence about a family member. Children use these books throughout the year for independent reading.

Beyond this in-class reading, teachers will want to support parents in reading to their children as well. There are many ways to do this; following are a few suggestions.

Nursery Rhymes. Although nursery rhymes have never been noted for the meaning that might be gained from them, they do help children discover rhythm, rhyming, and phonological awareness. Teachers can explore a single rhyme over time, and then a simple take-home book can be created so that children feel comfortable sharing the rhyme with their parents. If teachers help children create shoeboxes that can hold their books, there will be a safe place in their homes where children can keep their books and reread them to themselves and their parents.

Keep Books. *Keep books* are small, inexpensive books that children can explore in school and then take home. For preschoolers, there are simple books that focus on captions and nursery rhymes. They also have Spanish versions as well, so children can explore the books in both languages (see Figure 2.7 for sample English and Spanish pages from two of these books). These books are available from Ohio State University (*www.keepbooks.org*).

Literacy Prop Boxes. Neuman and Roskos (1993) have described boxes, based on themes, that teachers and parents created for children to explore at home. For example, in one set of boxes, they placed school-related items: chalk and a small chalkboard; paper, pencils, and crayons; and a few books (both narrative and informational text) about going to school. When children took the boxes home, parents shared the books with their children, and the children had enough props that they could play school. Through the literacy box structure, children heard stories and enacted the language and knowledge they gained from the books in their play.

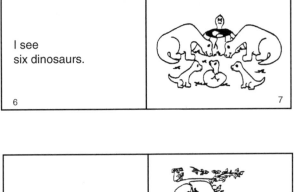

FIGURE 2.7. Sample pages from each of two keep books (one in English, one in Spanish).

Assessment of Reading Focused on Comprehension

The best way to explore the meaning that children are acquiring from reading or being read to is to have them retell a story (Goodman, Watson, & Burke, 1987). Having very young children draw or write about the books they have read or heard is not inappropriate; in fact, it is an excellent activity for young children to do to extend meaning and to further conversation about a book. It will just be very hard to decipher what they have written or drawn. For example, in Figure 2.8 is a picture

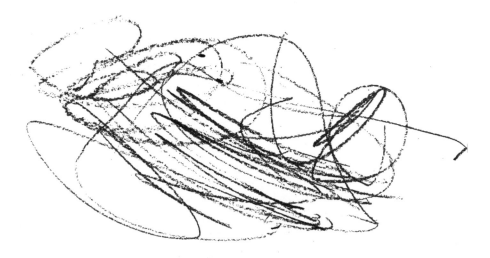

FIGURE 2.8. Noah's frog.

drawn by a young child about the book *Brown Bear, Brown Bear, What Do You See?* (Martin, 1967). When Noah was asked about his picture, he said it was the green frog in the book (the scribble was green with orange eyes), and he even drew the eyes. However, without Noah's help, most teachers would probably not have known what he drew.

When asking a child to retell a story, a teacher can observe whether the child retells it in order, mentions the characters or setting, and so on. Teachers can certainly nudge students through the retelling by asking, "Can you help me understand what happens next?" or "What did [character] do then?"

Below are two examples of the same child retelling the story *Spot's First Walk* (Hill, 1981) at the beginning and ending of his 4-year-old preschool experience. This book is about a dog that leaves home for a day and explores the neighborhood near him. On each page there is an illustration hidden under a fold that enhances the story. One of us (Diane Barone, the "I" in what follows) read the book to Carlos, and then I asked him to tell me about the story. In September, he told me about the book, although he only looked at the illustrations on the page to help him with this retelling.

September
Page 1: A little dog and a big dog.
Page 2: I see a dog crashing in the backyard.
Page 3: The dog scared the cat. The cat was hiding in the house. I see a bird chopping up dirt.
Page 4: I see another dog and a child and the chick is mad. The dog scared him.

His retelling continued in this way throughout the book. He identified what he thought was happening on each page and explored the feelings of the characters. There was never any carryover from page to page to create a story; rather, each page was a separate event. He also did not use any book language in this retelling. He just described what he saw, and his retelling was very dependent on the illustrations in the book to make sense of it.

In June, he retold the same story. This time he looked at each page carefully and often put his finger on the words, although he could not read extended text yet. However, he was aware that the words on the page carried meaning.

June
Page 1: Spot don't get lost.
Page 2: His mother says not in there. He meets a snail and he says hello.
Page 3: He sees a cat in there. He scares the cat. The cat got scared.
Page 4: Now he sees chickens. He sees a mama chicken and a baby chick.
Page 5: He says, "Who is that bird?" He saw a woodpecker.
Page 6: He smells some butterflies through the door. He smells flowers and a tree.

There were great differences between the September and June retellings of *Spot's First Walk*. The June retelling was continuous across pages. Carlos was telling a story this time. He was also using oral language, and he borrowed book language in his retelling, as noted in his quotes and his use of past tense. In addition, he used the sorts of connectors that appear in written text (e.g., *now* and *then*).

In this simple comparison of retellings, it is easy to see how this child was building his understanding of the story. There are many ways to evaluate retellings. Figures 2.9 and 2.10 provide two methods that a teacher might choose to evaluate the retellings of his or her students.

Book and Print Concepts

As children interact with books, they become aware of how books and print are organized, and this knowledge is important for them as they begin learning to read and write. Clay (1972) has developed an assessment, the Concepts about Print Test, which targets many aspects of books. Her test assesses children's knowledge of such concepts as book orientation (front and back), difference between illustrations and print, directionality of print, book terminology (e.g., *word*, *letter*), top and bottom of a page, and the beginning and end of a book. Although Clay used specific books that she developed for this assessment (called *Sand* and *Stones*), teachers can use most predictable, simple text to learn about a child's knowledge of a book and its structure.

Assessment of Concepts of Book and Print

Assessing book and print concepts requires a teacher to work one on one with a student. A teacher might read the book that he or she is going to use for the assessment to the whole class. Children like to know what the book is about before they engage in this assessment process. After this reading, the teacher takes the book and an assessment record (see Figure 2.11 for an assessment record) and interacts with each child. For very young children, probably only a few of a book's concepts will be explored. These concepts include the following:

- *Book orientation.* The teacher hands the book to the child and asks him or her to point to the front and back of the book. Then the teacher asks the child to point to the title of the book. If the child is able to do this, the teacher asks, "What is the purpose of the title?"
- *Differences between illustrations and print.* The teacher opens the book to the first page. Then he or she asks a child to point to the illustrations and then to the print. If the child is able to do this, the teacher has the child point to where he or she should start reading.
- *Directionality of print.* The child points to the first line of text. Then the teacher asks, "How should you read this line of print?" The child should make a sweep from the left to the right under this line. If the child can do this, then the

FIGURE 2.9
Assessment of Story Structure Retelling

Name _____

Characters _____

_____

_____

_____

_____

Plot events _____

_____

_____

_____

_____

Setting _____

_____

_____

_____

_____

Note. The teacher writes in what the child says, and then determines how many of the characters are named and how many events. The teacher also determines whether the events are in the proper sequence. The teacher can use this simple form, or he or she can create one that lists the characters and the many events. Then the teacher can just check these off as the child mentions them.

FIGURE 2.10
Assessment of Early Literacy Story Retelling

Name _____

____ Attending to pictures, not forming a story. (Child identifies illustrations on each page. There is no connected story.)

____ Attending to pictures, forming an oral story. (Child connects the story from one illustration to another. The story sounds like conversation.)

____ Attending to pictures, forming an oral and book language story. (Child connects a story from page to page. The child tells the story and then uses book language intermittently.)

____ Attending to pictures, forming a book language story. (Child sounds as though he or she is reading the story. A listener can understand the story without access to the illustrations.)

____ Attending to print. (Child knows that print carries the message.)

____ Actual reading. (When asked, "Can you read this?", child responds as follows:

    ____ Refusal (Child refuses because he or she does not know how to read.)

    ____ Aspectual reading. (Child reads text that is known and pretends to read the rest.)

    ____ Holistic reading. (Child's focus is on getting the words right, not meaning.)

    ____ Independent reading (Child reads the text.)

Note. This retelling evaluation is drawn from the work of Sulzby (1985). It is focused more on how the child retells a story than on the exact details shared.

FIGURE 2.11
Assessment of Concept of Book

Child's name _____   Date _____

Book orientation

_____ Able to point to front and back of book
_____ Able to point to title
_____ Able to identify purpose of title

Differences between illustrations and print

_____ Able to point to illustrations
_____ Able to point to print
_____ Able to point to where reading should begin

Directionality of print

_____ Able to show directionality of print on a page

Knowledge of beginning and end

_____ Able to point to beginning of the story
_____ Able to point to end of the story
_____ Able to point to beginning of text on a page
_____ Able to point to end of text on a page

Using book terminology

_____ Able to identify top and bottom of a page
_____ Able to point to a word
_____ Able to point to a specific word
_____ Able to point to a letter
_____ Able to point to a specific letter
_____ Able to point to lower-case letter
_____ Able to point to upper-case letter
_____ Able to identify a period
_____ Able to identify a question mark
_____ Able to identify an exclamation mark

teacher asks, "Where would you read the next line?", looking to see whether the child again moves to the left.

- *Beginning and end.* The child points to the beginning and end of the book.
- *Book terminology.* The child is asked to point to the top and bottom of a page. Then he or she is asked to point to a word. If the child can do this, then he or she is asked to point to a specific word. If the child can do this, then he or she is asked to point to a letter in the word. A teacher might also see whether a child recognizes upper and lower case. Following this exploration, the teacher asks questions about punctuation.

Importantly, most preschoolers will not know all the specific concepts of a book by the end of preschool. This knowledge continues to develop during kindergarten and into first grade.

Writing

In the 1970s, with the work of Clay (1975) and Read (1975), teachers and parents were made aware of the importance of children's writing even before it is conventional—or able to be read by someone other than the children themselves. These researchers, among others helped teachers and parents to understand the development shown within scribbles, to appreciate when children represent a word with an initial consonant, and to determine when they move to a full phonemic representation of a word (such as *red* for *read*). From this background, more recent researchers like Labbo (1996), Rowe (1994), and Dyson (1992) have demonstrated the importance of the social context surrounding writing. Each has detailed the support that peers give to each other as they engage in writing. For instance, they have highlighted how a nearby friend can suggest a character or show how to spell a word. Other recent, researchers (e.g., Richgels, 1995) have documented that when young children write, they also practice and develop phonemic awareness, in addition to learning how to convey a message.

Explorations in Writing

Young children do not begin their writing explorations with representations that others can read. Scribbling is the first form of writing that most children engage in, and now, thanks to the work of Temple, Nathan, Temple, and Burris (1993), teachers and parents can note developmental changes in scribbles. Children begin with uncontrolled scribbles—that is, random marks on paper. For very young children, discovering that they can make a mark is the most important discovery, and they often take this discovery to the walls of their homes or classrooms. Children can sometimes identify a scribble that they are making, although they may label it as something different each time they are asked. Following uncontrolled scribbling, children move to controlled scribbling. Here children make marks in a systematic way. Noah's picture, shared earlier in Figure 2.8, is an example of a controlled scribble. What is particularly interesting about this phase of scribbling is that the scribbles a child uses to represent writing soon look like the language that the child is familiar with. Here is where clear distinctions emerge between scribbles used for drawing (larger) and scribbles used for writing (tighter and smaller). Harste, Woodward, and Burke (1984) observed that children's scribbles in Arabic, Hebrew, and English had characteristics of each written language. That is, the scribbling shapes looked very much like conventional writing in that language. Children picked up the unique characteristics of writing that they saw in their communities.

During this time, children begin to use drawings to represent meaning as well. In Figure 2.12, Noah moved beyond a scribble to draw a clearer representation of a green goblin. He dictated what his drawing was, but it was not hard to know that it was a green person of some kind—very different from the green frog that he had drawn earlier.

Children move from drawings only, to drawings and writing, to just writing to shape their messages. In Figures 2.13 through 2.16, Kennady's writing from scribbling to sound–symbol relationships is shared. In Figure 2.13, she used circles with letter-like forms within her writing. When asked, she said, "I am writing letters." In Figure 2.14, she was still using the circle strategy, but the shapes within looked more like letters, especially *o* and *e*. She said that she "spelled Kasey," her friend. In Figure 2.15, she used a string of letters to represent her writing. She was not sure what she had written when asked. Then in Figure 2.16, she drew the Eiffel Tower and wrote *Paris* (as PRS). Here she demonstrated her ability to represent the most salient

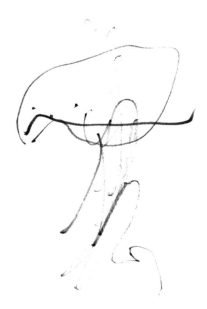

That's the green goblin.

FIGURE 2.12. Noah's green goblin.

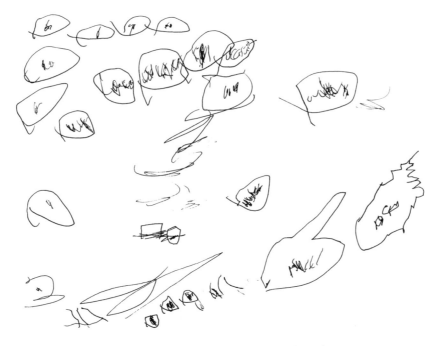

FIGURE 2.13. Kennady's writing with circles.

FIGURE 2.14. Kennady's circle and letter strategy.

FIGURE 2.15. Kennady's letter string.

FIGURE 2.16. Kennady's writing of *Paris*.

sounds in the word *Paris*. And she certainly demonstrated knowledge that the Eiffel Tower is in Paris; she could have made this connection because of her love of the *Madeline* books. These few examples demonstrate the knowledge that children develop by having opportunities to write.

After children leave scribbling and are using letter strings for writing, they typically use initial consonants; then they use both initial and final consonants; and then they include a vowel (Bear & Templeton, 1998). They also learn how to represent their names, as described earlier in this chapter.

In a previous section, it has been recommended that children have writing supplies in centers where appropriate. Here children can experiment with writing a bill, a shopping list, or a menu. They get a sense of writing in circumstances that are familiar to them outside school. Following are several other activities to develop young writers:

- *Journals.* Even in preschool, teachers can provide journals for young children. Children can draw, scribble, copy, and write messages in these journals. Teachers and parents can see each student's writing development by viewing these journals over time.
- *Responses to read-aloud text.* Teachers can offer children the opportunity to write or draw after a book is read aloud. If possible, the teacher can move among the children as they do their drawing and writing, and provide a dictated account to accompany the work. This was done with Noah's drawing of the green goblin. Children can then see their words represented in print.
- *Language experience activity.* A teacher brings something for children to talk about. It can be as simple as a stuffed animal, or as complex as a science experiment. Then a small group of students tell the teacher about what was brought. The teacher writes what the children said so that they again see talk converted to text. In preschool, it is important to include each child's name, as this may be the only word that a child can find. Below is a short example of a teacher's writing of this type, from a discussion centering on a fish that visited a preschool classroom:

> John says, "I see a big fish."
> Maria says, "I see it swim."
> Julio says, "What name?"
> Children say, "Yellow Fish."

Once the dictation was complete, the children read it with the teacher. The teacher pointed to the words as she read, but most children did not notice the speech-to-print match that she demonstrated. After this reading, she asked children to come to the chart and point to their names and to other words (e.g., *fish*). At a later time, she shared the book *Goldfish* (Harper & Randall, 1997) with them. In this book, they learned facts about goldfish and extended the knowledge they shared when seeing a goldfish.

- *Interactive writing.* As children develop some letter–sound concepts, teachers may encourage the children to help write a message. For example, a teacher may ask children about the things they eat for breakfast. As the teacher records each answer, children can be encouraged to add a letter or word to the chart (McCarrier, Pinnell, & Fountas, 2000)

• *Labeling items.* Teachers and children can label objects in the room. They can also label creations made by children with blocks or Legos. If a child creates a road, for example, it can have a label. If a child builds a building, the teacher can label it. In some preschools, children then draw what they have built in a journal, and the teacher again records what they have made. In this way, they have a record of this accomplishment, even though the original has had to be torn down.

Assessment of Writing

Assessment of writing is quite straightforward for young children. At first, more attention is paid to the way a child represents a message. Later on, the content of the message becomes more important. Figure 2.17 in an assessment form that can be used for writing.

Word Study

A discussion of word study may seem surprising in a chapter about developing literacy learners. However, in preschool, children learn important concepts about words that support their literacy growth; these include phonological awareness, letter knowledge, and sound–symbol relationships (all of which can be reinforced through concept sorting).

Phonological Awareness

There has been considerable research to support the importance of phonological awareness (Adams, 1990; National Reading Panel [NRP], 2000b; Snow et al., 1998). Many teachers confuse *phonological awareness instruction* with *phonics instruction.* Phonological awareness instruction is targeted to helping children recognize the individual sounds in *spoken* language. And children must be able to manipulate phonemes (the smallest sound units in words) before phonics instruction makes sense. This ability to manipulate sounds orally is one of the best predictors of later reading success (Stahl & Murray, 1994). There are multiple ways to develop phonological awareness; a few have already been discussed, such as reading to children, language experience, interactive writing, and independent writing. Following are other methods that teachers can use to help children develop this knowledge.

• *Rhyming.* Teachers can read rhymes to children and have them identify the words that rhyme. When children are comfortable with this, they supply a rhyming word—for example, "The hat is on the [cat]."
• *Identifying syllables.* Children clap the syllables in their names and in the names of their classmates.
• *Identifying onsets and rimes.* Here children identify the first consonant in a

FIGURE 2.17
Assessment of Writing

Name _____

Interest in writing

____ Child infrequently seeks out writing activities.

____ Child occasionally seeks out writing activities.

____ Child frequently seeks out writing activities.

Directionality

____ No pattern of left to right can be discerned.

____ On most occasions, the child starts at the left and moves right across the paper.

____ On all occasions, the child starts on the left.

Word representations

____ Uses uncontrolled scribbles.

____ Uses controlled scribbles.

____ Uses drawings.

____ Uses shapes, numerals, and letter-like representations.

____ Uses letter strings.

____ Can conventionally represent name.

____ Uses initial consonant to represent a word.

____ Uses several letters to represent a word.

____ Includes a vowel in the representation.

word and then the remainder of a word. If a teacher asks, "What is the first sound in *dog?*", a child will say *d*, and when the teacher asks, "What is the last sound in the word *dog?*", the child will say *og*. Importantly, this is done orally.

• *Phoneme identity.* Children recognize the same sound in multiple words. A teacher might ask, "How are *big, box,* and *bag* alike?"

• *Phoneme categorization.* Children identify which word does not belong in a series. For example, the teacher might ask, "Which word is different—*big, box, dog,* and *bag?*"

In phonological awareness instruction, children move from identifying the individual phonemes in words to being able to substitute and delete phonemes. For instance, a child tells what new word is created when the *p* is taken away from the word *pin*. Or he or she might be asked to tell what word is created when the *i* in *pin* is changed to an *a*. This type of oral manipulation of words is more difficult than simply identifying initial consonants or a word that is different.

Exploring Letters

Young children, especially after they recognize their names, enjoy exploring letters. They love to manipulate magnetic letters and to look through alphabet books. For preschoolers, it is best to use uncomplicated simple alphabet books like *Flora McDonnell's ABC* (McDonnell, 1997), where there is a simple illustration like a lemon for *L*, rather than the very sophisticated ones like *Tomorrow's Alphabet* (Shannon, 1995), where C is for *milk* because it will become cheese.

Following are some strategies to help children learn the letters of the alphabet:

• *Magnetic letters.* Each child can find the first letter in his or her name; the teacher can then ask the children to find other letters.
• *Finding letters.* Children cut the letter that has been identified from magazines and other sources.
• *Stamps.* Children use hand stamps to make copies of the letter that is the target of instruction.
• Matching upper- and lower-case letters. Teachers can use magnetic letters or simple puzzles that allow children to match upper- and lower-case letters.

Concept and Sorting

Concept sorting is introduced as a strategy to focus on all concepts surrounding words and letters (Bear & Barone, 1998). Developing literacy learners who are still not aware of letters or words in print can sort pictures by categories, so that they see the connections among the pictures. When children sort pictures, they are also developing vocabulary. For example, children are given about 12 pictures to sort with the teacher. The teacher establishes categories, such as animals and school things, and has children sort the pictures. First, the teacher picks up each picture and asks the children what it is. Then as a group, they decide where it should go—

with the school things or with animals. They do this for each picture. Then the teacher has pictures available for children to sort individually, using the same categories (see Figure 2.18). Children can use catalogues and magazines independently to find pictures of animals or school things to add to their first sort. They can tear or cut the pictures and glue them onto paper at a center. At the center where this activity takes place, there should be lots of conversation about the items being placed on each child's paper. To support this work, the teacher might want to read Richard Scarry's books and others like them that organize items and people into groups.

Young children who show that they are aware of letter representations and initial sounds connected to them might sort pictures that begin with *b* or *s*, for example. To return to Figure 2.18, children can identify the *snake* and *scissors* and then add them to the *s* group. They can also pull *book* for the letter *b* group. To facilitate this sorting, a teacher can provide a paper with two columns—one labeled *s* and the other labeled *b*. Children can then paste pictures in the appropriate columns (see Figure 2.19 for an example).

Assessment of Word Study

For most of the assessment of word study, teachers listen to children as they rhyme, manipulate phonemes, learn letters, and participate in concept sorts. Figure 2.20 is a form that teachers can use to record the development of their students in this area.

FIGURE 2.18. Pictures for a concept sort by categories (animals and school things).

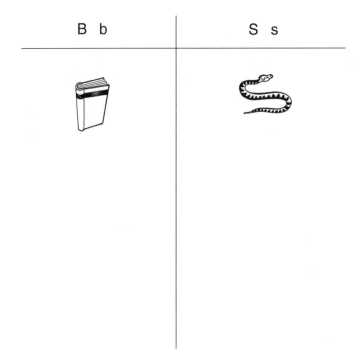

FIGURE 2.19. Two of the pictures from Figure 2.18, sorted by first letter (*b* or *s*).

Conclusion: Visiting a Preschool Classroom

In Becky Schneider's preschool classroom for 4-year-olds, children were involved in many activities simultaneously, and there was a steady hum of conversation. For example, when I (again, Diane Barone) visited, I noted some children looking at books in a library, a few children working on a computer creating drawings, others building with Legos, and a few writing in journals. I asked Mrs. Schneider to share her organization and to describe how she provided literacy instruction to her students. This is what she said.

Getting Started

"During the first week of school, we did a lot of playing—we played with manipulatives, we built towers with blocks, we painted. During this free-play time, I was able to teach the kids how to use all the centers and do some informal assessment with each of them. While children were playing at centers, I pulled some kids over and taught them how to use the computer or the tape recorder in the listening center. I also watched at the writing center to see how children recorded their messages. I checked on each child's knowledge of the alphabet. I asked whether they had favorite books. During this first week, we also started the alphabet that was on the wall in the classroom. Instead of buying one, the children created the letters. These were hung, and as we found pictures or drew pictures that began with a spe-

FIGURE 2.20
Assessment of Word Knowledge

Child's name _____ Date _____

Phonological awareness (teacher provides descriptions next to each category)

Rhyming _____
_____
_____

Identifying syllables _____
_____
_____

Identifying onsets and rimes _____
_____
_____

Phoneme identity _____
_____
_____

Phoneme categorization _____
_____
_____

Phoneme deletion _____
_____
_____

Letters (teacher writes letters that a child can identify—lower and upper case) _____
_____
_____

Sorting (teacher notes categories, letters, etc., that a child has explored) _____
_____
_____

cific letter, we attached them to the appropriate letter. It wasn't as pretty as a store-bought one, but the children owned it and recognized the pictures that they added.

"I am lucky that I have two rooms and an aide. So in one room, I have the library and a writing center close by, so that children can use books if they want when they write. In the other room I have the computer, blocks, puppet stand, dress-up area, and sand/bean table. These activities are noisier and are closer together, as the children often move among them. I see them create something with blocks and then get dressed up as monsters and knock them down. There is also one center where I put books and objects related to the theme we are investigating. Children like to explore at this center, and they often bring in objects or books to expand it.

"On the walls, I mainly hang students' work, but I have the alphabet and an environmental print wall. During circle time, children share words that they can read from the wall. They bring in all the environmental print—if I have 10 McDonald's wrappers, that is fine, because 10 different children brought them in. We have cereal boxes, candy wrappers, and tons of fast-food wrappers. It is the entire wall!"

A Typical Day

"Each day the children entered the room, said goodbye to a parent and hello to the class, and then started in their journals. This way, if children came late, they knew what to do. At this age, I was looking for them to create in their journals. I wanted them to have plenty of time to draw, scribble, or write. I went around to each child during this time and had him or her dictate what had been written or drawn. I read each word that children dictated to me as I wrote, as I wanted them to make the connection between the word they said and what I wrote. I had some children who wrote conventionally, so I just talked to them about their page. After they were done writing, I provided time for any child to share what he or she had written or drawn.

"Following journals and sharing, we interacted with the calendar. This time was focused on the days, numbers, and weather. After calendar time, I read a book related to our theme; then we sang and did movement activities. After this, it was center time. The children moved among three centers. At one, they worked with me on a literacy or math activity. At a second center, they engaged in an activity related to our theme with my aide. And the third center was for free-choice activity.

"The literacy activities in my center changed, but here are some of the things we did. We created class books with dictation. I read to the children, and we discussed the book. Then we reread it together. After we read it several times, it was in the library for them to explore. We sorted pictures and things by concept and initial-consonant sound. I took dictations from the children, and they read these as well.

"After centers, the children had a break and snack. Then I read to them again. The last 20 minutes of the day were free-play time. This was when I had a chance to interact with children one on one. Sometimes I assessed them, and at other times I supported them as they wrote at the computer or wanted a sign made for their Legos or block creations.

"Basically, this is how my class ran. Literacy was my main focus, and I used it as my tool for learning. Books and writing happened every day in the form of journals, writing center, and my teacher-guided center. Through books we explored themes and learned about the world."

Reflecting

Mrs. Schneider shared how she set up her class, her instruction, and her assessment as well. She spent a week or two establishing the environment and her expectations. She said, "Children were expected to be engaged at centers as they conversed with friends. By the second or third week of school, children were able, for the most part, to work independently in centers. They had ample time each day to participate in reading and writing and for their own personal exploration. By the end of the year, many of the children were beginning readers, in that they could read simple text independently. Other children recognized all of the alphabet letters and were beginning to understand sound–symbol relationships. All of the children ended the year with many experiences with narrative and informational text, writing, and word study."

Through this snapshot of Mrs. Becky Schneider's classroom, the interplay between the elements of literacy instruction is easily seen. Children talked, listened to stories, interacted with text, and wrote on a daily basis.

Chapter 3

DEVELOPING LITERACY
AND ENGLISH LANGUAGE LEARNERS

I hate English! Mei Mei said in her head in Chinese. . . . In New York in school,
everything happened in English. Such a lonely language. Each letter stands alone and
makes its own noise. Not like Chinese.

—LEVINE (1989), *I Hate English!*

Mei Mei, like millions of English language learners (ELLs) across the United States,
comes to a new school environment in which a new language—English—is spoken.
Like Jim in *Will I Have a Friend?* (Cohen, 1967), ELL children are also looking for
friends at their new schools—and, in their cases, friends who share a common language
with them. In many situations, it may be relatively difficult for an ELL child
to find a friend who speaks the same language.

According to the U.S. Department of Education (2002), between 2001 and
2002 the total K–12 enrollment growth was 12%, whereas for students with limited
English proficiency (LEP), the enrollment growth was 95%. In 16 states, there was
more than 200% enrollment growth for LEP students between 1992 and 2002. In
addition, between 2001 and 2002, the K–12 total enrollment growth for the three
states with the largest K–12 enrollments—California (6.2 million), Texas (4.2 million),
and New York (2.9 million)—was 10.5%, 17.6%, and –5.3%, respectively.
The LEP students' enrollment growth in the three states, however, was 40.2%,
81.3%, and 44.3%, respectively. In these three states, Spanish, Vietnamese, Chinese,
Hmong, and Korean are common native languages of LEP students.

Across U.S. schools, additional support for LEP students varies from self-
contained bilingual instruction to self-contained English as a second language
(ESL) instruction. Some LEP students receive pull-out ESL instruction, while others
get push-in ESL instruction. The nature of the support for ELL children is
affected by such factors as politics (e.g., Proposition 227 in California and Proposition
203 in Arizona; Gutierrez et al., 2002), budgetary cuts, the rapidly increasing
number of ELL children with varied native languages, and the limited number of
teachers who are prepared in the theories and pedagogy of teaching ELL children. It

is likely that teaching the majority of ELL children, and in particular teaching them to be literate in English, has already or will soon become the responsibility of teachers in mainstream classrooms (Au, 2002; Neufeld & Fitzgerald, 2001).

Linguistic, Social, and Academic Challenges for ELL Children

What Do These Challenges Mean for ELL Children?

One may argue that all young children coming to school for the first time face the linguistic, social, and academic challenges that ELL children do. The challenges that ELL children experience, however, are unique. For many ELLs, the school environment may be the first place in which they are totally immersed in English with the absence of a native language. This excessive and sudden exposure to a new language can be frightening to young children. (We suggest to teachers of ELLs, "Just imagine that you, an adult, are in a place where an unfamiliar language is spoken and you are expected to understand it.") Furthermore, ELL children are expected and pressured to master, in a short period of time, the spoken English language, which native English-speaking children have taken years to develop (Ashworth & Wakefield, 1994). At school, ELL children must learn to speak *and* write a whole new language whereas their native English-speaking peers come to school to practice and improve their spoken English, as well as to learn the written language.

Although both ELL children and native English-speaking children make adjustments in order to become part of a new classroom community, the process of ELL children's becoming socially accepted by their peers is further complicated by their LEP status. Tabors (1997) has described this process as a "double bind" (p. 35). In other words, in order to be socially accepted by his or her English-speaking peers, an ELL child must be proficient in English and be able to communicate with his or her peers in English. In the meantime, the ELL child can develop his or her English proficiency *only* through communicating with his or her English-speaking peers. To put this another way, in order to communicate with peers, the ELL child needs to be accepted by his or her peers—and vice versa.

The academic challenges ELLs face are even more overwhelming. On top of trying to become part of a new classroom community, and learning to read and write in English (which is a new language to them), ELL children are also using English to learn in various content subjects. In other words, these children are expected to develop academic language while developing their communicative language. Cummins (1986) has referred to communicative language as *basic interpersonal communicative skills* (BICS) and academic language as *cognitive academic language proficiency* (CALP). BICS usually take ELL children 2–3 years to develop, while CALP requires 5–7 years for children to develop. The reason for this time difference is that children are usually exposed to a larger amount of communicative language than of academic language, both at school and at home. Some examples of BICS are talking with peers on the playground and understanding classroom routines. Examples of

CALP include responding to a book that has been read and presenting a research report.

What Do These Challenges Mean for Teachers?

The linguistic, social, and academic challenges that ELL children face during their first few years of schooling are interrelated, complex, and overwhelming. Research has indicated that ELL children follow patterns and processes of language and literacy development similar to those of their native English-speaking peers, and that helpful instructional strategies for native English-speaking children can also be effective for ELL children (Barone, 1996; Freeman & Freeman, 2000; Hudelson & Serna, 2002; Perez, 1998). The unique linguistic, social, and academic challenges for ELL children, however, complicate these patterns and processes, and teachers need to take these challenges into consideration during literacy instruction for these children. Furthermore, teachers need to be knowledgeable about beginning stages of ELL children's language development. Figure 3.1 provides an overview of this development and can be used as an assessment form.

Coming to Know ELL Children

In order for teachers to become acquainted with children from backgrounds different from their own, Nieto (2002) suggests that teachers "need to make a commitment to become *students of their students*" (p. 217; emphasis in original). What this means is that teachers must learn about their students' cultural, linguistic, and academic backgrounds. Although most schools require parents of ELLs to complete a home language survey that includes children's native language and the medium of communication at home, the survey often fails to provide classroom teachers with information that is unique to ELL children. For example, two children who both speak Chinese, but in two different dialects, will have literally no common language to communicate with each other. If their teacher has learned only from the survey that both children speak Chinese, the teacher may not understand why these two children do not talk to each other in the classroom. Figure 3.2 lists the areas about ELL children's backgrounds that are often not included in a home language survey. Information about siblings and friends, for example, may come in handy when teachers are looking for someone who can translate. Furthermore, knowledge of an ELL child's native language—in particular, the similarities and differences between English and the native language—can help a teacher understand why the child has difficulty with certain aspects of oral and written English language (Cary, 2000).

According to Cummins's (1989) *interdependence hypothesis*, to the extent that a child's native language and English share some underlying similarities, skills and strategies related to the native language can be transferred to learning in English, although the degree of transference will vary across different languages. For example, if a Spanish-speaking ELL child has mastered concepts about print in Spanish (an alphabetic language), he or she will probably grasp these concepts in English

FIGURE 3.1
Beginning Stages of Language Development

Name _____ Date _____

Silent/nonverbal stage

____ Using gestures and body language

Early production stage

____ Using telegraphic speech ("Water" for "I want to drink some water")

____ Combining words ("I water now" for "I want to drink some water now")

____ Using formulaic speech ("I am fine" in response to "How are you today?")

____ Using simple sentences to express basic needs and wishes ("I want to go to the movie")

____ Understanding simple commands

FIGURE 3.2
ELL Parent Survey

BACKGROUND INFORMATION

Student name in English: _____

Student name in native language: _____

Native language: _____

Dialect of native language: _____

Student age and birth date: _____

Preschool experiences

   In home country: _____

   In United States: _____

Grade levels of siblings: _____

Grade levels of friends: _____

Favorite things (e.g., food, sports, etc.): _____

_____

Holidays celebrated: _____

ORAL LANGUAGE

Fluency in native language	Fluency in English
____ Using telegraphic speech	____ Using telegraphic speech
____ Combining words	____ Combining words
____ Using formulaic speech	____ Using formulaic speech
____ Using simple sentences to express basic needs and wishes	____ Using simple sentences to express basic needs and wishes
____ Understanding simple commands	____ Understanding simple commands
____ Using productive language	

WRITTEN LANGUAGE

Literacy experience in native language	Literacy experience in English
____ Being read to	____ Being read to
____ Understanding of concepts about print	____ Understanding of concepts about print
____ "Pretend" reading	____ "Pretend" reading
____ Songs, chants, nursery rhymes	____ Songs, chants, nursery rhymes
____ Conventional reading	____ Conventional reading
____ Enjoyment of reading	____ Enjoyment of reading
____ Drawing pictures and scribbling	____ Drawing pictures and scribbling
____ Writing own name	____ Writing own name
____ Writing words to partially match a picture	____ Writing words to partially match a picture
____ Writing words to completely match a picture	____ Writing words to completely match a picture
____ Writing only words	____ Writing only words
____ Enjoyment of writing	____ Enjoyment of writing

more easily than a Japanese-speaking ELL child will, because Japanese is a non-alphabetic language and does not follow the same directionality.

Learning about an ELL child's native language can start with the child's parents. Parents often appreciate a teacher's efforts to learn about their native language, which results in additional respect for the teacher (International Reading Association [IRA], 2001). Community members and international students in nearby universities and colleges can also be resources. Still other sources of information about ELL children's native languages are children's books written in one or several native languages. A website, the Center for the Study of Books in Spanish for Children and Adolescents at (*www.csusm.edu/campus_centers/csb*), provides information on children's books written in Spanish and in both English and Spanish. *The Usborne First Thousand Words in Japanese* (Amery & Cartwright, 1995) provides some background knowledge about Japanese. *Hu Is a Tiger: An Introduction to Chinese Writing* (Goldstein, 1995) describes the Chinese writing system and provides some examples of Chinese characters. In *Table, Chair, Bear: A Book in Many Languages* (Feder, 1995), accompanying an English label for an object on each page are the corresponding labels in 12 different languages (i.e., Korean, French, Arabic, Vietnamese, Japanese, Portuguese, Lao, Spanish, Chinese [Mandarin], Tagalog, Cambodian, and Navajo). *Who Says a Dog Goes Bow-Wow?* (De Zutter, 1993) invites readers to experience saying "Bow-wow" in 10 different languages. Finally, with a click of a mouse, teachers can gain access to various native languages on the Internet. One interesting and useful website is the Southern California Multi-Language Station (*www.kscitv.com*). Selecting 1 of the 14 languages on the homepage, readers will be able to read a description of a TV show in English and in a native language.

Learning about ELL children's native languages also allows teachers to experience the discomfort, anxiety, frustration, or lack of self-confidence that these children go through when they come to a school where English is the only language spoken. To sample these feelings, teachers can read the short paragraph in Figure 3.3 that is written in English and translated into Chinese; they can then jot down the similarities and differences they notice between English and Chinese.

Creating a Nonthreatening, Language- and Print-Rich Classroom Environment

Welcoming ELL Children

Creating a nonthreatening classroom environment (Krashen & Terrell, 1983) starts with a teacher's smile and interest in ELL children and their native languages. Importantly, on the first day of the school, the teacher welcomes all children and their parents with a smile, and pays close attention to the conversation in a native language between an ELL child and an adult or adults. Even though the teacher may not understand a word in such a conversation, paying attention to their communication (rather than frowning and walking away from the child and adults) sends a powerful message: The teacher cares about and respects each child, shows an inter-

FIGURE 3.3
Learning about Chinese

English:

Mei Mei, like millions of English language learners (ELLs) across the United States, comes to a new school environment in which a new language—English—is spoken. Like Jim in *Will I Have a Friend?* (Cohen, 1967), ELL children are also looking for friends at their new schools—and, in their cases, friends who share a common language with them. In many situations, it may be relatively difficult for an ELL child to find a friend who speaks the same language.

Chinese:

像成千上萬在美國學習英語的孩子,美美來到一個新學校環境裡,

學習一種新語言--英語。像我會有一個朋友嗎?一書中的吉姆 (Cohen,

1967),學習英語的孩子也想要在他們的新學校裡尋找朋友。對他們

來講,他們要尋找會講同樣母語的朋友。在許多情況下,他們也許相

對地不容易找到講同樣母語的朋友。

Similarities:

Differences:

est in the language that the child is able to speak, and thus provides a welcoming environment!

In addition to welcoming smiles, a classroom needs to be an environment that is not totally unfamiliar and strange to ELL children. Many parents of young ELL children have noted that during the first few months of the school year, their children often feel lost and afraid, because they have lost control of the world that is familiar to them. This unfamiliarity can result from the absence of native languages, the massive presence of the English language, unknown classmates, and complicated classroom routines. To create a relatively familiar classroom environment for ELL children, teachers can ask parents to bring print materials or environmental print in a native language (e.g., menus, books, newspapers), as well as photos about the children's life experiences (e.g., family gatherings) or pictures reminiscent of the children's home countries or cultural experiences (e.g., holiday celebrations). All of these materials are posted around the classroom. Such materials not only help bring ELL children's familiar world to the classroom, but also provide native English-speaking children in the classroom with opportunities to learn about other cultures and languages (Au, 2002).

For some ELL children, a familiar world can exist only when they see their familiar objects. A teacher may need to allow an ELL child to bring an object (e.g., a stuffed animal, a small birthday present) that comforts him or her (in the same way that a cozy blanket makes a young child not afraid during the night). This special object may also become a faithful listener for the ELL child when he or she wants to speak a native language and later to practice speaking English. Each child's object can become the first show-and-tell item that holds special meaning.

Developing a Language- and Print-Rich Classroom

A nonthreatening classroom does not exclude the presence of language and print in both English and native languages. A language- and print-rich classroom provides ELL children with opportunities to become comfortable and familiar with English, and to explore its functions and conventions (which may share similarities with a native language). To create a language- and print-rich environment, teachers need to start at a personal level and then move on to a more academic level. Here are several suggestions.

• Paste a picture of each child in the classroom next to the child's name label on the desk. At the beginning of the school year, English names do not make much sense to ELL children, but pictures do.

• Post the first names of all children on the wall, and avoid last names. In some languages (e.g., Chinese, Korean), a family name or surname is not called a *last* name, as in English; it is written before the first name. It would be confusing to ELL children if both the last name and the first name of each child were listed. Alphabetize first names, so that the names can provide a point of reference while teaching letter names and sounds of the alphabet. Also, paste each child's picture next to his or her first name.

- Give each student a name tag to wear, so that all children can learn their peers' names. Ask parents to write ELL children's names in their native languages below or above their English names, if the native and English names differ.

- Label the classroom, but do not overwhelm ELL children. Start with the most important words that ELL children need to know in order to survive the classroom routines (e.g., *desk, table, book, pencil,* and *crayon*). Introduce five labels per week, and review old labels frequently as new labels are introduced. Create a word wall for the labels. For each English label on the word wall, include as many equivalents in children's native languages as possible (see Figure 3.4 for one set of examples). These help bring familiarity to the classroom and may also help children better understand English labels if they have mastered sight words in a native language.

- Decorate the classroom with children's writing samples. Post book jackets of high-quality children's literature. Have books of varied topics and interests accessible to students throughout the classroom, not just in the library area.

- Most important of all, keep in mind that a language- and print-rich classroom is an environment where every child is encouraged to interact with peers, and to write, read, listen to, and evaluate various texts.

Familiarizing ELL Children with the Classroom Routine

A nonthreatening, language- and print-rich classroom is also characterized by children's familiarity with classroom routines. The classroom routines in U.S. schools are not always similar to those in ELL children's preschools or schools in their home countries. Even if the children were born in the United States, their parents may have described their own experiences with school routines in their home countries to the children, who thus may not know about classroom routines in U.S. schools.

FIGURE 3.4. An English label with labels in children's native languages on the word wall.

Becoming familiar with classroom routines is crucial to ELL children's participation in various language and literacy events.

Many teachers in kindergarten classrooms use a combination of pictures and words to display the daily schedule on a board or in a pocket chart. Displaying the daily schedule is not enough, however. Teachers need to draw children's attention to how the class moves from one activity to another as described on the schedule. During the first several weeks of the school year, Cindy Chon explained her schedule to her kindergartners, half of whom were non-English-proficient. The daily schedule was displayed in the pocket chart, and there was a clock next to the schedule. For each activity, Mrs. Chon displayed a card giving the time for that activity (e.g., 8:10–8:25), a card with a picture of the activity (e.g., a calendar or reading a book), and a card with the word for the activity (e.g., *calendar*). Following is some of her discussion with her students:

> MRS. CHON: Good morning, boys and girls! It is 8:10 (*pointing at the clock and then the 8:10–8:25 card*). It is our calendar time (*pointing at the calendar next to the board, and holding up the appropriate picture card and word from the pocket chart*). [The class then engaged in the calendar time activity.]

> MRS. CHON: (*After the class finished the activity*) Now we are finished with our calendar time (*pointing at the calendar, holding up the picture and word cards, and turning the cards over*). It is 8:25 (*pointing at the clock and the 8:25–8:50 card*). It's our read-aloud time (*holding up the book to be read, together with the appropriate picture and word cards from the pocket chart*). [The class then engaged in the read-aloud activity.]

> MRS. CHON: (*At the end of the day*) Who remembers what we learned first today? (*Setting the clock to 8:10 and pointing at the clock; some children raised their hands to volunteer.*) José [a beginning ELL child], who is your friend? [Mrs. Chon always asked two children to come up to arrange the cards for the schedule.]

> JOSÉ: Lan [another beginning ELL child].

> MRS. CHON: Good! (*Talking to both José and Lan*) What did we do at 8:10 (*pointing at the clock*)?

> JOSÉ AND LAN: (*Turning over the picture card of a calendar and the word card*)

> MRS. CHON: What did we do?

> JOSÉ: (*Pointing at the calendar*)

> MRS. CHON: (*To Lan*) We had calendar time, right (*pointing at the calendar*)?

> LAN: (*Nodding his head*) Ca-ca.

> MRS. CHON: Calendar. At 8:10, we had our calendar time (*pointing again at the clock, the calendar, the time card, and the word card*).

In this example, Mrs. Chon not only helped children learn about the daily routines of her classroom, but also invited ELL children to practice oral language and interact with print. Familiarizing children with the routines in Mrs. Chon's class-room became a language and literacy activity for the children.

Providing Comprehensible Input in Oral and Written Language

When teachers use comprehensible input (Krashen, 1985) during instruction and communication with ELL children, they adjust their speech to the level that ELL children can understand. Teachers also adjust the difficulty level of a written text so that ELL children can comprehend the text.

Oral Language

Slowing Down Speech

The most important way for teachers to provide ELL children with comprehensible input is to slow down their speech (Echevarria, Vogt, & Short, 2000). Teachers who are native English speakers seldom realize how fast their speech is. The rate of speech that seems normal to native English speakers may be considered too fast by ELL children, who may just hear a series of sounds. As Mei Mei in *I Hate English!* (Levine, 1989) describes, "Each letter stands alone and makes its own noise. Not like Chinese." Teachers can slow down their speech by enunciating each word clearly and by repeating key words and sentences. It is especially important for teachers to slow down their speech when explaining and providing directions, because how much ELL children understand what teachers have said directly affects their performance. Teachers may increase the speed of their speech as their ELL children's proficiency level increases. Although speech at a reduced rate is compre-hensible input, ELL children also need to be exposed to English at a normal rate, which is more natural and authentic. Teachers can achieve a balance of slowed speech and authentic language by speaking at a normal rate and then at a slowed rate for beginning ELL children. When repeating speech at a slowed rate, teachers include key words and phrases, if necessary.

Using Objects, Pictures, and Gestures

In addition to slowing down their speech, teachers can use objects, pictures, and gestures to accompany their talk (Cary, 2000). For example, while going through her daily routine for calendar time, Mrs. Chon frequently referred to objects. She pointed at the clock and the calendar while saying, "It is 8:10. It is our calendar time." Referring to objects can also help ELL children understand a concept that is difficult to explain, even with slowed speech. For example, in helping ELL children grasp the concepts of *smooth* and *rough*, teachers may ask children to feel the surface of a desk while saying "smooth," and to feel the carpet while saying "rough." Although not all objects can be available to accompany speech, teachers can use pictures. A picture of snow-covered mountains provides some background information about snow for ELL children from countries with warm climates.

In a similar way, gestures add clarity to speech. For example, a teacher can make a sad face to show children what the word *sad* means, or use *total physical response* (TPR; Krashen & Terrell, 1983) to show children various behaviors related to literacy activities throughout the day. Telling an ELL child to read a book silently may be confusing. If the teacher opens a book and uses TPR to demonstrate the act of reading silently, an ELL child will have a better chance of understanding how to follow the teacher's direction. Similarly, while saying, "Go to the writing center," the teacher demonstrates the command by actually walking to the writing center.

Avoiding Idioms

Teachers' speech that is comprehensible to ELL children is also free of idioms (Echevarria, Vogt, & Short, 2004). Idioms are often culturally bound and difficult for ELL children to understand. For example, few native English speakers can explain why the idiom "easy as pie" is used to describe easiness, when making a pie is actually not easy for many people. In many other cultures, the idioms similar to "easy as pie" seem to make more sense. In Thai, easiness is expressed by "easy as peeling a banana," and in Chinese by "easy as turning your hands." In classrooms with ELL children, teachers should avoid using idioms as much as possible.

Using Simple Commands

Another way to make speech comprehensible is to use simple commands rather than requests. The request "Can you please open your book?" is confusing to ELL children, because the request is in the form of a question. Children respond to the request with a "yes" or "no" rather than performing the act of opening a book. If the simple command "Please open your book" is used, children will not be confused.

Written Language

Comprehensible input in a second language for ELL children, as Krashen (1993) has noted, must also be provided in written language. A text that is comprehensible to ELL children contains language and content/concepts that are not overwhelming to these children. For example, *Shapes, Shapes, Shapes* (Hoban, 1986) has pictures of various shapes that children see in their environments (e.g., a chair and a manhole cover), but there is not one word of English in the book. Another book, *The Shapes of Things* (Dodds, 1994) is also about shapes, but it has several clauses on one page: "A square is just a square, until you add a roof, two windows and a door, then it's much, much more!" Although both books focus on the concept of shapes, the second book, *The Shapes of Things*, will be more overwhelming and at times threatening to an ELL child than the first book, *Shapes, Shapes, Shapes*.

In providing comprehensible input, teachers also need to take into consideration ELL children's understandings of the concepts discussed in books. Although some concepts (e.g., colors) are universal, others are culturally bound. A U.S. breakfast includes food ranging from cold cereals to hot cereals to eggs and bacon. A breakfast can be cooked or not cooked. In other parts of the world, like in China, everything for a breakfast, such as soy milk, porridge, and steamed or baked buns, is cooked. So the concept of *breakfast* in English may entail types of food and methods of preparation different from those in Chinese. Given the culturally specific nature of certain concepts, a text whose language is comprehensible to ELL children can still be difficult for them to understand. Taking the issues of both language and content/concepts into consideration, Freeman and Freeman (2000) and Gibbons (2002) suggest that teachers need to provide students with books and other reading materials that are predictable, familiar, and interesting; that include high-quality illustrations or other visual aids; that integrate content and language; and that provide authentic language.

Predictability

A predictable text has repetitive or cumulative patterns, and often rhyme and rhythm as well. When ELL children are read a predictable text, they are exposed to the same linguistic pattern multiple times. For example, in *Brown Bear, Brown Bear, What Do You See?* (Martin, 1967), children hear and see the linguistic pattern "[adjective(s)] + [name of an animal], what do you see?" on every page. Their increasing familiarity with this recurring linguistic pattern is more likely to allow them to join in with the teacher in shared reading of the text. A predictable text also provides ELL children with a sense of security, as they can anticipate what types of sentences they are going to hear and see on the following pages.

Familiarity

The predictability of a book's language increases its familiarity to children. Other aspects of a book's familiarity come from its content or concepts. As mentioned earlier, content/concepts are often culturally bound, and a book whose concepts are familiar to native English-speaking children may seem strange to ELL children. For example, in *The Mouse Mess* (Riley, 1997), the foods the mouse ate—cornflakes, syrup, cheese, and juice—may be unfamiliar to ELL children from Asian countries, where mice often eat rice. To increase the familiarity of a book, teachers need to be aware of ELL children's prior knowledge, and to supplement this knowledge if children lack information on the content or concepts presented in the book. The following are different types of books that may bring familiarity to ELL children.

• *Bilingual books.* Children's native language helps make an unfamiliar book written in English familiar to them. *In My Family/En Mi Familia* (Garza, 1996), written in both English and Spanish, adds familiarity to the text through Spanish and through descriptions of family events similar to those Spanish-speaking children have experienced.

- *Books reflecting native cultures.* In many cultures, there are folktales and other stories similar to those in U.S. English culture. If children are exposed to books in English that tell stories reflecting their native cultures before they are read the English-culture versions of the same stories, they may feel less intimidated, because they have some prior knowledge about the stories. Some examples of these books are *Lon Po Po: A Real Red Riding Hood Story from China* (Young, 1989) and *The Three Little Javelinas* (Lowell, 1992).

- *Books with environmental print.* Miss Bindergarten Stays Home from Kindergarten (Slate, 2000) includes many types of environmental print that children see in their own classroom, such as children's name tags, labels for the cubbies, and words on the bulletin board.

- *Books about survival.* When books describe situations similar to those that children may have been going through themselves (e.g., going to kindergarten, going to a doctor's office, and learning a new language), they may be interested in finding out how the characters in the book deal with the situations (Hadaway, Vardell, & Young, 2002). For example, Slate's (1996) *Miss Bindergarten Gets Ready for Kindergarten* describes how the kindergarten children and Miss Bindergarten are getting ready for their first day of class: "Adam Krupp wakes up. Brenda Heath brushes her teeth. . . . Miss Bindergarten gets ready for kindergarten."

- *Books adapted from children's TV shows and movies.* Although some books based on children's TV shows or movies may be above ELL children's English proficiency levels, the illustrations in the books mostly resemble what they have seen in the TV or movie sources. This prior experience increases the familiarity of these books. Having TV- and movie-based books available to ELL children motivates them to interact with print (see Table 3.1 for a list of such books).

- *Books with the same concept/theme.* Books with the same concept (e.g., counting, weather) or the same theme (e.g., good vs. evil, as in three little pigs fighting a bad wolf) increase familiarity for children, thus helping them focus on meanings rather than linguistic features of the books (Freeman & Freeman, 2000). Same-theme books can be used during read-aloud, shared reading, guided reading, and other reading activities.

- *Books written by the same author.* After children have read several books by the same author, they become relatively familiar with the storylines, the linguistic patterns, and the style of illustrations (Krashen, 1985, 1993). For example, after children have had some prior experiences with *Brown Bear, Brown Bear, What Do You See* (Martin, 1967), the linguistic patterns in *Polar Bear, Polar Bear, What Do You Hear?* (Martin, 1991) should not be too unfamiliar to them. Children who have been read *If You Give a Mouse a Cookie* (Numeroff, 1985) are more likely to be familiar with the pattern of the storyline in other books by Numeroff, such as *If You Give a Moose a Muffin* (1991), *If You Give a Pig a Pancake* (1998a), *If You Take a Mouse to the Movies* (2000a), and *If You Take a Mouse to School* (2002). In a similar way, after ELL children have read one version of *The Three Little Pigs*, they may have had some prior knowledge about other versions of the same story.

TABLE 3.1. Books Adapted from Children's TV Shows or Movies

Beechen, A. (2001). *The wild Thornberrys: The cat's meow.* New York: Simon Spotlight.
Bourgeois, P. (1997). *Franklin's bad day.* Toronto: Kids Can Press.
Bridwell, N. (1988). *Clifford's birthday party.* New York: Scholastic.
Cousins, L. (1999). *Maisy's pool.* Cambridge, MA: Candlewick Press.
Daugherty, G. (2002). *Sagwa, the Chinese Siamese cat: Acrobat cats.* New York: Scholastic.
Daveport, A. (1998). *Teletubbies: Go, Po, go!* New York: Scholastic.
Dowdy, L. C. (1997). *Barney goes to the dentist.* New York: Barney.
Egan, C. (2002). *Lilo and Stitch: Say cheese!* New York: Random House.
Gold, R. (2001). *Rugrats: Phil and Lil go to the doctor.* New York: Simon Spotlight.
Mooney, E. S. (2000). *The PowerPuff Girls: Snow-off.* New York: Scholastic.
Muldrow, D. (1999). *Pokemon counting book.* New York: Golden Books.
Redmond, D. (2001). *Bob the builder: Bob's birthday.* New York: Simon Spotlight.
Santomero, A. C. (1998). *Blue's clues: Blue skidoos to the farm.* New York: Simon Spotlight.
Sesame Street. (1997). *Little Ernie's animal friends.* New York: Random House.
Smith, G. (2001). *SpongeBob SquarePants: The good, the bad, and the krabby.* New York: Golden Books.
Snyder, M. (2000). *Dragon tales: Ord and the shining star.* New York: Random House.
Wasserman, R. (2000). *Search for Scooby snacks.* New York: Scholastic.
Wilson, S. (2002). *Dora the explorer: Little star.* New York: Simon Spotlight.
Zoehfeld, K. W. (1997). *Pooh's first day of school.* New York: Disney Press.

Illustrations and Other Visual Aids

Illustrations in books and pictures in environmental print logos provide contextual clues to support the written text. In *Cars! Cars! Cars!* (Maccarone, 1995), an informational book that describes different types of cars, there are two groups of cars on the first page. Under the first group (just one car) is the phrase "One car," and under the second group is the phrase "Two cars." There is "1" written on one car and "2" on another car. On another page, the phrase "Yellow car" is written under a yellow car, and the phrase "Blue car" is under a blue car. The illustrations explain the text, and the text is placed under the illustrations consistently across all pages. The supportive nature of the illustrations, and the consistency in the positional relationship between a picture and a text, help increase the familiarity of the book.

In a storybook, illustrations play an even more important role in helping ELL children comprehend the text. On the first page of *If You Give a Mouse a Cookie* (Numeroff, 1985), accompanying the text "If you give a mouse a cookie . . . " is a picture of a boy giving a mouse a cookie. On the second page, the picture of the boy opening the door to his house, and of the mouse running toward the door, supports the text "he's going to ask for a glass of milk." On the third page, the picture of the mouse drinking from a glass of milk while the boy is holding the glass accompanies the text "When you give him the milk . . . " It is important for teachers to keep in mind that not all illustrations support text. Some pictures may look appealing, but they may not be supportive of the text. This can be true for a book with too much text on one page, and with pictures that are not illustrative of the text.

Engagingness

A text that engages children possesses predictability, familiarity, and supportive illustrations/visual aids. More importantly, it invites children to think actively about the story or information while they are being read to or in independent reading. An engaging text has an interesting story plot or information related to children's life experience, invites children to predict and to confirm or disconfirm their predictions, allows them to make connections, and provides them with an opportunity to play with language and have a good laugh. Following are some examples of engaging texts.

- *Text with an interesting plot.* In *If You Take a Mouse to School* (Numeroff, 2002), children are interested in finding out what a mouse will do in a school when he is taken there.
- *Text with interesting information.* In *I Love Trucks!* (Sturges, 1999), simple text with about five words on most pages provides children with information about various trucks they see in their environment.
- *Text allowing for prediction.* In *The Little Mouse, the Red Ripe Strawberry, and the Big Hungry Bear* (Wood & Wood, 1984), the simple story with one or two sentences on most pages invites children to predict how the mouse will hide the ripe strawberry that he has found from the big hungry bear, and eat it himself.
- *Text allowing for making connections.* In *What Daddies Do Best; What Mommies Do Best* (Numeroff, 1998b) and *What Grandmas Do Best; What Grandpas Do Best* (Numeroff, 2000b), simple text with one sentence on each page helps children think about things that they often do with their parents and grandparents, thus engaging children in making a text-to-self connection.
- *Text with fun language.* Dr. Seuss's books for beginning readers, as well as *Sheep Out to Eat* (Shaw, 1992), *Sheep Trick or Treat* (Shaw, 1997), *Sheep in a Shop* (Shaw, 1991), and other sheep adventure stories by Shaw, allow children to listen to the rhythm and rhyme in each text, and have a good laugh at the silly stories.

Authenticity

An authentic text has language that children hear, see, and read in their environments both at school and at home. While in many states decodable texts have become part of literacy curriculum, teachers need to find texts with authentic and natural language to supplement the literacy curriculum.

In summary, a text that facilitates ELLs' language and literacy development needs to have a good combination of predictability, familiarity, supportive illustrations, engagingness, and authenticity. Teachers can use Figure 3.5 as a guide for selecting books for ELL children, and also to check for a wide range of books in the classroom. The more "Yes" boxes checked, the more books with comprehensible input there are available to use with ELL children.

FIGURE 3.5
Book Selection Guide for ELL Children

	Yes	No
Predictability		
The book has repetitive patterns.		
The book has cumulative patterns.		
The book has rhyme and rhythm.		
Familiarity		
The book is bilingual.		
The book reflects native culture.		
The book has environmental print.		
The book is about survival.		
The book is adapted from a children's TV show or movie.		
The book is one of several books with the same concept or theme.		
The book is one of several books written by the same author.		
Illustrations/visual aids		
The book's illustrations support the written book.		
The book has a consistency in positional relationship between illustration and print.		
Engagingness		
The book has an interesting plot.		
The book has interesting information.		
The book allows for predicting.		
The book allows for making connections.		
The book has fun language.		
Authenticity		
The book has language children hear, see, and read in their natural environments.		

Scaffolding ELL Children's Language and Literacy Learning

Like the corresponding section of Chapter 2, this section is organized around language and literacy learning and teaching in the areas of oral language, reading, writing, and word study. All these four areas, however, are integrated into actual teaching and learning (IRA, 2001). Reading aloud, for example, provides ELL children with comprehensible input of the oral language; it helps children become familiar with the linguistic units of the English language (i.e., phonemes, words, phrases, sentences, and connected discourse). Comprehension can be taught through a follow-up activity on the book (e.g., sequencing events), and children can practice writing through their responding to the book read. Finally, word study can focus on identifying words in the book that start with a target sound (e.g., words starting with the /t/ sound). Many activities presented in Chapter 2 can effectively help ELL children with teachers' scaffolding (Vygotsky, 1978). When teachers scaffold children's learning, they support children in terms of providing comprehensible input, modeling, and inviting children to participate.

Oral Language

Oral language development is most crucial to ELL children. Whereas their native English-speaking peers have not been pressured to develop oral language, ELL children have to develop both their basic communicative skills and some academic language within a short period of time. These children urgently need extensive exposure to authentic and high-quality oral language within various social settings. The following are some activities that support ELL children's oral language development.

Reading Aloud

Reading aloud benefits ELL children in many of the same ways that it does for native English-speaking children (Cunningham & Allington, 1999; Hadaway et al., 2002; Krashen, 1993). With the unique needs of ELL children, however, teachers' scaffolding is needed. Here are some suggestions:

- Start with a book that provides ELL children with comprehensible input (see Figure 3.5 for the guide on selecting books). Use a big-book version of the book, so that children can see the text and pictures.
- Do a picture walk through the book before reading it. A picture walk allows children to get a sense of what the book is about, thus helping them activate or build their prior knowledge (Fountas & Pinnell, 1996).
- Talk about the book conventions (e.g., front cover, author[s], illustrator[s], title page, and back cover) before reading. Read the book with a slowed speech rate during the first reading; then resume a normal rate of speech gradually during subsequent readings. This provides ELL children with an opportunity first to hear English words clearly and later to be exposed to authentic English speech.

- Select a few key content words that are central to the book after the first reading of the book. For example, in the book *Rains* (Kalan, 1978), the word *rains* appears on most pages. Write the word *rains* on a board or on a card for the word wall, and use a highlight tape to highlight the word in the book. Before the second reading of the book, review the word *rains*. During each subsequent reading of the book, highlight other content words, such as *house, grass, road,* and *car.* Highlight one or two words during each reading of the book. Because these key words are explicitly supported by the illustration of the book, their meanings are relatively easy for children to grasp. While pointing at these words in the book during each reading, also point at the picture that each word represents (e.g., *rains* for the rains across the page).

- Encourage children to make connections between the text and themselves. For children who are at the silent nonverbal stage of language development, give them pictures with phrases or sentences. For example:

  - After reading *Rains* several times, model how to respond to the book by holding up a picture with a happy face and the sentence "I like rains" under the face. Also nod the head while saying, "I like rains."
  - Next model the response "I don't like rains," by shaking the head and holding up a picture with a not-so-happy face and the sentence "I don't like rains" under the face.
  - Then ask two children to come up to the front to demonstrate how they would respond to the book. Each child is asked to pick up a picture with a happy face or with a not-so-happy face. As you say, "I like the rains," nod the head and hold up one child's hand with the picture of a happy face. As you say, "I don't like rains," shake the head and hold up another child's hand with the picture of a not-so-happy face.
  - Conduct a guided practice with children, using one of the two picture cards and the body language (i.e., nodding the head or shaking the head).

- For children who are at the early production stage, encourage them to respond to the book. Incomplete sentences or sentences in broken English should be acceptable. If they are shy or feel uncomfortable with sharing in the class, ask them to whisper their responses to a buddy or to you (the teacher).

Acting Out a Story

When children act out a story that has been read to them, they are given a chance to demonstrate their understanding of the story through actions. Acting out is a useful strategy for children who are at the silent/nonverbal and early production stages (Herrell, 2000). For example, during acting out the story *The Very Hungry Caterpillar* (Carle, 1967), each child in a group of seven children is given a card with a day of the week (e.g., *On Monday*) and props (e.g., one apple or two pears). The teacher reads the story from the beginning. When the teacher gets to "On Monday," the first child with the *On Monday* card says "On Monday" if he or she is verbal, or holds up the card if he or she is at the nonverbal stage. Then he or she acts out eating an apple. The teacher continues by saying, "But he was still hungry." Each of the remaining six children takes turns saying the words on the card or holds up the card, and then acts out eating the food. The teacher says the rest of the story till the last sentence, "He was a beautiful butterfly!", which the children in the audience say chorally.

As children's English proficiency increases, the teacher decreases the number of words he or she says during acting out. Gradually, the teacher changes the strategy from acting out a story to Readers' Theatre, during which children mostly read their script adapted from a book and do some action. The process should start with predictable or pattern books, as they are easy for the teacher to convert a text to a script and for children to produce sentences with a linguistic pattern. Books like *Brown Bear, Brown Bear, What Do You See?* (Martin, 1967), *Polar Bear, Polar Bear, What Do You Hear?* (Martin, 1991), and *There Was an Old Lady Who Swallowed a Fly* (Taback, 1997) are fun for children to use in Readers' Theatre.

Play Centers

Literacy-related play centers as described in Chapter 2 are crucial for ELL children to develop communicative skills for varying social settings. Teachers start with the centers that are most familiar to children, such as a house and a classroom. They furnish each center with props, and most importantly with print materials (e.g., cereal boxes, newspapers, and utility bills for a house). Teachers encourage parents to bring props and print items unique to ELL children's cultures and languages, and invite parents to be coplayers in the centers. Utilizing funds of knowledge (Moll, 1994) from the community enriches the multicultural and multilingual experiences of all children in the class, and also makes the classroom a more familiar environment for ELL children. Vukelich, Christie, and Enz (2002) describe different roles that a teacher can take at a play center, ranging from a stage manager who prepares materials for the center to a coplayer who participates in the play with children. For ELLs, it is important that teachers take on the role of coplayers, so that they can model for children how to communicate in a certain setting. In particular, teachers model for children the formulaic sentences used in one particular setting, such as the expressions used in a store: "Do you want the dress or shorts? Do the shorts sound okay?"

Media Center

In a media center, children can listen to the tapes of the books that teachers or others have read to them. Listening to the tape and reading the book allow children to match sounds with words and to learn to read with expression. Encourage children to point at words while listening. A buddy system for children enables them to share or discuss what they have heard. Teachers can include a TV/VCR in the media center, so that children can watch their favorite TV shows or movies. Keeping the mute button on, so that captions appear on TV, allows children to see the words while they are watching. A computer in the media center will also be very helpful to children (see Chapter 5). Ideally, teachers can have books adapted from TV shows and movies available in the listening center. Children can listen to a book on tape, watch the show or movie from which the book is adapted, and visit the website that features the show or movie. Multiple sources of linguistic input with the same content make the information familiar and predictable.

Assessment of Oral Language

As discussed in Chapter 2, assessment of children's oral language requires the teacher to observe children during various literacy events. For ELL children who are at the silent or nonverbal stage, their oral language output will be none or minimal. However, they are often good observers of how and when language is appropriately used. Xu (1996) documented the literacy experience of a Tagalog-speaking kindergartner, Emily, in an English-only classroom. She used different strategies during the process of becoming proficient in oral language and learning about English written language. Emily's evolving interaction patterns and strategies included (1) the no-response pattern in conjunction with the observing strategy; (2) the active response pattern in conjunction with the observing and imitating strategies; and (3) the active initiation pattern in conjunction with the observing, imitating, and confirming strategies. Therefore, assessment of ELL children's oral language needs to include their behaviors. Figure 3.6 is a form that can be used in this assessment.

Reading

Scholars in the fields of second-language acquisition (Cummins, 2002; Krashen, 1993; Krashen & Terrell, 1983) and of literacy research (Au, 2002; Fitzgerald & Noblit, 1999; Neufeld & Fitzgerald, 2001) have stressed that literacy instruction in a second language should focus on helping children construct meanings, not just on helping them learn the surface linguistic features of the second language. That said, the instructional strategies and materials discussed in Chapter 2 can also be applied to ELL children if their unique needs are taken into consideration.

Using Wordless Books

Wordless books present little linguistic challenge to ELL children, as there is no English print in such books. Children can form their own story based on the illustrations of a wordless book (Flatley & Rutland, 1986). They can tell the story in a native language (which can later be translated into English by parents or community members) or in English, using words, phrases, or sentences (depending on their English proficiency level). Therefore, children at various stages of oral language development can participate in telling a story based on a wordless book (Hadaway et al., 2002; Xu, 2003). See Table 3.2 for a list of wordless books.

FIGURE 3.6
Assessment of ELL Children's Oral Language

Stages and characteristics	Examples	Settings
Silent/nonverbal stage		
Observed behaviors (e.g., nodding, moving closer to the book)		
Observed strategies (e.g., imitating, repeating)		
Early production stage		
Telegraphic speech		
Combining words		
Formulaic speech		
Using simple sentences		
Understanding simple commands		
Productive discourse stage		
Communicative speech (BICS) (e.g., "Can I borrow your black crayon? I can't find mine")		
Academic language (CALP) (e.g., "I like the story because it reminds me of . . . ")		

TABLE 3.2. Wordless Books

Baker, J. (1991). *Window*. New York: Greenwillow Books.
Bang, M. (1980). *The gray lady and the strawberry snatcher*. New York: Simon & Schuster.
Banyai, I. (1995). *Zoom*. New York: Viking.
Briggs, R. (1978). *The snowman*. New York: Random House.
Carle, E. (1973). *I see a song*. New York: Crowell.
Day, A. (1991). *Good dog, Carl!* New York: Simon & Schuster.
Mercer, M. (1992). *A boy, a dog, and a frog*. New York: Dial Books.
Spier, P. (1982). *Rain*. Garden City, NY: Doubleday.
Tafuri, N. (1984). *Have you seen my duckling?* New York: Greenwillow Books.
Veitzman, J. P. (1998). *You can't take a balloon into the Metropolitan Museum*. New York: Dial
   Books.
Veitzman, J. P., & Glasser, R, B. (2000). *You can't take a balloon into the National Gallery*. New
   York: Dial Books.
Ward, L. (1992). *The silver pony: A story in pictures*. Boston: Houghton Mifflin.
Wiesner, D. (1991). *Tuesday*. Boston: Houghton Mifflin.
Wiesner, D. (1998). *Fire fall*. New York: Lothrop, Lee & Shepard Books.
Wilson, A. (1999). *Magpie magic: A tale of colorful mischief*. New York: Dial Books.

While children are telling the story, the teacher can write down the words, phrases, or sentences on Post-it Notes and then tape each note on its corresponding page. Or the teacher can type text for each page on a sentence strip and then place each strip under its corresponding page. If a wordless book has been read frequently across a period of time, both the teacher and children may be surprised to learn that the amount of language used in the story has been increased, that words and sentence patterns in the story have become more diverse, and that the quality of the story has been improved. The following example shows how Maria Lopez, a kindergarten teacher, used *Do You Want to Be My Friend?* (Carle, 1971) to facilitate her students' comprehension. Her class included native English-speaking children and ELL children at the nonverbal and beginning stages.

MS. LOPEZ: Boys and girls, today we are going to read this book, *Do You Want to Be My Friend?* (*holding up the book and pointing at the title*).

MING: Book?

MS. LOPEZ: Yeah, this is a book with no words. Let me show you (*turning through the pages for a picture walk*). We are going to make a story. To put words in here, here, here . . . (*referring to the blank space on each page*). Then this book will be like this one (*turning through the pages of the book* The Very Hungry Caterpillar [*Carle, 1967*]).

MING: Oh.

ROSA: Writing the book?

MS. LOPEZ: Yes, we are writing the book. [After reading the title and talking about the author/illustrator, Ms. Lopez read the sentence on the first page where there is a mouse and partial picture of an animal's tail, "Do you want to be my friend?"] What is this (*referring to the mouse*)?

MIEN: M-M-M-, not like *cat*.

MS. LOPEZ: A mouse. You are right. A mouse does not like a cat (*writing down* mouse *on a Post-it Note and sticking it next to the mouse*). What is this (*referring to the partial picture of an animal's tail*)? (*After waiting for a minute and noting that nobody was responding*) Think (*referring to her head*). What is this?

GARY: A brush.

MS. LOPEZ: Good thinking. It looks like a brush (*writing down* brush *on a Post-it Note and pasting it next to the tail*). Any other answers? (*After seeing Maria touch her hair*) Good thinking. It could be hair, Maria. It looks like hair, a ponytail (*writing down* hair *on a Post-it Note and pasting it next to the tail*). Any more answers? (*Silence*) I'm going to turn the page. Are you ready? (*Turning the page*) Now it is a . . .

DING: Tail.

CLASS: Oh, no!

MS. LOPEZ: It is a tail! It's okay. We had fun guessing (*turning to the previous page and pasting the Post-it Note with* tail *next to the tail*). [After the teacher and the children labeled all the animals during two periods of reading and language arts block time, they went back to the first page to add more sentences.]

MS. LOPEZ: What can we write on this page (*referring to the page where the mouse is asking the horse, represented by its tail, a question*)?

MING: Mouse say this (*referring to the sentence in the speech bubble*, "Do you want to be my friend?")

MS. LOPEZ: You are right. The mouse is saying this sentence (*referring to the sentence*).

TRAVIS: He is asking a question.

MS. LOPEZ: How do you know he is asking a question?

TRAVIS: Here (*referring to the question mark*).

MS. LOPEZ: Good. You are right. A question mark tells you this is a question. We ask a question, but not say a question. What should I write on the Post-it Note?

MING: Mouse ask the question, here (*referring to the question in the speech bubble*).

MS. LOPEZ: Good. The mouse asks the question, "Do you want to be my friend?" Who is he asking?

DIEN: The tail.

MS. LOPEZ: We know whose tail this is (*pointing at the tail*). Right?

TON: Horse.

MS. LOPEZ: Yes. The mouse is asking the horse, "Do you want to be my friend?" (*writing down the sentence on the Post-it Note and pasting it on the page*).

In this example, Ms. Lopez scaffolded her kindergartners' learning in several different ways, and integrated into the read-aloud teaching reading strategies, concepts about print, and vocabulary words. Ms. Lopez created a supportive environment "where ELL students' brainpower is fully acknowledged and activated" (Cummins, 2002, p. viii).

- Ms. Lopez reviewed concepts about print through comparing this book to another one and talking about the question mark.
- Ms. Lopez encouraged her ELL children to participate in the lesson through the activity of labeling the animals.
- Ms. Lopez provided positive and constructive feedback to children's responses through paraphrasing in correct English.
- Ms. Lopez encouraged children to predict, and to confirm or disconfirm their predictions, thus teaching them two important reading strategies—predicting and rereading the previous text.

Using Graphic Organizers

In addition to engaging children in discussing a book, another way to facilitate their comprehension is to use various *graphic organizers*. A graphic organizer visually represents a complete story structure (i.e., a beginning–middle–end cluster) or part of the story structure (e.g., a character map). Both types of organizers provide some support for ELLs to organize their thoughts about the book, thus enhancing their comprehension. When using graphic organizers, teachers need to start with the ones that help organize a whole story (i.e., a beginning–middle–end cluster). With the support of this type of graphic organizer, children have a holistic picture or main idea of the story. Teachers later move on to the graphic organizers that focus on the details of one particular story elements (e.g., a character map or a Venn diagram). These organizers invite children to examine certain story elements in depth. For example, a teacher first uses a beginning–middle–end cluster to help children get the main ideas in *The Three Little Pigs* (Galdone, 1970). Later, the teacher uses a Venn diagram to compare and contrast the first two little pigs with the third little pig, thus allowing children to explore the characters in the story.

Assessment of Reading

To assess ELL children's comprehension through retelling of a book, teachers can use Figures 2.9 and 2.10 in Chapter 2. However, not all ELL children are ready to retell a book they have heard. Children at the silent/nonverbal stage and at the early production stage may provide little information about the book. Being unable to retell the book does not mean that children have not comprehended it, however.

The following are some ways to assess comprehension of ELL children at either the silent/nonverbal or the early production stage.

Retelling the Story in a Native Language. Teachers need to allow some ELL children to retell a story in their native language. A teacher can tape-record a child's retelling, and then ask parents or community members to translate the retelling. Although it is time-consuming to assess children's retelling in a native language, the effort is worthwhile. Through the process, a teacher gets some ideas about a child's comprehension. The child has an opportunity to participate in the assessment just as his or her peers do, and thus gains a sense of self-confidence about his or her own ability to understand the book.

Sequencing the Story Events. Teachers can copy the pictures in a story that represent key events in the book. For example, for the book *The Three Little Pigs* (Galdone, 1970), the pictures of key events include the following: (1) The mother pig sent the three little pigs away; (2) the first little pig built a house of straw; (3) the wolf blew down the house; (4) the second little pig built a house of sticks; (5) the wolf blew down the house; (6) the third little pig built a house of bricks; and (7) the wolf couldn't blow down the house. A teacher can ask an ELL child to sequence these pictures. The teacher can also encourage the ELL child to draw pictures of the events in a story to retell the story. As the child's English proficiency level increases, the teacher writes down short sentences describing the events on sentence strips and asks the child to sequence events.

Retelling about a Character through a Character Map. To assess an ELL child's understanding of a character in the story, a teacher can ask the child to describe the character through a character map with a picture of a character in the middle. The child then draws pictures related to the character. For *The Three Little Pigs* (Galdone, 1970), the picture in the middle of a character map can depict the three little pigs or the wolf, depending on from whose point of view the story is told.

Retelling an Informational Concept through Graphic Organizers. As noted earlier, it is important to introduce informational books to ELL children, even if they are in the beginning stages of English proficiency; it is equally essential to assess their understanding of concepts in such a book. A concept map or a flow chart can be used for the assessment. In a concept map, the teacher draws or writes the concept in the middle. For example, for the book *Shapes, Shapes, Shapes* (Hoban, 1986), the teacher draws a shape (such as a circle) or writes down the word for that shape (*circle*) in the middle. The child draws pictures of objects from the book or from his or her environment that have the shape of a circle. In a flow chart, a child draws pictures to sequence events in a story, to describe the changes that occur (e.g., the life cycle of a butterfly), or to document a cause-and-effect relationship (e.g., the heat causes people to sweat).

Writing

ELLs follow similar patterns and processes in their development of reading and of writing. Like reading instruction, teaching ELL children to write should begin with providing children with opportunities to be immersed in and to interact with print, in English and/or in a native language. Through these experiences with print, children come to understand the functions of writing in various social settings. This foundation is necessary for children to learn about the conventions of written language.

Figures 3.7, 3.8, and 3.9 are three writing samples from a Chinese–speaking ELL preschooler, Charlie. In Figure 3.7, he drew a picture of his mom and dad. Later, in Figure 3.8, Charlie copied down the name of a *Pokemon* character, Diglett, to label his drawing of the character. Charlie's teacher, Jane Johnson, often cut out environmental print items from words and pictures related to a theme the children were learning. She introduced the words to the class and talked about the pictures. In the month of May, before the end of the school year, Ms. Johnson introduced the class to Mother's Day in May and Father's Day in June, along with a small box of words and pictures related to both days. On Charlie's card for his dad (see Figure 3.9), Charlie pasted the picture of a heart, the phrase "Happy Father's Day," and the word *love*. Using the word *love*, he copied down the rest of the phrase "I Love You Dad" from one of the environmental print items. The three writing samples illustrate an ELL child's developmental process of writing—that is, from a picture, to a picture with a label, to a picture with a message. Although Charlie copied all the words from the environmental print items, he did use them appropriately in his writing. In addition, the content of Charlie's writings all focused on his life experiences (i.e., his family and his interest in *Pokemon*).

FIGURE 3.7. Charlie's first writing sample: "Mom and Dad."

FIGURE 3.8. Charlie's second writing sample: "Diglett."

FIGURE 3.9. Charlie's third writing sample: "I Love You Dad."

Many of the activities for supporting children's writing development described in Chapter 2, and the assessment form provided there (see Figure 2.17), can be effectively used with ELL children, if teachers keep in mind the following suggestions:

• *Model concepts about print in English.* Not all aspects of concepts about print in English apply to those in children's native languages. For example, as noted earlier, not all languages have the same directionality as the English language. Both Chinese and Japanese can be written from top to bottom and right to left. In addition, in several languages, each word/character has the same shape (e.g., a square or a rectangle) and the same length. See each word in the following sentences, each of which means "The dog barked at an elephant":

Korean: 개 는 코 끼 리 에 짖 었 다
Chinese: 狗在對大象咆哮了

After each character there is a space. Each English word in the sentence "The dog barked at an elephant," however, has a different shape and length. Word boundaries in English may be a difficult concept for children whose language has words that are all roughly the same shape and length. Teachers need to model concepts about print through the activities of language experience approach, shared writing, and interactive writing. Across these activities, the teachers gradually release their responsibility as people who write for the children, who eventually hold a pen and write for themselves.

• *Make print accessible to children.* As discussed earlier, teachers need to create a language- and print-rich classroom for ELL children. Displaying print around the classroom is not enough, and it is important to make print accessible to ELL children—for example, when a teacher writes words related to a theme the children are studying, draws a picture for each word, and puts these words on a word wall so that children can refer to the words during their writing (see Figure 3.10). If a child is looking for a word for his or her journal and is not sure about which word to use, the picture for each word on the word wall provides him or her with some clue to the word. Also placed in a writing center should be boxes of words and pictures cut out of environment print items that have been categorized into different themes/topics (e.g., fruit, meat). If possible, words and pictures related to children's native languages should be included in the boxes.

• *Focus on linguistic patterns.* Written language is different from oral language in terms of its structure, word choice, and decontextualized nature. Like learning to read, learning to write is not an easy task even for native English-speaking children. The additional challenge that ELL children face is that they need to deal with the differences between English and a native language. One of the differences is sentence structure. For example, in Spanish, an adjective modifying a noun comes after the noun. "Red car" in English will be "car red" in Spanish. In Korean, an object in a sentence comes before a verb. "I go to school" in English will be "school I go to" in Korean. Focusing on linguistic patterns in English can be done through explicit

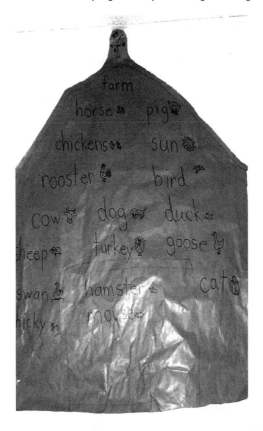

FIGURE 3.10. Farm animal words in Catherine McBride's classroom.

teaching after reading activities, in addition to free journal writing. For example, in *ABC, I Like Me!* (Carlson, 1997), the basic sentence structures are "I am awesome," "I have big dreams," "I love to giggle," and "I can jump and juggle." The teacher can choose one sentence structure at a time to work on with the children. In their journals, children can write a sentence starting with "I am . . . " and draw a picture that matches the sentence. Later, the teacher can move on to more complicated sentence structures with different tenses (e.g., past tense, third-person singular, and present progressive tense).

Word Study

Phonological awareness (e.g., phonemic awareness, rhyming words) and alphabetic knowledge can be more challenging for ELL children than for native English-speaking children, again because of the differences between English and a native language. As discussed earlier in this chapter, teachers' knowledge of ELL children's native languages can be very helpful in figuring out why certain linguistic concepts are hard to some children speaking one particular native language. While doing activities presented in Chapter 2, teachers need to keep in mind the following:

- The phonological system of some languages is very different from that of English. First of all, not all phonemes in English exist in other languages. Two different English phonemes, /b/ and /v/, are the same phoneme in Spanish, /b/. The phoneme /th/ is not in Spanish and Chinese. Moreover, not all languages can be segmented at a phoneme level, as English can. In Japanese and Chinese, for example, the smallest unit of sound is a syllable, not a phoneme. Each word/character is a syllable. The concept of rhyming words is also not universal. In English, the rhyming words *cat*, *sat*, *bat*, *mat*, and *pat* share the same rime (or word family), *-at*. In Chinese, the concept of rhyming words does not exist. The concept of homophones, however, is an important one. The homophones with the syllable *ma* include 媽 (*mother*), 麻 (*linen*), 馬 (*horse*), 螞 (*ant*), and 罵 (*scold*). In addition, the concept of beginning, middle, and ending sounds in an English word may be confusing to some ELL children. For instance, the English word *book* has beginning (/b/), middle (/oo/), and ending (/k/) sounds. Its equivalent in Korean, 책, has a sound for the letter in the upper left position, a sound for the letter in the upper right position, and a sound for the letter at the bottom.
- Alphabet books can help children learn about letter names and sounds (Hadaway et al., 2002). Some alphabet books with too much print, however, will overwhelm ELL children. Alphabet books with simple labels for objects should be used at first. Two examples are *Animals A to Z* (McPhail, 1989), where each page depicts animals and gives their names under the pictures (e.g., *ant*, *armadillo*), and *Eating the Alphabet: Fruits and Vegetables from A to Z* (Ehlert, 1989), where each page depicts a group of fruits and vegetables whose names start with the same letter (e.g., *artichoke*, *avocado*, *apple*, *apricot*, *asparagus*). Teachers can later introduce children to alphabet books that are more interactive and have some print on each page, such as *Chicka Chicka Boom Boom* (Martin & Archambault, 1989), where each alphabet letter (in alphabetical order) climbs up a coconut tree.

Conclusion: Visiting a Kindergarten Class

Catherine McBride's kindergarten class had 15 non-English-proficient and 5 beginning English speakers. The native language of all 20 of these students was Spanish. Her classroom was language- and print-rich: On display were environmental print, books of various topics and interests, class writings (e.g., a chart on farm animals and a chart on a bird's body parts), students' individual writings, and a science center for children to explore life cycles of different animals (e.g., chickens). Mrs. McBride described how she supported her students in developing English language proficiency and literacy skills while valuing their strengths in Spanish.

At the Beginning of the School Year

"At the beginning of the year, I relied on a great deal of Spanish for clarification and instructions. My kindergartners had not been in a setting like school before. I keep a daily routine, so that the children know what to expect and what is expected of them. Once the routine is established, I speak to them in English and only clarify in Spanish when necessary. Body language is important as well. For example, if I ask a child to count the days on the calendar, I hand the child the pointer so that the child understands what is being expected of him or her, even if he or she is unsure of all of the words on the calendar. If the child is still unsure, I repeat the request, and I may start counting with him or her or even help him or her point at the calendar. Many times I ask another child or let him or her pick another child to collaborate with on a task.

"The children are always allowed to speak in Spanish, but I often ask them to attempt what they said in English as well, and then I repeat the correct structure as if clarifying, but not correcting. This makes them feel successful that they communicated something in English, and they immediately hear the correct structure.

"My English language development (ELD) lessons at the beginning of the year include school survival skills. I teach the children how to ask questions to take care of their needs, like going to the bathroom, getting a drink of water, getting a pencil, and so on. I use a lot of simple commands in the form of games, like Simon Says, Bingo, and Pair Share to practice verbs and other vocabulary. I use songs and patterned books for repetition of vocabulary and language structures. Repetition in a group seems to be a huge key to getting them comfortable attempting English. They feel like part of the capable group and are more likely to take risks on their own."

Throughout the School Year

"I teach thematically. High-interest themes allow for ongoing lessons using repetitive vocabulary and language structures. Thematic teaching also creates ongoing interests in the subject and lends itself to deeper exploration, which in turn leads to expanded vocabulary and language learning. I have a science center in my room, which has several different purposes. The first is for the children to learn to be responsible for taking care of a pet. The second is for them to learn about the animals and different things related to these animals. Another one is to create a high interest and have something hands-on and meaningful for the children to see, touch, play with, and explore, to increase their realm of experiences. And finally, of course, the idea is to generate language from the children.

"I try to add something new to the science center that goes along with each theme. In the spring, we had an aquarium with caterpillars that the students found (and that I ordered) at our local science store. We talked about caterpillars as a group, and much was discussed excitedly in Spanish. This gave the students a base of understanding, and then I introduced the new vocabulary in English. We created a word wall of 'butterfly words' (and I drew pictures next to the words for reference). We made a KWL chart [see Chapters 6 and 7 for more on these charts], and I brought out a 'special book basket' of butterfly and insect books. I used these books for read-alouds followed by much discussion. The children browse during their free reading time through the book box, and make their own 'butterfly discoveries.' We observed the caterpillars daily and watched them change, grow fat, make chrysalises, and then turn into butterflies.

"I modeled writing and drawing in my journal, and they followed my lead. I put the butterfly aquarium on the journal writing table, so that they could draw the caterpillars in their journals. We wrote a long story about butterflies and how they change during interactive writing [see Figure 3.11], and then made our story into a class big book as well as individual little books to take home. We became 'butterfly experts.' The children brought plants and flowers they picked on the way to school to feed their caterpillars and butterflies. One day we all went outside and sat in a big circle, said goodbye, and set the butterflies free. ELD lessons included structured phrases and sentences about what we knew about butterflies, what we liked, what butterflies have and do, and how we felt about them. The theme with a high interest made the children want to talk about their experiences."

Reflection

"In my teaching, I highly value children's native language, their life experience, and their efforts to learn English. I try to make reference to and to teach cognates. For example, *Mom* is similar to *mamá* in Spanish, and *lion* is similar to *león* in Spanish. Using cognates makes it easier for the children to learn and remember the words in English and Spanish. I also make references to things the children already know, such as language structures. For example, the Spanish *a la playa* can be directly translated as 'to the beach.' I also teach the children how to say in English the phrases they use most frequently in Spanish.

"In my class, the children must never be made to feel ashamed that they do not understand or that their attempts to speak in English are not good enough. They should always feel supported and capable, and a strict rule in my room is that we don't laugh at others or hurt others' feelings. I believe that once children feel they can't do something well, they stop trying.

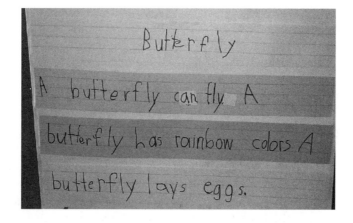

FIGURE 3.11. Interactive writing on butterflies.

"My biggest challenge this year was that my students had no opportunity to interact with English-speaking peers for any part of the academic day. An added challenge was the Open Court Phonics program that I was forced to teach for 45 minutes per day. This was a waste of time, because the content of the program was not comprehensible to my non-English-speaking children at all. I addressed these challenges by using my time very wisely, practicing the flexible teaching methods, and teaching language and literacy through content. I also went to ELD training, and I discussed things with and asked for advice from peers, professors, and administrators. Mostly importantly, I researched effective methods for ELD, and began my master's program in reading in search of ideas to make me a more expert teacher for my ELL children."

Chapter 4

BEGINNING LITERACY

"Well, here we are, Junie B.," he said. "*First* grade. At *last.*"

My stomach had flutterflies (*sic*) in it. Also, my arms had prickly goose bumps. And my forehead had drops of sweat.

"I am a wreck," I said.

Daddy smiled very nice.

"There's nothing to worry about, Junie B. I promise," he said. "You're going to *love* first grade. Just think. There is a whole roomful of brand-new friends just waiting to meet you."

He ruffled my hair. "Are you ready to go in now?" he asked. "Hmm? Are you ready to begin your first-grade adventure?"

—PARK (2001), *Junie B., First Grader (at Last!)*

Beginning readers, like Junie B., are often overwhelmed at the task before them. Although they have played with and explored many concepts about print, they are now making the important realization that they must attend to the print and thus begin the adventure of becoming independent readers. Beginning readers are typically in kindergarten to second grade. This level is characterized by the beginning of the orchestration of many early literacy behaviors. For example, beginning readers have typically developed concepts about print, concept of word, and alphabet recognition. They have some knowledge of sound–symbol relationships, sight words, and phonological awareness. However, due to their limited knowledge in these areas, reading and writing are laborious tasks.

Children who are beginning to read and write independently are, in a way, fragile. They have just enough knowledge to read and write the simplest text, yet the further development of this knowledge is essential to their growth. Teachers and parents need to carefully support and encourage these children as they extend their limited knowledge about literacy. For example, beginning readers can successfully read a simple, predictable text. However, they will need support to move to less structured text. Similarly, a child who writes "The cat is brown" will need support to add more words to this writing. Children who write letter by letter, rather than in phrases, tire easily and are frequently disappointed in their limited production.

This beginning time can be described as a period of reciprocal development: The skills and behaviors children bring to the text enable them to read and write, and the reading and writing of text strengthens these skills. This chapter examines these reciprocally developing areas of beginning literacy in reading, writing, and word study through exploring key developments and successful instructional strategies.

Reading

What is the best way to teach beginning readers? Bond and Dykstra (1967) attempted to answer this question in their massive and comprehensive First Grade Studies. As described in Chapter 1, this research project compared all the methods of reading instruction being implemented at that time. The conclusion they drew was that there is no one best method for teaching beginning reading. The National Reading Panel (NRP, 2000a) also tried to answer this question from the perspective of considering what research had shown to be most effective. However, the NRP's research synthesis did not provide a simple answer to this question either. Perhaps this is because learning to read is a complex process that includes the orchestration of many skills, and what appears to be a simple question is actually extremely complex.

The NRP identified several areas in its conception of reading. These included the alphabetic principle, fluency, comprehension, and vocabulary. All of these areas, as well as others not mentioned by the NRP (e.g., sight words, literature, and home literacy experiences), are essential components of beginning reading.

The Alphabetic Principle

The alphabetic principle is by far the most highly debated area in beginning reading. These debates have a rich history, with many seminal publications attempting to resolve the debate (see, e.g., Adams, 1990; Chall, 1967). Although it may appear that this controversy has been over whether or not to teach the alphabetic principle, the heart of the debate has usually centered on what method (e.g., phonics) is best for teaching the alphabetic principle, or on the sequence of that teaching (e.g., before formal reading instruction). Yet, arguably, most would agree that the alphabetic principle is an integral part of beginning reading. That is, the notion of how sounds map onto print is essential in reading. In terms of the reciprocity of beginning reading, knowledge of the alphabetic principle is necessary to learn to read, yet this knowledge is also strengthened as children begin to read.

This notion of reciprocity as it applies to the alphabetic principle in a sense neutralizes the phonics debate. From a more balanced perspective, phonics instruction should take place as children are learning to read, with the caveat that this knowledge develops as children are given experiences with text.

Stahl (2001), using language borrowed from Durkin, defines *phonics* as "any approach in which the teacher does/says something to help children learn how to decode words" (p. 335). There are numerous approaches to teaching phonics; viewed through a broad lens, these can be classified as *analytic* and *synthetic* approaches. Analytic approaches have children analyze sounds in words. That is, they start with a word and take it apart. An example of this approach is the study of word families, in which children may explore the *-at* word family by looking at a number of words that are in that family. Synthetic approaches begin with learning letter–sound relationships and blending them to create words. Thus words are introduced first by individual sounds. For example, the word *cat* is taught by first reviewing the three sounds /c/ /a/ /t/. Then, after the children say each sound, they blend the three sounds together.

Chall's (1967) study as well as the findings of the NRP (2000a), concluded that one type of approach is not superior to the other. Furthermore, the NRP report suggested that phonics instruction is most effective in kindergarten and first grade.

In considering the most effective way to teach phonics, Stahl, Duffy-Hester, and Stahl (1998) propose the following principles:

1. Good phonics instruction should develop phonological awareness.
2. Good phonics instruction should provide a thorough grounding in the letters.
3. Good phonics instruction should *not* teach rules, need *not* use worksheets, should *not* dominate instruction, and does *not* have to be boring.
4. Good phonics instruction provides sufficient practice in reading words.
5. Good phonics instruction leads to automatic word recognition.
6. Good phonics instruction is one part of reading.

Phonics instruction, which can be synthetic or analytic, can also be both inductive and deductive. Historically, within a deductive approach, students were taught rules and then provided with opportunities to apply these rules to unknown words. However, this method was called into question by the work of Clymer (1963/1996). That is, in his landmark study, he found that only 28 out of 45 generalizations taught were actually useful when these criteria were applied: (1) They were true at least 75% of the time; and (2) there were at least 20 words to which the generalization could be applied. A deductive phonics lesson might involve children's decoding lists of words, typically on a worksheet. For example, the phonics rule "When two vowels go walking, the first one does the talking" would be introduced, and then the students would find other words with long-vowel digraphs. However, Clymer found that this particular generalization was only true 45% of the time! For example, the rule does not hold up in words like *bear* or *thread*.

Thus more contemporary, inductive approaches to phonics involve looking at patterns in words and determining the similarities or discovering the generalizations. Two methods that use this approach are word study (see the section on word study later in this chapter) and making words (see, e.g., Cunningham & Hall, 1994). Both approaches are hands-on and allow children to discover English orthography. An example of lesson in making words is given below.

Making Words

The teacher gives all the children the magnetic letters or letter cards *a*, *t*, *p*, *s*, and *b*. He or she then puts *a* and *t* together to make *at*, and instructs the children to do the same. The teacher then models placing a *b* at the beginning of the word to make *bat*. He or she next asks the children to replace the *b* with a *p* to make *pat*, and then to reverse the *b* and *t* to make *tap*. The lesson continues with the teacher modeling many words and eventually increasing the number of letters in the words. The children are also provided opportunities to make their own words. This particular example involves the teacher's modeling. However, in subsequent lessons, the children are more involved in making the words, as in the following example: The teacher gives the children the letters *i*, *p*, *r*, *s*, and *t*.

> TEACHER: I would like you to make the word *pit*.
> Now change the beginning sound to make the word *sit*.
> Next I want you to take off the *t* at the end and put a *p*.
> What word did you make?
>
> CHILDREN: *Sip*.
>
> TEACHER: What letter can we change to make the word *rip*?
> Now put a *t* at the beginning of the word.
> What word did we make?
>
> CHILDREN: *Trip*.
>
> TEACHER: Let's see who can figure what word we can make using all of the letters.

In this lesson, the children are actively engaged in making words. They are asked both to figure out what words they make as they change letters, and to change letters on their own to make new words. The final challenge is to use all of the letters to make one word.

Regardless of the approach or combination of approaches used, the ultimate goal in phonics instruction is to provide children with knowledge they can use to decode unfamiliar words. However, phonic knowledge is only one means to an end. That is, in addition to phonic knowledge, children need other strategies to enable them to decode—namely, context clues.

Context Clues

Teaching beginning readers to use context clues is imperative, because they tend to overrely on phonic knowledge in their decoding. Rather than asking children to sound out an unfamiliar word, a better strategy would be to ask them, "What word would make sense?" This question requires them to use all three cuing systems: *semantics*, *syntax*, and *grapho-phonics* (Goodman, 1993). The semantic cuing system is enacted by considering meaning; the syntactic cuing system is enacted by considering the word type and placement; and the grapho-phonic cuing system is enacted by considering the sounds and symbols in the word. So if a child is not sure of the word *house* in the sentence "I found the dog in the house," the teacher may ask the child to read the sentence and think about what might make sense. The child may respond *yard*. After complimenting the child for thinking of a word that might make sense at the end of the sentence, the teacher then asks the child to look at the word and think about the beginning sound. At this point the child may come up with the word *house*.

Teachers at DuQuoin Elementary School in southern Illinois use Our Helping Hand (see Figure 4.1) to provide children a reminder of the strategies they can use to decode unfamiliar words. The teachers introduce each strategy by reading a text aloud and modeling how they use that strategy to decode. They focus on one strategy at a time for several days. They remind the children to use that particular strategy and give them a great deal of praise for doing so.

Decodable Text

Decoding, for beginning readers, is an intensive task that consumes many of their cognitive resources. Although one approach to alleviate these cognitive demands is the use of decodable text, there is no research base on its effectiveness in beginning reading instruction (Allington, 2002a). That is, it is not clear whether decodable text actually makes the reading process easier for beginners. However, decodable text is becoming quite popular in basal reading series. Perhaps what it most interesting about decodable text is the way in which it is defined: Any text can be considered decodable, as long as a given number of words can be decoded on the basis of what has been previously taught. For example, if the word family *-ig* has been introduced, then children may encounter stories about a pig that does the jig in a wig.

In many ways, the decodable text of today is a recycled version of the controlled-vocabulary text of the past. That is, the limitations of word choice in cre-

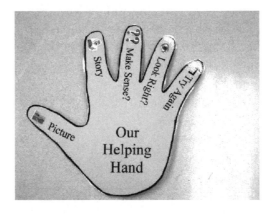

FIGURE 4.1. Our Helping Hand.

ating the text compromise the content of the text. Although Hoffman, Roser, Salas, Patterson, and Pennington (2000) did find that the use of decodable text was positively related to decoding ability, it was also negatively related to fluency. It would seem the best way to choose text for beginning readers would be to strike a balance among decodable text, predictable text that has ample picture clues and repetitive language, and authentic children's literature. In this way, decoding can be taught through text, as well as in the context of other literacy skills.

Sight Words

In addition to supporting children in their beginning reading efforts through appropriate text, it is necessary to build their sight word knowledge. *Sight words* are words that can be recognized automatically. Clearly, the more sight words that are in the text, the less cognitive energy children need to expend in decoding.

The development of sight word knowledge is also reciprocal. That is, children learn sight words through numerous encounters with words, yet bringing sight word knowledge to text enables children to be successful readers. Often the sight words selected for instruction are those from lists of high-frequency words, such as *it, the*, or *with* (see, e.g., Fry, 1980). These words are often displayed in the room on word walls. Teachers can then easily reference these words.

Another successful strategy for sight word instruction is the *language experience approach* (LEA; Stauffer, 1980). The LEA is a technique for beginning reading instruction in which the children dictate text to the teacher. The story can become a text for instruction, as children read their own language with great ease. The process begins by engaging the children in dialogue about a particular topic. A stimulating, engaging, and concrete topic tends to elicit more language from the children.

Upon completion of the dialogue, the teacher takes dictation on the topic. It is important for the teacher to write exactly what the children say, as that is what they will read. The following is a partial example of a completed LEA text in which the students in a first-grade class shared their favorite experience after visiting a local apple orchard.

> Ethan said, "I liked the slide!"
> Parker said, "The hay ride was fun!"
> Bryce said, "I can't wait to eat my apples!"
> Shaneice said, "I liked picking apples."

The class then reads the text several times. The teacher makes copies of the text for each child so that they all may practice the text. The teacher can then ask the children to identify words they recognize in the text. These words can be placed on note cards and used to begin children's sight word banks. Children can review these words and use them in writing or in word sorts.

Although the LEA is an effective strategy in developing sight word knowledge, it is far more multifaceted. The text children create through the LEA tends to be effective in supporting beginning readers. They can read this text fluently, as it is so familiar to them.

Fluency

Perhaps one of the most noticeable characteristics of beginning readers is their lack of fluency. They tend to read word by word, and thus their reading sounds very choppy. Due to their limited but growing knowledge, this type of reading should be expected. And it is when they move past this type of reading that they are actually transitional readers. Still, it is very important to work on fluency during this time period. One strategy for teaching fluency is modeling it through read-alouds. Children need to hear fluent reading on a daily basis. The LEA is another strategy that works well with beginning readers to develop fluency. Other strategies for developing fluency—repeated reading and wide reading—are detailed in Chapter 6.

Beginning readers' word-by-word reading, limited sight word knowledge, and rudimentary decoding skills all take resources and energy away from their comprehension. Thus it is imperative that comprehension instruction be another focus in beginning reading instruction.

Comprehension

Instruction in comprehension for beginning readers can occur through reading and listening. Often the simple text that beginning readers can read independently lacks substance. Therefore, it is necessary to read more difficult text aloud to beginning readers and incorporate comprehension strategies. For example, the *directed listening–thinking activity* (DLTA) is a strategy that can be used to teach comprehension while reading aloud to children. The DLTA method helps children set a purpose for reading, actively listen for comprehension, and react to the text. It can be used with both narrative and expository texts. The first step of the DLTA involves prediction: Children are asked to make predictions about the text, based on the title and pictures. The teacher then reads to a predetermined point in the text and asks the children whether their predictions were confirmed or not. It is essential that the children use text to support their answers. This strategy is considered cyclical, as once this discussion takes place, the teacher then asks the children to make new predictions and the process begins again. Upon completion of the reading, a discussion and reaction to the text occur.

Another successful strategy for developing comprehension through listening is a teacher *think-aloud*. The teacher models comprehension processes through sharing thoughts as he or she reads. Consider the following example:

> That night Max wore his wolf suit and made mischief of one kind and another. . . . Boy, I can really visualize Max. He's in this monster suit and he's chasing after his dog with a fork in his hand. I think he's really starting to act crazy. I wonder what made Max act like that. . . . Hm-m-m . . . I bet he was getting a little bored and wanted to go on an adventure. I think that's my prediction. (Pressley et al., 1992, p. 518)

The teacher in this example was using visualization and prediction to model how a good reader interacts with text. In addition to teacher think-alouds, children can use think-alouds on their own as a strategy to improve comprehension.

Although the strategies discussed to this point focus mainly on listening comprehension, it is also essential to teach comprehension while the children are reading. In addition to comprehension strategy instruction, *guided reading* (Fountas & Pinnell, 1996) provides a framework for teaching strategic reading. Guided reading involves supporting children though text by helping them develop strategies for text processing. Fountas and Pinnell (1996) suggest the following elements for guiding the reading process before, during, and after reading.

Before reading, the teacher selects an appropriate text and introduces the text or sets a purpose by engaging the children in a discussion. What takes place during reading is the heart of guided reading. At this point the teacher carefully listens to the children read and takes note of strategies they use. The teacher can intervene to help children with difficult text by helping them to problem-solve. The prompts in Figure 4.2 can be used during guided reading (see also Clay, 1979).

Guided reading concludes with an after-reading activity; for example, the class may talk about the story by sharing personal responses. The teacher can also use this opportunity to return to the text to discuss problems the children have encountered while reading. During guided reading, children may work on their decoding skills; however, guided reading centers the focus on comprehension.

*   *   *

In addition to comprehension instruction, vocabulary, genre diversity, and response to literature are equally important for beginning readers. However, Chapter 6 provides an overview of these strategies for transitional readers. It is essential to consider that these strategies are also very successful with beginning readers.

Clearly, beginning reading instruction requires a balanced approach that teaches children to orchestrate many skills. Figure 4.3 is a checklist that may be useful in tracking beginning readers' oral reading.

Writing

Beginning writers are also fragile in their development. Their limited but ever-growing knowledge of print makes writing another laborious task. They tend to write letter by letter, and often lose their message as they focus on the individual letters within words. For this reason, it is necessary to vary the types of writing in which beginners engage to include (1) independent writing, (2) dictation, and (3) interactive writing.

Independent Writing

In order for young children to develop as writers, it is useful to begin by creating a sense of community. A community of writers is a place where children feel safe

FIGURE 4.2
Guided Reading Prompts

Strategy: What the child does

Prompts to foster strategic reading: What the teacher says or does

Meaning cues

"Does it make sense?"
"Try it again."
"Read it again, say _____, and read on."

Structure cues

"Does it sound right?"
"Try it again and think about what would sound right."

Visual cues

"Does it look right?"
"It could be, but look at [first letter, last letter, middle letters]."
"Do you know another word like that?"
"What word would you expect to see?"

Confirming

"Were you right?"
"How did you know what it was?"
"Why did you stop?"
"What did you notice?"

Reinforcing self-corrections

"Good, you found the tricky part."
"I liked the way you figured that out."
"Good, you fixed it yourself."

Promoting independence

"What could you try?"
"Can you find the tricky part?"
"Try that again."
"Something's not quite right. Can you find it?"

FIGURE 4.3
Checklist for Oral Reading Development

Name _____	Date _____				
Decoding strategies					
Uses picture clues					
Uses context clues					
Uses knowledge of sound–symbol relationships					
Skips word—reads to the end of the sentence					
Rereads sentence					
Asks for help					
Other strategies					
Reads fluently					
Reads with expression					
Attends to punctuation					
Self-corrects					
Takes risks					

and secure to take risks, make mistakes, and seek assistance. And it is a place where children have time to write, share, listen, take chances, support, and offer feedback to one another. It is also important that children have a sense of ownership. Children need to feel that their writing belongs to them, that they have control over it, and that they are allowed to make decisions on what they think is best. Calkins (1994) suggests that young writers be given both choices and time.

Children need to take responsibility for their own ideas and writing. Choices may include topic selection, genre, length of the piece, the time to confer with peers, the way they will go through the process, the time they will spend on a piece, the audience they will appeal to, and the time and place where they will share their piece.

Allowing children opportunities to evaluate their own writing can increase their sense of ownership over their writing. With beginning writers, a simple checklist can be used to help them think more critically about their work. Figure 4.4 is such a checklist; it requires children to evaluate only a few aspects of their writing.

Children also need to be given time to write. There is no craft or skill that does not require time, effort, and practice. Children will become better writers when they are provided many opportunities to write. In addition, when children are provided with time and choices in their writing, they will explore and experiment with different genres and the many purposes of writing. For example, consider Figure 4.5, which depicts Stephanie's experiment with writing a news script. In this piece of writing, Stephanie has demonstrated her willingness to take a risk and experiment with a different genre. She shows her command of the function of print as a means to communicate to an audience. She clearly understands how TV news reports are written and how to make the transition to the next reporter.

However, when children are not quite as willing to experiment and are bogged down with the intensive task of writing, which at this stage is very similar to their reading (i.e., word by word), they often return to what Clay (1975) referred to as the *generative principle*. In the early stages of writing, this refers to children's using a limited number of symbols, combined in different ways, to generate pages of text. As it recurs with beginning writers, it takes on the form of self-selected sentence stems. For example, a child may write:

> I like my mom.
> I like my dad.
> I like Mrs. Rose.
> I like . . . [and continue to name every child in the class].

Children tend to do this because it is much easier; thus, with beginning writers, it is imperative that they are encouraged to take risks and use writing as a means of communicating. Teachers can stretch children's writing from these simple frames to the more complex sort of text shared in Figure 4.5.

FIGURE 4.4
Writing Checklist for Children

____ My sentences make sense.

____ I have used ending punctuation (. ? !).

____ I have used capitals in the right places.

____ I have circled words I may have misspelled.

Title: _____

Author: _____

Date: _____

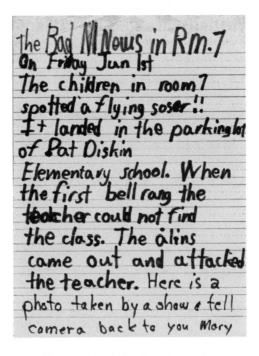

FIGURE 4.5. Stephanie's writing.

Dictation

Taking dictation is a practice that should continue with beginning writing. This practice allows children to express themselves freely without feeling daunted by trying to compose all they want to express. Dictation can occur through the LEA, in stories written on a wall chart, and as written responses to text the children have read.

Dictation also does not need to be a paper-and-pencil or chart paper task. Using a computer to record students' thoughts, and then projecting these thoughts with a liquid crystal display projector, truly enhances this approach. The children can see the text as it is coming across the screen. Furthermore, with just one click of the print button, the text is copied for their personal reading.

Interactive Writing

The interactive approach to teaching writing combines independent writing and dictation. The children and the teacher literally share the pen. Figuratively, this practice allows them to co-construct a message. Literally, children can write what is comfortable for them. For example, a child who is still only writing beginning sounds can be asked to contribute some of these to the text, while a child who can write a number of sight words may be asked to write an entire word.

Interactive writing can be used at any time of the day and for any subject. That is, it does not have to focus solely on writing. For example, Figure 4.6 depicts a sample of interactive writing used in concert with teaching reading comprehension. Upon completion of reading a story, a first-grade class created a chart that depicted the elements of the story. Rather than filling in the chart herself, the teacher used this as an opportunity for interactive writing.

The process of learning to become a writer requires a great deal of nurturing from teachers and parents. The focus of instruction at this stage ought to be on the messages children are conveying. Furthermore, the context of and models for children's writing require thoughtful consideration. For example, the following are excerpts from a first-grade student's journal, where the purpose for writing was to share thoughts and feelings:

1/31: I have 3 ressis bot all of the 3 ressis i was lole not evin Dana or Micah. [I have 3 recesses but all of the 3 recesses I was lonely not even Dana or Micah.]

2/1: My mom wat to my class it was fun ixsap i wasint in that group i was in the ferst group! [My mom went to my class today. It was fun except I wasn't in that group. I was in the first group.]

2/4: I will eat Bare Bare Bagls today they are dlishs I love Bare Bare Bagls. [I will eat Berry Berry Bagels today. They are delicious. I love Berry Berry Bagels.]

The next example is a story written by the same child. However, this time the focus was different. This child spent a great deal of her reading time in school involved in the Accelerated Reader (AR) program. Thus her construct for her story (see Figure 4.7) was colored by this exposure. In addition, she wrote a quiz to go with the story, as shown in Figure 4.8.

These examples highlight the importance of creating a community of beginning writers—a place where there are many purposes and types of writing, and where young writers are encouraged to explore writing genres and many purposes to writing. They also show how young children's writing conforms to the texts they are exposed to, as seen in Figures 4.7 and 4.8.

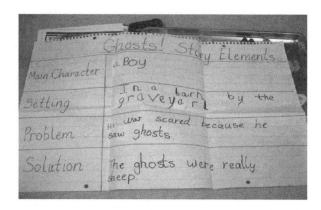

FIGURE 4.6. Interactive writing.

The Pig And The Cat
By KMM

Once upon a time there was a pig and its name was Kim. She always dressed herself in pink. One day she was walking on the road and she met a cat named Joe. He was wearing a blue tee-shirt and red shorts. She said, "What is your name?"

Joe said, "My name is Joe and what's your name?"

"My name is Kim. Do you want to go to the Carnival next week?"

"Yes, I would love to," said Joe.

"What time would you like to meet?" asked Kim.

"About 2:00," said Joe.

They met at the carnival the next week.

"What do you want to go on?" asked Kim.

"Let's go on the Satellite!" said Joe.

"Okay!" said Kim.

So they went on the Satellite.

"Let's go on it again!" said Kim.

So they went on it again. Then they went on the Twirl. Then they went on the Merry-Go-Round. Then they got something to eat. And then, they went on some more rides. When they were getting ready to leave, they bought cotton candy.

"I had a fun time!" said Kim.

"I did too!" said Joe.

"Let's go home," said Kim.

So they went home. That's how the story of Pig And The Cat Goes.
THE END!

FIGURE 4.7. Story written in the tradition of the AR program.

The Pig And The Cat Quiz

1. What was the cat's name?
   a. Bob
   b. Joe
   c. Carrie
   d. Michelle

2. What was the Pig's name?
   a. Kim
   b. Amy
   c. Stu
   d. Dan

3. Where did they meet?
   a. gas station
   b. grocery store
   c. Walmart
   d. Carnival

4. What was the first ride they went on?
   a. Twirl-a-whirl
   b. Pony
   c. Satellite

5. What did they buy before they left?
   a. cotton candy
   b. a drink
   c. pizza
   d. a cookie

FIGURE 4.8. Quiz to go with the story in Figure 4.7.

Word Study

For beginning readers and writers, the study of words is pivotal to their development. Their word knowledge, as described by Ehri (1998), is *partial alphabetic*. That is, they tend to rely on only a few letters—usually beginning and ending sounds—when reading words. For example, they read *kitten* by using the /k/ and /n/. This means that they do not have fully bonded representations for words, and they are not fully decoding words. Thus they truly benefit from instruction at the word level.

In writing words, children at this phase of development are characterized as using a *letter name* strategy (Bear, Invernizzi, Templeton, & Johnston, 2004). That is, they use the names of the letters to write. They believe that there is a one-to-one correspondence between letters and sounds, and they use their alphabetic knowledge to make those determinations. In addition, their knowledge of short-vowel sounds is rudimentary in its development; they often systematically confuse these sounds, again in relation to their letter name knowledge.

The following examples are common spelling patterns among beginning readers and writers:

- *jen* for *chin*
- *jiv* for *drive*
- *sap* for *step*
- *hep* for *ship*

As is evident from these spellings, each sound (and blend) is represented by one letter. The process works as follows: A child will say the word, and then break it down into individual phonemes. The child will then try to find a single letter name that sounds like the sound he or she is making. If the child says /ch/ or /dr/ long enough, it begins to sound like /j/. For the vowel sounds, the child relies on where the sound is articulated. For example, the place in which the short sound of /i/ is articulated is the very same location as where the letter name *e* is articulated. Thus the child uses that knowledge to name the sound.

The Primary Spelling Inventory (Bear et al., 2004) is an assessment tool that was developed to look more specifically at the spelling behaviors of children in the letter name phase. The first eight words—*fan, pet, dig, rob, hope, wait, gum,* and *sled* (p. 301)—target short-vowel sounds, with a few long vowels and one blend. Rather than administering Bear et al.'s Elementary Spelling Inventory to beginning readers and writers, teachers will find that this primary inventory can provide much more insight through the greater number of words at this letter name level.

Once the Primary Spelling Inventory has been administered, instructional decisions for word study can be made. For example, depending on the types of errors children make, word study at this stage may focus on short-vowel sounds, blends, and/or digraphs. For children at this phase, it is useful to make word study a concrete and a hands-on activity. The following is an example of a closed word sort focusing on the short-vowel sound /e/.

The teacher begins by brainstorming a list of 10–15 words with short /e/. The words should be consonant–vowel–consonant (CVC) words that are identifiable to the children and belong to different word families (e.g., *beg, bet, met, den, red, jet, bed, leg, peg, pen, men, pet, ten, led*). Next the teacher writes the words on individual note cards and provides copies for all the children. He or she then models the sort:

-eg	-et	-ed	-en
beg	bet	red	den
leg	met	bed	pen
peg	jet	led	men
	pet		ten

While modeling, the teacher draws attention to the patterns in the words or word families. The children then practice sorting independently. Also, it is useful for the teacher to say the words and have the children sort them in order for them to hear the sounds along with seeing the patterns. Children may then be asked to examine the books they are reading and find additional words that can be placed into the various groups.

The major goal of word study at this level is to focus on the initial consonant and what follows. Children learn to recognize and write many words, because they become flexible in changing initial and final consonants to make new words (e.g., *bat* becomes *can*). This foundation later allows them to examine less predictable long-vowel patterns.

Conclusion: Visiting a First-Grade Classroom

Susan Heape teaches first grade at DuQuoin Elementary School, which is in a rural area in southern Illinois. She has 15 years of teaching experience, with the past 9 years in first grade. Although there are very few students from culturally or linguistically diverse backgrounds at the school, the poverty level is just under 50%. Mrs. Heape has been trained in Reading Recovery and uses that knowledge as a guide to approaching literacy instruction. In addition, she has completed the necessary graduate coursework in reading and literacy to obtain the state's reading endorsement.

She views this education as important preparation for her teaching position in first grade. Mrs. Heape places an extraordinary emphasis on her literacy instruction. In fact, she recently completed a self-directed course in which she revamped and rebuilt her entire literacy curriculum to focus on best practices. She blocks the entire morning for literacy instruction, using Four Blocks (see, e.g., Cunningham, Hall, & Sigmon, 2001) as a framework.

The day begins at 8:00 A.M. with the usual opening activities of attendance, lunch count, and calendar. Yet, shortly after, Mrs. Heape has a brief reading time with the class, often using a shared reading approach. This morning reading tends to involve simple text, such as chart stories and poetry. At 8:45, the class leaves for the reading room to participate in Reading Team Time (see Chapter 9 for a detailed discussion of the reading room concept).

The class spends 30 minutes in Reading Team Time, where they are divided by ability into four small groups. On Mondays and Wednesdays, the children participate in guided reading, and new, leveled books are introduced. The focus on Thursdays is on word-level activities. Every other Tuesday, *running records* are taken on each student. In running records, the teacher marks exactly what students say when reading a passage. If they say *men* for *ten*, the teacher marks this miscue. Running records are useful to determine the strategies that students use while reading and the level where they can read successfully (Clay, 1993a). On the other Tuesdays, the focus is on writing. One day, during a Reading Team Time visit on a Thursday, the children were doing an activity with making words. The children were grouped by ability, and this lesson was geared to their level. Following the making-words lesson, the students all read leveled text. Mrs. Heape listened to their reading, prompting them with cues when needed. The exciting part of Reading Team Time is that it is additional reading instruction time for the children. That is, it does not replace their classroom instruction.

At 9:15, the children return to the classroom. They spend 30 minutes on a word-level activity. This may include making words or word wall activities. The first-grade teachers all use the same words for the word wall, and they introduce five new words each week. These same words are also included on the word wall at Reading Team Time. Often they play games with words on the word wall. For example, Mrs. Heape may say, "I am thinking of a word wall word that starts with *l* and rhymes with *bike*" (the target word is *like*). Another game they play is Rhyming Bingo. That is, rather than marking a word she calls out, the children must mark a word that rhymes with it. Mrs. Heape finds this to be a successful game to help the children transfer their word learning.

Following recess, from 10:00 until 11:00, the children participate in guided reading. Mrs. Heape varies the grouping she uses during this time from week to week. Some weeks, the class reads a text together and they spend a good deal of time with comprehension activities, such as KWL (see Chapters 6 and 7), story mapping, webbing, and story elements. The class also participates in choral reading and repeated readings. The texts they use often relate to the themes they are studying in science and social studies.

During other weeks, Mrs. Heape divides the class into four groups—the same groups they are in for Reading Team Time. However, due to the ongoing and continual assessment practices used, these groups are flexible, and children move based on their development. Mrs. Heape meets with two groups each day twice a week (i.e., groups 1 and 2 on Monday and Wednesday, and groups 3 and 4 on Tuesday and Thursday). During this time, she introduces new books, listens in while the children read, and prompts them as needed.

In introducing new books, she often focuses on words with which they may struggle. For example, they were reading a book that used the word *sausages* in reference to hot dogs. Mrs. Heape said, "This little boy calls hot dogs *sausages*. What do you expect to see at the beginning of that word? Let's clap it. Is it a long word or a short word? Can you find the word *sausages?*" These strategies are successful in help-ing them think about and identify the word prior to reading.

Mrs. Heape also takes time at the end of the lesson to review and capitalize on strategy instruction. For example, when reading a book for the first time, Todd made two self-corrections: (1) He started to say *ocean* and corrected to *sea*; and (2) he first said *woods* and corrected to *forest*. When he finished reading, Mrs. Heape said, "I was so proud of something you did two times while you were reading this book. On page 2 you started to say *ocean*, but you changed it to *sea*. How did you know that? I am glad to see you are checking to see if the word looks right. You did the same thing on page 4. At first you said *woods*, but you noticed it didn't have the right let-ters and you changed it to . . . " Todd replied, "*Forest!*"

Mrs. Heape has created a system for documenting these types of episodes, along with other progress and difficulties she observes. She has a notebook with a page for every child. She jots these types of things down on Post-it Notes and places them on each child's page. She then uses this information to reflect on her children's devel-opment and plan for further instruction. Figure 4.9 provides a sample of the types of information she records. Mrs. Heape truly uses her guided reading time to focus on the strategies her beginning readers are using and modifies her instruction accord-ingly.

The children who are not working with Mrs. Heape during this time are involved in centers. Interestingly, they are heterogeneously grouped for centers. This provides the children with opportunities to work in different groups, as well as keeping the number of children in each center lower. There are centers for journal writing, science and math activities, tubs with children's books/library, working with words/magnetic letters, and blocks. Mrs. Heape values the time the children spend in centers, as she believes they need opportunities to learn through play as well as instruction.

Amy:

<u>9/10</u> struggled w/Bubbles (1.4)—"Bigger, bigger, bigger"—I couldn't get her to see they were the same words. She listens to others to get the words—stays a bit behind

<u>10/1</u> do/can self-corrects—was cross-checking

<u>10/2</u> good 1:1. Told her things and frost and many. Prompted for pumpkins. Inserted the and self-corrected. Really looking at print.

<u>10/21</u> noticed she has been working on word wall words and writing #s at home

<u>11/6</u> not recognizing word wall words in print—up/under, ?/went

<u>11/12</u> seems to now get end and beginning

<u>11/13</u> maybe not

<u>11/14</u> still confused

<u>12/8</u> Greedy Cat (6) very difficult. Can't make connections between words with spelling patterns. Worked on -at and -ar words with making letters.

FIGURE 4.9. Sample teacher observations.

Then, at 11:00, Mrs. Heape does an interactive writing lesson. The first day back from winter break, Mrs. Heape informed the children that they would be having show and tell later that week, and each of them could bring in a gift they had received for the holidays. She suggested that they write a letter to their parents informing them of the show and tell. She used interactive writing to draft the letter on chart paper (see Figure 4.10). As shown in Figure 4.10, Alex was writing the word *bring*. Yet he was unsure of how to spell the word. Mrs. Heape asked him what word on their word wall sounded like *bring*. Alex replied, "*Thing*." Mrs. Heape wrote *thing* on the paper next to their letter. She said, "Since you know how to spell *thing*, how would you spell *bring*?" Alex then correctly added the word *bring* to their letter.

Finally, to close out the morning, Mrs. Heape focuses on writing from 11:15 to 12:00. She devotes this time alternately guided writing and to writers' workshop. When writers' workshop is the focus, she begins with a mini-lesson. The children then work on their writing while she circulates around the room, helping as needed. Each workshop session closes with a few children who have signed up to share their work.

In guided writing, the class members often brainstorm ideas together. They then use these ideas to complete their independent writing. The web in Figure 4.11 is one they created for ideas on writing New Year's resolutions. Mrs. Heape had the students brainstorm different resolutions they could make that related to family, friends, and school. They all began writing, "I resolve to . . . "; they were then free to complete the sentence as they desired. They then could explain their resolutions or add others. One student, Dillon, wrote, "I resolve to listen to my teacher every day." Dillon extended an idea from the web.

After lunch, Mrs. Heape reads aloud to the children. She uses this time to read chapter books that are more difficult than those the children can read independently. She often models comprehension strategies at this time by sharing her thinking with the class, having them make and discuss predictions, and stopping to talk about words.

FIGURE 4.10. Alex engaged in interactive writing.

FIGURE 4.11. Writing web.

Reflections

As is true of many teachers, the one thing Mrs. Heape would like more of is time. She finds it very difficult to fit everything into one day. This is, in part, the reason why she has such flexibility in her scheduling. She has found that by varying the type of instruction from week to week, she can accomplish more than if she tried to fit everything into a single week.

Mrs. Heape made a major change to her teaching this year by modifying her guided reading time. In the past, she used that time in the more traditional Four Blocks way, focusing solely on comprehension strategies. Yet she came to realize that she was losing sight of the children. Since she only worked closely with one group each 9 weeks during Reading Team Time, she wasn't feeling keenly aware of where all of her children were in their reading development. This year, she has continued the guided reading groups in her classroom and is alternating those with her other guided reading. She has found this to be a major improvement in her teaching.

In her ninth year of teaching first grade, Mrs. Heape seems very confident in what she is doing. She has made numerous changes throughout the years and seems genuinely pleased with her current curriculum. When she was asked about the changes from the three-reading-group basal reader structure she began with to what she is currently doing, she said, "I like the way we are able to meet the needs of each child, and it is not the same old thing." Of course, she would love to have more time to spend talking with the children about what they are reading, and working with them on a one-on-one basis.

Chapter 5

EARLY LITERACY AND TECHNOLOGY

The sign on the computer read, "The computer is closed today." The preschool director made this decision after months of agonizing over what she observed as children "zoned out" while passively engaged in computer activities. The problem the director faced arose from the way in which technology was narrowly conceived of and used in this particular classroom. That is, the computer, through the use of drill and practice software, was being used to support the isolated learning of discrete skills seemingly required for traditional literacy—that is, singular book literacy. In many ways, this type of computer use reflected a reading readiness perspective. From such a perspective, learning to read is viewed as the accumulation of certain skills in a hierarchical manner. That is, learning to read begins with first learning letters and letter–sound relationships. Then that knowledge is used to read words, which leads to reading sentences and finally connected text. However, this perspective situates children as passive consumers of literacy knowledge. In addition, as technology continually redefines the nature of literacy, technology use in classrooms must be viewed from a wider perspective—one that recognizes multiple literacies (Karchmer, Mallette, & Leu, 2003). As described by Luke (2000), *multiple literacies* draw on a range of knowledge in which readers make meaning of the linguistic, audio, and visual representations created by new technologies. The New London Group's (2000) similar notion of *multiliteracies* refers to the skills necessary for communication within a global community.

Multiple Literacies in a Preschool Classroom

Rather than close down the preschool computer permanently, however, Janna Keller (an extraordinary teacher) opted to change the focus. A new computer had recently been donated to her classroom. Rather than installing any of the old drill and practice software, Janna chose at first to leave the computer with the only software installed, Microsoft Word. The rationale behind this decision was to provide opportunities for children to become more actively engaged in the use of technology while also becoming producers of literacy.

The first step in getting the children more actively engaged was to expose the children to Microsoft Word. Special attention was paid to what the children already knew and how to expand upon that. Children quickly became familiar with such functions as return, delete, space, caps lock, changing fonts, and the arrow keys. The children in this classroom had varying degrees of literacy knowledge. Thus their use of the word-processing software and their experimentation with print were closely related to their developing knowledge. However, this type of experimentation required a knowledgeable teacher who understood the roles she needed to assume in play and in scaffolding literacy learning. Janna assumed the role of a more knowledgeable other as she interacted with the children. She intervened in their play when she saw opportunities to support their learning. Yet she also afforded the children opportunities to make their own discoveries. Consider the following examples from Janna's classroom.

JANNA: Would you like to type your name?

MEG: (*Typing g, m, a*) That's for Kate (*pointing to a, which is found in her sister's name*).

JANNA: That's for your sister. Can you do your own name?

MEG: Okay (*hitting the spacebar and typing M E G*).

A little later, Mallory was sitting at the computer typing strings of letters.

JANNA: What are you typing, Mallory?

MALLORY: Nothing (*laughing*).

JANNA: What does this say?

MALLORY: It says nothing.

JANNA: Would you like to type some sentences?

MALLORY: Mmm?

JANNA: You could tell me a sentence (*reaching for paper from the writing center*), and I'll write them, and then you can type them on the computer.

MALLORY: Yeah! Okay!

JANNA: Okay, what's the first sentence?

MALLORY: "The cat rode a bike."

Janna wrote the sentence and Mallory typed it. The sentence was typed in all caps and lacked a period at the end; however, Mallory demonstrated her knowledge of concept of word by placing spaces in between the words. Janna introduced the period, first by adding it to the sentence on the paper, and then by showing Mallory the period key and explaining that this key should be struck at the end of a sentence. Mallory decided to do another sentence.

MALLORY: "Mallory has a cat named Grace." (*Mallory typed the entire sentence, again in all caps, and omitting the word* A.)

JANNA: What comes at the end of this sentence?

MALLORY: The dot (*typing a period*).

Mallory noticed that there was a green line between the words *HAS* and *CAT*. Janna read the sentence and pointed to the words exactly as she had typed them.

JANNA: (*Reading*) "Mallory has cat named Grace."

MALLORY: Oh!

JANNA: The computer is telling you you made a mistake.

MALLORY: Oh! A!

JANNA: You can use this arrow key to go back and add the A.

MALLORY: Um, no, that's okay. Okay, next one. "My dog loves running."

Meg entered the area and sat next to Mallory.

MEG: What'cha doing?

MALLORY: Typing sentences.

MEG: Can I type?

MALLORY: Not now, Meg. I have to finish this sentence.

MEG: Oh, okay.

Mallory typed the sentence successfully, only asking whether the letter *L* at the beginning of *loves* was an *L* or an *I*. She continued to space correctly between words, and remembered to add the period at the end of the sentence.

MALLORY: Okay, Meg. Now it's your turn. Do you want Janna to write for you?

MEG: No, I want to type.

When Meg began typing, a red line appeared under her word

MALLORY: That word is spelled wrong.

This example elucidates the changing nature of literacy. Using a word-processing program to compose text, the children made new discoveries about literacy beyond those typically made with the use of paper and pencil. Mallory was beginning to develop knowledge about the construction of print through computer technology. For instance, in just one session, Mallory learned that the computer could tell her when she spelled a word wrong. However, clearly important to the success of this learning experience was the role of the teacher. Janna was able to scaffold this literacy experience for Mallory by providing enough support for Mallory to be successful. In addition, she was able to step back and allow Mallory to scaffold Meg's learning.

Although Microsoft Word provided these preschool children with opportunities to produce literacy, the type of literacy was still singular, albeit much broader. The next two vignettes are more illustrative of how children can become producers of multiple literacies. At this point, the Kid Pix Deluxe software was installed on the computer to provide the children with opportunities to continue being producers of literacy, while at the same time using what could be considered a more developmentally appropriate program.

Brockton and Tyler had been playing at the computer, using Kid Pix Deluxe. They had been taking turns adding fire stamps and raindrop stamps to the screen. Tyler chose to leave the area. Miriam and Kelsi entered the area shortly afterward. Brockton cleared the screen but went back to the stamps, choosing fire and raindrops again. Miriam exclaimed, "It's raining!" Brockton kept adding more raindrops to the picture, but did not say anything. Miriam began to sing, "It's raining, it's raining," to the tune of "It's Raining, It's Pouring." Kelsi began to sing also. Brockton was becoming annoyed with the singing. He chose the fan icon, made a circle with it, and then began another (see Figure 5.1). The girls continued to sing the entire time. Brockton finally turned to the girls and, exasperated, he said, "It's a 'brella! It keeps you from getting wet."

In this context, the children were involved in "electronic symbol making" (Labbo & Kuhn, 1998, p. 79). Although the symbols being used were not text, they represented an additional sign system made available to the children through technology. Here the symbol making by Brockton elicited the construct of rain, and the two girls connected the rain to a song. Yet, when Brockton could no longer take their singing, he used another symbol to suggest subtly that they need not sing any more. His choice of creating the umbrella demonstrated his sophistication in symbolic play. His explanation of the symbol did not explicitly direct them to stop sing-

FIGURE 5.1. Brockton's fan to stop the rain (or at least the singing!).

ing; rather, it was implied. In this preschool classroom, the computer was thus transformed from a machine children stared at while passively engaged to a tool for active play. The next vignette provides another illustrative example of electronic symbol making connected to dramatic play.

The class invited a group of firefighters to visit the school. After viewing the truck, sitting in the driver's seat, and asking the firefighters questions, the children returned to the classroom. Kyle, Michael, Trevor, Isaiah, Westin, Sierra, and Isheng became involved with building a fire truck in the block area. The fire truck was completed in the block area, and the play began. Fires were announced, and the children climbed aboard the truck. Michael and Kyle were the drivers (see Figure 5.2).

They proceeded to the adjoining dramatic play area to put out the fire, carrying blocks for oxygen tanks and thin blocks for hoses. Meanwhile, Tyler and Brockton chose to go to the computer area. Brockton entered Moopies on Kid Pix Deluxe (in this software, the Moopies function enables children to create moving pictures). He chose the fire icon and placed fire stamps at several points around the screen by holding the mouse button down and moving the mouse.

> BROCKTON: I'm a firefighter! Oh, no! There's fire everywhere! We have to put it out! (*He paused and then clicked the raindrop icon.*) Hey, there's water! (*He made fire truck siren noises and added more raindrops.*)

The firefighters from the block and dramatic play areas heard Brockton's sirens. Kyle, Isaiah, and Michael moved to the computer area to investigate. They interacted with Brockton and Tyler momentarily. Brockton cleared the computer screen. He and Tyler left with Kyle and Michael to go to the fire truck in the block area. Isaiah stayed and became interested in the computer. He clicked the fire icon and placed fire stamps all over the screen. He then clicked the raindrop icon (see Figure 5.3).

FIGURE 5.2. Michael and Kyle driving the fire truck.

FIGURE 5.3. Isaiah's fire and raindrop stamps.

> ISAIAH: I'm putting out the fire! (*He made a noise similar to water coming from a hose.*)

Isaiah got up from his chair, picked up his firefighter "hose," and began to pretend he was using it to put out the fire on the screen. The firefighter play was still occurring in the block and dramatic play areas. Isaiah headed to the block area.

> ISAIAH: Kyle, I have a fire.
>
> KYLE: What?
>
> ISAIAH: I have a fire for ya. It's on the 'puter.
>
> KYLE: Hey, there's another fire in this room! (*The children proceeded to the computer area to put the fire out.*) Okay, this one is out. (*The screen still had the fire and raindrop stamps.*) Let's go.

Isaiah cleared the computer screen and then clicked the fire icon again. The other children returned to the block area, but Kyle paused to watch Isaiah add fire stamps to the screen.

> KYLE: Hey, we can make another fire.
>
> ISAIAH: Yeah! (*He added more fire stamps.*)

Kyle and Isaiah returned to the block area to take the fire call, get on/drive the truck, and put the fire out at the computer. This occurred three more times.

These anecdotes provide the opportunity to see literacy from a transactional perspective: technology transforming literacy (Reinking, 1998) and literacy then transforming technology. Clearly, though, this transformation occurred as a result of an *envisionment* by Janna and the children: "When individuals imagine new possibilities for literacy, transform the function or the structure of existing technologies to construct this vision, and then share their work with others, an envisionment has occurred" (Leu, Kinzer, Coiro, & Cammack, 2004, p. 1593). The children discovered that their symbolic play could be broadened to include semiotics, and then transformed the technology by making it an integral part of their play. The computer, which once was viewed in this classroom as a machine that occupied children as they passively worked, had become an authentic and dynamic component of their dramatic play and literacy learning.

The nature of early literacy as described in this chapter thus far is clearly broader and more encompassing than traditionally defined literacy. Yet this is only the beginning. The Internet and other forms of information and communication technology (ICT) continually redefine literacy, and the construct of literacy is expanding into what are thought of as *the new literacies*:

> The new literacies of the Internet include the skills, strategies, and dispositions necessary to successfully exploit the rapidly changing [forms of ICT] continuously emerging in our world for personal growth, pleasure, and work. These new literacies allow us to use the Internet and other [forms of] ICT to identify important problems, locate information, analyze the usefulness of that information, synthesize information to solve problems, and communicate the solutions to others. (Leu et al., 2004)

Although some may argue that the complexity of these new literacies precludes their use in early grades, Karchmer et al. (2003) suggest just the opposite. Young children need to learn not only to read and write, but to navigate, integrate, and evaluate the Internet as part of their early literacy learning. The new literacies of today require a closer look at how we view early literacy learning, along with new methods of early literacy instruction. In the remainder of this chapter, we will look more concretely at these new early literacies.

Rethinking Concepts about Print

The work of Marie Clay (1982) highlighted the importance of concepts about print in early literacy learning. However, these concepts about print are closely aligned with book literacy. As we have begun to recognize that book literacy does not quite capture the literacy behaviors prevalent in homes in this diverse society (Heath, 1983; Purcell-Gates, 1996), we must now also rethink how these concepts about print change with ICT. For example, the notion that text is read from top to bottom is not always accurate in hypertext, where readers jump from one page to another in the order that suits their purposes. Thus, in addition to learning concepts about print as related to books, children now need experiences in learning how to navigate hypertext, where the order is not necessarily linear.

Another timeless tradition in early literacy learning is the notion that print carries meaning, and therefore is what people read. Yet ICT changes this idea as well. Web pages are created with multiple sign systems that are often integral to meaning. That is, text and animation often work together in creating meaning. For young children, this means that in addition to learning to read the text, they must now learn to read multiple sign systems.

Concept of word also takes on a new dimension. What once was an obscure white space to signify the boundary between two words can now be enhanced with a physical movement, hitting the space bar. As the example with Mallory demonstrated, space is made more concrete with word boundaries that are more tactile.

As Karchmer et al. (2003) have suggested, these new literacies in no way replace book literacy; rather, they expand upon it. Concepts about print still represent important discoveries in early literacy learning. However, the new concepts about print are equally important, especially since today's infants are the first generation of children born to parents who had exposure to the Internet in high school and college. Interestingly, children ages 2–5 constitute the fastest-growing group of Internet users. In 2000, only 6% of children ages 2–5 had Internet access, while in 2002, 35% did (Fitzgerald, 2003). Certainly, the use of the Internet by this age group is a matter of parent choice, yet this trend shows that more children will be entering school with a much broader construct of concepts about print.

Young Literacy Learners and the Internet

Web resources are specifically targeting parents with children in this age group. For example, Nick Jr. (*www.nickjr.com*) has games, stories, music, and activities designed for parents and children to experience together. This website provides an illustrative example of new early literacies. The hypertext, animation, words, and icons are all integral to the design and function of this website. Children who are exposed to interactive resources such as this one are taking part in new literacy experiences. Furthermore, these experiences are designed for adult and child interactions. Thus, similar to storybook reading, navigation of web resources is becoming a common practice in *some* homes.

An important caveat here is that not all homes have Internet access, and thus not all children are having these types of literacy experiences. For example, in 2001, the rate of Internet use in households with annual incomes of $15,000 or less was 25%, while the rate of Internet use in households with annual incomes of $75,000 or greater was 78.9% (National Telecommunications and Information Administration [NTIA], 2002). This is further complicated by the growing number of Internet users in the 3–8 age group—that is, 7.2% in 1997 and 27.9% in 1999 (NTIA, 2000). The *digital divide* (Lebo, 2003), is thought by some to be lessening, as the rate of Internet growth among poor and minority households is greater than the rate of growth in affluent households; however, as evidenced in the statistics just given, the disparity is still quite large.

Thus the digital divide in particular, and the digital future in general, are becoming increasingly important issues to consider in the earliest stages of literacy learning. As it is already documented that children from advantaged homes have far greater access to the Internet and are learning many important skills at home rather than school (Warschauer, 2003), it is necessary to consider the skills that these children will be *bringing* to school as well. If we seek to bridge this disparity, it is essential to rethink the nature of early literacy instruction from a perspective that considers these new, multiple literacies.

Rethinking Early Literacy Instruction

Concepts about Print

Building on the knowledge base of successful early literacy teaching, we can broaden the approach of shared book reading. As Holdaway (1979) suggested, children make many discoveries as they interact with readers in the lap-reading context. It is conceivable, then, that the same will be true for children who participate in interactive Internet experiences. An instructional approach that can mirror those interactions may be shared web page reading. Web pages can be projected, and teachers can think aloud as they navigate through them. Children can participate in the decision making, and in turn can see the consequences of text navigation and discover the attributes of nonlinear text. In addition, children have opportunities to learn how multiple sign systems work together to create meaning.

In considering how to complement this experience with a shared writing approach, teachers can use a shared hypertext writing approach. Children can experiment with hypertext by creating classroom web pages, where they make decisions about hyperlinks and about text and graphic arrangements. For example, Mr. Fontanella's kindergarten class web page (*www.jsd.k12.ak.us/hbv/classrooms/Fontanella/fontanejhbv*) is a wonderful resource in which he provides his kindergarten students with opportunities to be active creators of new early literacies.

Beginning Reading Instruction

Beginning reading instruction is a topic that has been under scrutiny for some time. Major research and political endeavors have attempted to cast light on what constitutes effective instruction for beginning readers. For example, the NRP's (2000b) subgroup reports identified the areas of alphabetics, fluency, comprehension, teacher education, and computer technology as those most essential to understanding beginning reading instruction. Although the NRP has been heavily criticized for its definitions of research and criteria for inclusion of studies in its analyses (Allington, 2002a; Cunningham, 2001), most would agree that the topics themselves are indeed all essential to understanding beginning reading instruction. However, the panel's focus was also extremely narrow, suggesting that equally important areas were not considered (Pressley, 2001).

Interestingly, it seems that computer technology was one of the areas that received the least attention from the NRP. Though the panel was unable to reach any research-based conclusions, it did suggest the following:

> Despite the fact that there were no experimental instructional studies on this topic that met the NRP criteria, the application of hypertext concepts to reading and reading instruction seems to have a great deal of potential. The use of hypertext and hypermedia

on the Internet almost mandates the need to address this issue in reading instruction. (NRP, 2000b, p. 6-9)

The role of the Internet in beginning reading instruction can be thought of as providing support to beginning readers. That is, the multiple sign systems that constitute the text can aid these readers. Karchmer (2001) has found that teachers of beginning readers value the extra support provided on web pages, because it helps readers decipher difficult text. For example, the graphics, audio, and video features can serve as aids that are similar to graphic organizers, yet richer and more descriptive. Thus beginning readers can view complex content beyond their reading levels.

Instruction in New Literacies

Perhaps the easiest way to begin instruction in new literacies is to join an Internet project. The Lightspan Network Internet Project Registry (*www.gsn.org*) and Classroom Connect's Teacher Contact Database (*www.connectedteacher.com/ teacherContact/search.asp*) provide teachers with opportunities to join other classrooms in Internet projects. These resources give detailed information about each type of project, learning goals, intended age group, duration of projects, and information on how to participate. Internet projects can be a first step in acquainting young children with the capabilities of new literacies. Furthermore, they can give young children an apprenticeship in participation in the global community.

For example, Susan Silverman (*www.kids-learn.org*) creates at least two new projects each year that are aligned with the New York Standards of Learning. The projects often focus on a piece of children's literature. For example, the Cinderella Around the World project was introduced during the fall of 2001 and was co-created with Pattie Knox. The classes that participated in this project read one version of *Cinderella* and then completed a writing activity (e.g., a book review, Cinderella comparisons, and graphic organizer). Ms. Silverman and Ms. Knox posted all of the work on the Internet project page (*www.northcanton.sparcc.org/ ~ptk1nc/cinderella*) for other classes to view and learn from.

Another essential area of instruction in new literacies is navigating the Internet. Finding information on the Internet can be frustrating and difficult for young children, due to the many skills necessary for navigating the Internet successfully. These skills include (1) narrowing a topic; (2) reviewing for accuracy and readability; and (3) constructing meaning from the nonlinear text and multiple sign systems. These types of skills can best be learned through hands-on experiences and teacher modeling.

Certainly, one possible problem in this instruction is the fear of ending up on an inappropriate site or page. This can be overcome by using search engines designed for children. For example, Ask Jeeves for Kids (*www.ajkids.com*) is a search engine in which children can submit key word search phrases and be linked only to children-friendly web resources. Yahooligans (*www.yahooligans.com*) is another search engine designed for children. These engines and others help make navigation an efficient process, while also only linking to resources that are considered acceptable for children. In addition, directories for children are also screened and linked to only appropriate resources. Examples of such directories include Great Sites for Kids (www.ala.org/greatsites) and Berit's Best Sites for Children (*www.beritsbest.com*).

Finally, instruction in new literacies must maintain a focus on evaluating Internet text. That is, children need to learn from the onset to be critical of what they read on the Internet. Karchmer et al. (2003) have suggested the following guidelines:

- Who created the information at this site?
- What is the background of the creator?
- Knowing who created the site, can you determine why they created it?
- Can you locate a link that tells you what this site is about? What does it say the purpose of the site is?
- When was the information at this site created?
- How recently was the information updated?
- Where can I go to check the accuracy of this information?
- Are the sources for factual information clearly listed so I can check them with another source?
- If the sources are not clearly listed, how confident can I be about the information at this location?
- Knowing who created this site and what the stated or unstated purpose is, how does this probably shape the information or the activities here?
- What biases are likely to appear at this location? (p. 189)

Final Thoughts

The construct of early literacy has evolved considerably in the last 30 years. Much of what we have learned about early literacy during this time has come from careful observation and documentation of young children's literacy behaviors. That is, we have learned that young children have many and varied types of literacy experiences long before formal schooling. Thus we see the need to recognize and value these experiences as foundational in their literacy learning. We now need to acknowledge that these experiences are changing. It is almost astonishing to consider that children ages 2–5 constitute the fastest-growing group of Internet users. Yet, given this knowledge, it is essential for early literacy instruction to become a broader construct reflecting new early literacies.

Chapter 6

TRANSITIONAL LITERACY

"I liked *The Lion, the Witch, and the Wardrobe*," Matilda said. "I think Mr. C. S. Lewis is a very good writer. But he has one failing. There are no funny bits in his books."
—DAHL (1988), *Matilda*

Matilda, being an extraordinary young reader, provides a window into the thinking about books that is characteristic of transitional readers and writers. They no longer just focus on text and literal comprehension on a first reading; they move beyond these basic levels of knowledge to a richer, fuller understanding of story. And sometimes, as Matilda does when she complains, "There are no funny bits in his books," they find themselves critical of the author's craft as well.

Transitional readers and writers may be present at any grade level, but typically they are most frequently seen in second through fourth grades. These students prefer to read silently (Pressley, 2000), and they read and write more fluently. When transitional students write, they represent short-vowel words correctly for the most part; however, they often confuse their representations of long-vowel, single-syllable words (Bear, Invernizzi, Templeton, & Johnston, 2004). For example, they may spell *road* as RODE or ROED. They are different from developing and beginning literacy learners, in that they have abandoned their one-letter-for-each-sound strategy and are now willing to record two letters for one sound, as seen in the OE for *road*.

Important Concerns of Transitional Students

When children are developing or beginning literacy readers and writers, their development is quite remarkable and easy to observe and document. They quickly move from recognizing and writing their own names, to knowing alphabet letters, and then to reading and writing simple words and messages. However, when children move into the transitional phase, their development is subtler and not as easily observable. This is a time when students are consolidating much of what they have learned and becoming more automatic with reading, writing, and word knowledge (Bear & Barone, 1998). They also move from considering only short picture books or predictable text for reading to books that are organized by chapters and have less picture support. In writing, they explore ideas not so familiar to them, such as personal narratives, and they move to longer, more complex texts about these less familiar topics and ideas (Graves, 1994).

Exploration of new genres in reading and writing is the first important concern for transitional readers and writers. As they move to chapter books in reading or writing, transitional readers and writers may not feel as successful or self-assured as they did in the past. Early attempts at writing a chapter book, for example, may end in failure or frustration, as they find it difficult to build a cohesive text (Calkins, 1986). To sustain these more complex literacy endeavors, students need to acquire persistence as they strive for success. Importantly, teachers have to support students as they stretch from their current levels of literacy knowledge and understandings, so that they develop the persistence and determination required to surmount initial failure in gaining new competencies.

A second concern centers around the more subtle development characteristic of the transitional phase. Students expend much energy as they consolidate previous knowledge and move to more complex literacy understandings. Literacy growth is not as dramatic or rapid; students slowly develop new skills to deal with the additional complexity and variability. For example, students are expected to read chapter books that are sustained over several days of reading, rather than completing a book in a single reading session. They need to remember what was read on previous days as they engage in each new day's reading. Writing a story or informational piece also extends over several days, as students add to and revise their longer texts. They acquire strategies so that they can pick up writing on successive days and productively continue it. And, finally, word study is more complex than the simple alphabetic mapping of sounds and letters that students engaged in previously. Now students explore long-vowel patterns, which are not as consistent in representation as short vowels. For example, long *a* may be represented with *ey*, as in *they*; or *a*, consonant, and *e*, as in *cake*; or *ea*, as in *break*; or *ai*, as in *rain*; or *eigh*, as in *eight*; and so on.

A third concern centers on the consolidation of previously learned literacy knowledge. It takes time for students to move beyond a word-by-word reading strategy to more fluent reading. As beginning readers and writers, students often feel a great sense of accomplishment in how many books they can read and how many stories they can write. Now they may elect to reread a book several times, so that they can read more fluently and understand the text more completely. Because of this need to be more fluent and understand text, they often enjoy series books and pick books by series number. In these books, the only changes are in the plots, as the characters are seen in each story in the series. In writing, students often replicate series books or other texts that they are reading. They write chapter books or books about insects, whales, or dinosaurs, for example. They find comfort in repeating the same format as they learn to write longer texts.

The instructional focus of transitional readers and writers thus moves from knowledge of books, literal comprehension, and mapping sound–symbol relationships to fluency, inferential understandings, silent reading, extended writing, and exploration of patterns in single-syllable words. Importantly, teachers need to find time in their instructional schedule for these longer explorations in reading, writing, and word study. Students require time to read and write independently, for instance, and they also require time with their teacher to extend their knowledge and practice of comprehension strategies for narrative and informational text, fluency strategies, and other instructional skills (Raphael, 2000).

Reading

This section is organized around the three key issues of reading growth for transitional readers: developing fluency, extending comprehension, and developing vocabulary. Although each of these components is presented separately, they overlap, and each supports the others synergistically. For instance, students who have rich vocabularies understand text and also read more fluently.

Fluency

Chall (1996) has stated that one of the primary advances in literacy development is made when students move from carefully and slowly sounding out each word as they read to reading words rapidly, accurately, and with expression. Once students move to more fluent reading of the majority of texts they encounter, they can focus on meaning, rather than just literal comprehension. Fluent reading is considered to encompass three components (1) accuracy in decoding; (2) automaticity in word recognition; and (3) appropriate use of stress, pitch, and phrasing (Kuhn, 2003). These components, when orchestrated, allow a reader to use his or her supply of attention to focus on comprehension, rather than on deciphering individual words (Perfetti, 1985; Stanovich, 1980). In addition to word knowledge, the third component extends the focus from single words to students' reading in phrases that make sense, rather than using cumbersome phrasing that does not support meaning getting (Kuhn, 2003).

As teachers and students work on building fluency, they often consider benchmarks to note progress. Good, Simmons, and Kame'enui (2002) have described benchmark goals for students in the primary grades. These goals are based on students' reading grade-level materials. So, for example, if a student is able to reach the benchmark number of words per minute, but he or she is reading in a below-grade-level text, the student is considered in need of an intervention to build fluency. Following are benchmark goals for fluency:

> Spring, first grade: 40 words correct per minute in grade-level material
> Spring, second grade: 90 words correct per minute in grade-level material
> Spring, third grade: 110 words correct per minute in grade-level material

Importantly, Good et al. (2002) note that these are goals for *all* students within a grade. If a student falls significantly behind these benchmark goals, then they recommend intervention for that student.

Beyond providing time for students to read independently, there are several strategies that teachers can use to develop fluency in reading. Following are some of these strategies. They require direct instruction at first, but then students can engage in them independently.

Repeated Reading or Rereading of the Same Text

The strategy of repeated reading is best used with students who decode accurately, but read at a very slow rate. A teacher selects text that is at the high end of a student's instructional level (i.e., a level where he or she can read with approximately 95% accuracy). For the first reading, the teacher times the student as he or she reads 100 words, and records any miscues that the student produces. After the reading, the teacher reviews the miscues with the student. Then the teacher and student mark two charts (see Figure 6.1), which show the child's reading speed and miscues. (The chart for miscues may not be needed for older students or more accurate readers.) The teacher and student can continue this process together, or the student can independently reread the passage on successive days until he or she can read about 100 words per minute with 2 or fewer miscues. (When students read independently, they need a stopwatch to keep time. This is a good activity for a student to engage in with a partner who can keep time and note miscues.) Once this goal is reached, another passage can be selected at the same instructional level. The teacher and student can decide when this level is too easy, and this process is then repeated with more difficult text.

In addition to this more formal approach to rereading, teachers can use simpler strategies. In a small-group reading session, the teacher and students may orally read a text together. This strategy, known as *choral reading*, allows the teacher to model fluent reading as students imitate his or her reading (Rasinski, 1998). Another strategy that uses the teacher as a model is *echo reading*. During this process, the students orally read slightly behind the teacher and again imitate the teacher's fluent reading. And a final strategy that builds on modeling of oral reading, has students listen to text that has been tape-recorded. Without a teacher's direct support, students can hear fluent reading. After listening to a tape-recorded text, students can silently read the text without this support.

Readers' Theatre

Another strategy that is engaging to students and builds fluency is Readers' Theatre (Martinez, Roser, & Strecker, 1998–1999). As with the other strategies that develop fluent reading, students can select narrative, poetry, or informational text to serve as a script for a Readers' Theatre presentation (Allington, 2001; Hoyt, 2000). The simplest way to have students participate in Readers' Theatre is to use scripts that are already available. Basals and Internet resources (e.g., *aaronshep.com/rt* or *www.teachingheart.net*) offer teachers simple scripts. Teachers just need to make copies for students so that they can practice their parts. The second method is for students to develop the scripts themselves from material that they are reading, so that

FIGURE 6.1
Charts for Rereadings: Words per Minute and Miscues

Name _____

Book _____ Genre _____

Words per minute	Practice sessions									
	1	2	3	4	5	6	7	8	9	10
100										
90										
80										
70										
60										
50										
40										
30										
20										
10										
Miscues	Practice sessions									
	1	2	3	4	5	6	7	8	9	10
10										
9										
8										
7										
6										
5										
4										
3										
2										
1										

they can perform it. This process is more extensive, as students need to convert text to a play format. Readers' Theatre does not rely on props or costumes; it is grounded in students' expressive and fluent reading. Students practice their parts several times, thus gaining fluency and expression through rereading and practicing. They then perform their script for a class audience.

Book Series Reading

As students become more competent readers, they often elect to read multiple books by the same author. This reading allows students to develop fluency, because most of these books retain characters, and the only significant differences are in the plots (as noted earlier). There are numerous book series available to students (see Table 6.1).

Teachers and students may track progress in fluency by using the charts in Figure 6.1. A teacher may also want to use a fluency rubric periodically throughout the year, to track fluency for individual students more generally. Figure 6.2 presents a rubric that can be used to monitor fluency growth. It can be used when a student reads a 100-word, grade-level passage with the teacher, and speed and miscues are recorded.

TABLE 6.1. Series Books for Transitional Readers

Title	Author
Amber Brown	Paula Danziger
Amelia Bedelia	Peggy Parish
American Girls	Various authors
Animal Emergency	Emily Costello
Arthur	Marc Brown
The Baby-Sitters Club	Ann Martin
The Boxcar Children	Various authors
Cam Jansen	David Adler
Captain Underpants	Dav Pilkey
Commander Toad	Jane Yolen
Dinotopia	Various authors
Franklin	Paulette Bourgeois and Brenda Clark
Frog and Toad	Arnold Lobel
Hank the Cowboy	John Erickson
Henry and Mudge	Cynthia Rylant
I Want to Be	Various authors
In My Neighborhood	Various authors
Julian	Ann Cameron
Junie B. Jones	Barbara Park
The Magic School Bus	Joanna Cole
Magic Tree House	Mary Pope Osborne
Nate the Great	Marjorie Sharmat
Ramona	Beverly Cleary

FIGURE 6.2
Fluency Rubric

	Not fluent—1	Moderately fluent—2	Fluent—3
Accuracy	Below 90%	90–94%	95–100%
Pace	Hesitates often Many pauses Many repetitions Choppy	A few hesitations Some pauses Some repetitions Relatively smooth	Few hesitations Few pauses Few repetitions Smooth
Phrasing	Word-by-word reading Ignores punctuation	Phrases read and some word-by-word reading Ignores some punctuation	Phrases read in meaningful chunks Punctuation is not ignored
Expression	Monotone reading	Some expression	Appropriate expression used when reading

Comprehension

With developing literacy and beginning literacy students getting the main elements and ideas presented in a story or informational text is sufficient. When students move into the transitional phase of literacy development, teachers are still concerned that the students grasp the literal elements of a text, but they also nudge them to richer and deeper levels of comprehension. Students are supported in making connections between their personal and world experiences and the text, as well as intertextual connections among the various texts that they are reading.

Following are several strategies to help students move beyond literal comprehension in both narrative and informational text. Although strategies for narrative and informational text are separated, many of the strategies can be used with either form of text.

Narrative Text Strategies

Written Response. Students can be asked to provide a written response to what they have read. Typically, students write in a notebook each day following reading. When starting this strategy, some teachers feel more comfortable giving students specific writing assignments. For example, students can be asked to write a summary, describe the characters or plot, or look for interesting words. If students are reading the same book and then meeting for discussion each day, a teacher may choose to give each student in the book club group a specific task for writing. This type of organization requires that students are reading the same pages in the same text. Following are some of the roles that group members can be given:

- *Discussion director*—This person thinks up good discussion questions to use with the group.
- *Passage chooser*—This person records important passages in the pages just read. He or she then shares them with the group for discussion.
- *Connector*—This person is responsible for making connections between the world, other books, or personal experiences with the section of text just read.
- *Word wizard*—This person finds interesting or confusing words for the group to explore.

Although the types of written responses described above are quite structured, students can also write freely about their reading. They might be encouraged to use a strategy known as the *double-entry draft* (Barone, 1990). In this strategy, students copy down a portion of text that they felt was interesting, important, or confusing to them on the left side of their paper. Then on the right side, they write why they chose this portion of text. In Figure 6.3, Amy wrote about a part in a *Ramona* book where Ramona and Beezus eat tongue for dinner. Amy had clear feelings about the possibility of eating tongue and asked her teacher for her feelings as well. The dialogue between the reader and teacher is clear in this response. In Figure 6.4, Sam responded to the single word *homework*. This word triggered a personal connection

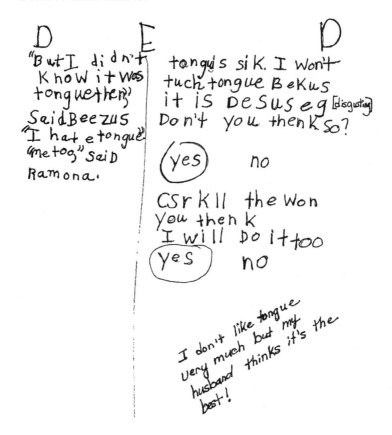

D E D

"But I didn't Know it was tongue ether" Said Beezus "I hate tongue me too" Said Ramona.

tongu's sik. I won't tuch tongue Bekus it is Desus eg [disgusting] Don't you thenk so?

(yes)   no

Csr kll the Won you thenk I will Do it too

Yes   no

I don't like tongue very much but my husband thinks it's the best!

FIGURE 6.3. Amy's writing about Beezus.

for him to the stresses of completing homework for school. As can be seen in these two entries, the structure of the double-entry draft supported the students in moving away from literal comprehension to more interpretive understandings.

When students read independently and share in book club groups with or without the teacher, teachers may want to employ a self-assessment form that can be used by the students on some occasions. Figure 6.5 is such a self-assessment form.

Sketch to Stretch. A technique called *sketch to stretch* helps students move beyond literal comprehension by having them think more seriously about theme (or other elements, such as characters, setting, or plot) (Harste, Short, & Burke, 1989). Students can work alone or with their book club group. Following is the process for the sketch-to-stretch activity:

1. Students read a portion of a book. Following reading, they write in a response notebook and then discuss the section with their group.
2. Typically, the teacher then helps readers think about the theme that has been shared in the book they are reading. They may also brainstorm ways to represent this theme.
3. Students then draw the theme or meaning that they have gained from the

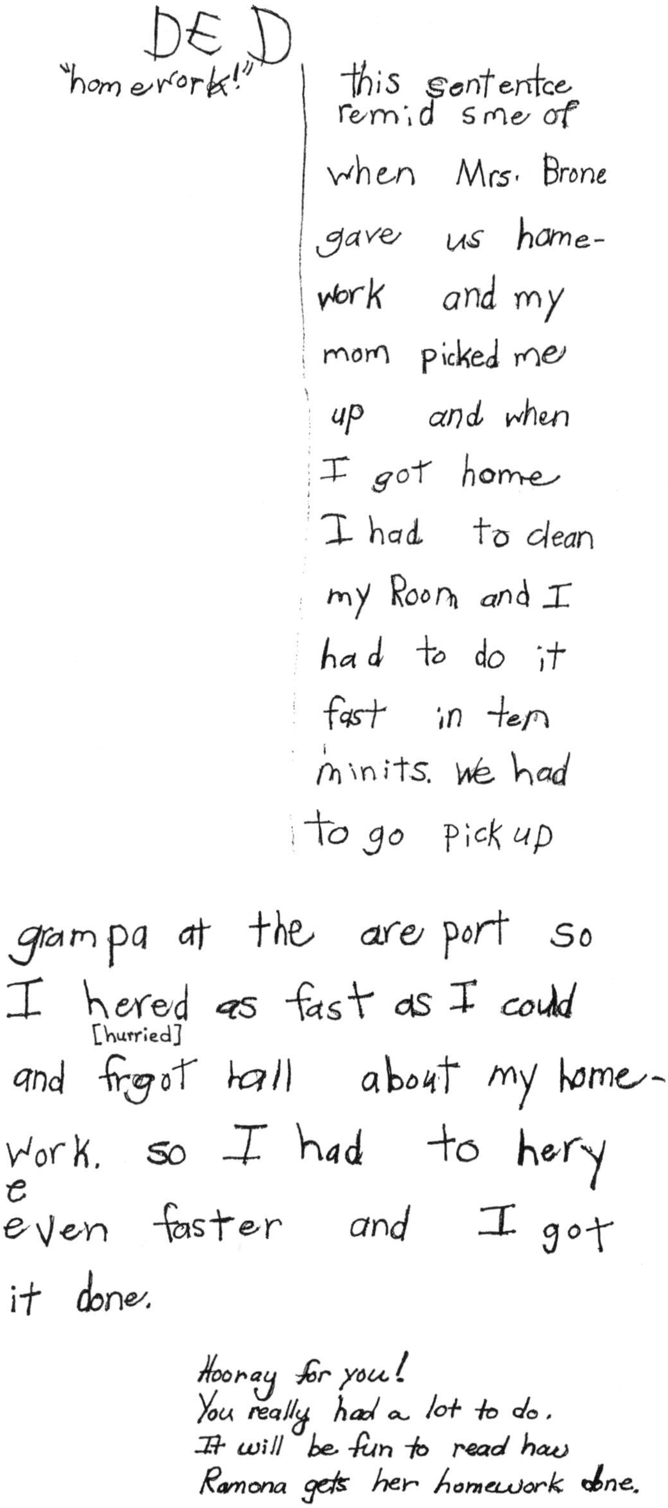

DED
"homework!"

this sontentce remid sme of when Mrs. Brone gave us home- work and my mom picked me up and when I got home I had to clean my Room and I had to do it fast in ten minits. we had to go pick up

grampa at the are port so I hered as fast as I could
[hurried]
and frgot tall about my home- work. so I had to hery
e
even faster and I got it done.

Hooray for you!
You really had a lot to do.
It will be fun to read how
Ramona gets her homework done.

FIGURE 6.4. Sam's writing about homework.

FIGURE 6.5
Self-Assessment Rubric for Children

Name _____

Book _____

Assessing Myself during Book Club

Things I did	Date	Date	Date	Date	Date
I read the assigned pages.					
I wrote in my response notebook.					
I was the discussion director.					
I was the passage chooser.					
I was the connector.					
I was the word wizard.					
I shared during book club.					
I listened to other members of my book club.					

narrative text. Importantly, students do not just draw their favorite part of the story; this activity is focused on the more abstract qualities of text.

4. Students share their sketches (if they are working individually) and discuss them.
5. Students can add to or revise their sketches.

Question–Answer Relationships. Raphael (1986) has developed a strategy in which students discover the requirements posed by a comprehension question, thus allowing them to see the difference between literal and inferential comprehension. Her strategy helps students learn where they might find the answer to a question: on the page, between the lines, or beyond the text. Teachers can help students write questions modeled on these distinctions for the books they are reading, or teachers can pose questions and facilitate the answering process with students. Raphael suggested that teachers give students feedback on the way they categorize a question immediately; start with shorter texts and move to longer ones; begin with simple questions and move to more complex ones; and start with direct instruction and move students to considering or writing questions independently. The four question types are these:

1. *Right there.* These are literal questions that can be answered right in the text. For example, "Who is the main character?" or "Where does the story take place?"
2. *Think and search.* These are inferential questions that expect students to find an answer in more than one place in the text. For example, if the text is Dahl's (1988) *Matilda*, "What kind of person is Matilda?"
3. *Author and me.* These are inferential and application-level questions that expect students to combine their thoughts with the author's. For example, "Why did Matilda's parents not like reading?"
4. *On my own.* These questions are application and evaluation questions that expect students to come up with their own ideas. For example, "Why do you think it was so easy for Matilda to learn to read?"

Dialogical-Thinking Reading Lesson. The dialogical-thinking reading lesson format was designed by Commeyras (1990) to teach critical thinking skills centered on moral, social, or political issues. In this format, students revisit text for clarification or validation, consider multiple interpretations, and evaluate these interpretations. First, students silently read the same text. Following this reading and a discussion, the teacher, and later students, pose a question that has multiple interpretations. Students support their interpretations. This strategy is not a quiet one; students passionately engage in it as though it were a debate. Following is an example from *Matilda*. The teacher poses this question: "Is Miss Honey a good teacher?" Students may respond as follows:

Yes, she is.
1. She understands the fears and worries of her students.
2. She tells Miss Trunchbull that Matilda is a genius.
3. She prepares her students for the weekly test.

No, she isn't.

1. She never smiles.
2. She gives her students workbooks and practice books.
3. She always asks the students to recite in front of each other.

Informational Text Strategies

Informational text comprehension carries with it a whole different set of expectations from those accompanying narrative text. Students are not trying to understand a plot or the motives of interesting characters; rather, they are reading to learn about interesting phenomena, such as countries, animals, or events. This kind of reading requires that they carefully attend to details in text, consider information presented in tables and figures, and vary their reading rate depending on the reading task. For example, if they are surveying a chapter in a textbook, they may scan it to get a general sense of what it is about. However, if they are reading to find out the details about spiders, they will probably slow down to make sure that they get the required details.

Moreover, informational text has many different structures that students must come to recognize. These include (1) description, (2) collection, (3) causation, (4) problem–solution, and (5) comparison. Students who are aware of these various structures will understand text better. Vukelich, Evans, and Albertson (2003) demonstrate how teachers can help students uncover the structure of informational texts and then create graphic formats to facilitate learning this information. For example, when students are reading text that is a description, they create a cluster. However, if the text compares two things (e.g., a frog and a toad), they will be better off using a Venn diagram. Following are several strategies that can be used to help transitional readers acquire fundamental and advanced knowledge about a topic of study in informational text, and the structure of informational text as well:

KWL. KWL is a strategy used before reading to activate students' knowledge about a topic and to help them form questions that will guide their reading (Ogle, 1989). The letters KWL stand for "what we already know" (K), "what we want to find out" (W), and "what we have learned" (L). When this strategy is first introduced, the teacher records the comments of students on a KWL chart. He or she also reconvenes students when the L part is recorded. However, this strategy can also be done by small groups of students or individual students. Figure 6.6 is a brief KWL chart created by second graders when they studied bison.

Anticipation Guides. Anticipation guides also help students build background knowledge before they engage in reading (Head & Readence, 1986). To create the guide, teachers create statements that are true and false. Students then decide whether each statement is accurate or inaccurate. Following this discussion, students read a text to discover whether their decisions were correct. Importantly, when teachers create statements, they should focus on the central knowledge that

K	W	L
What we know	*What we want to learn*	*What we have learned*
• Bison are like buffaloes.	• How big are they?	• They live in herds.
• They live in the West.	• Who are their enemies?	• They are buffalo and are big and make the ground shake.
• They have horns.	• Are they still alive?	• Native Americans hunted bison.
• They eat grass.		• Settlers moving West killed most of the bison.
		• They now live in parks.

FIGURE 6.6. KWL chart for bison.

they expect students to gain. After students read the text, teachers will want to re-convene the discussion centered on the statements and have students verify with text whether each statement was accurate or not. An example of an anticipation guide comes from the reading that second-grade students were going to do about orangutans (Marchetti, 2001):

Orangutans live in nests in trees.
Orangutans like rain.
Orangutans live with other orangutans.
Orangutans eat fruit, nuts, flowers, and bugs.

Clusters, Venn Diagrams, and Other Graphic Organizers. *Clusters* are diagrams that allow students to organize their thoughts (Bromley, 1996). Clusters can either be organized or unorganized, and can be used before, during, and after reading. An unorganized cluster lets students record information without classification. In an organized cluster, students group their information by topic area. For example, students can write the word *bison* in a circle and then, on spokes coming from the circle, write the facts that they learn about bison for an unorganized cluster (see Figure 6.7). Or this same information can be organized as seen in Figure 6.8.

Students can also use other graphic representations during and after reading to better understand the connections between the structure of an informational text and the information they are trying to gain. For example, a Venn diagram is perfect

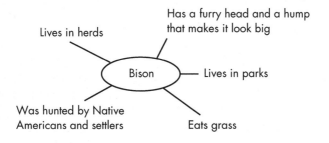

FIGURE 6.7. Unorganized cluster about bison.

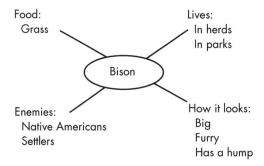

FIGURE 6.8. Organized cluster about bison.

when the text focuses on comparison. For a learning sequence such as the life cycle of a butterfly, a student can create a chart or map with each event in the sequence noted (Vukelich et al., 2003).

Data Charts. Data charts build from the cluster strategy. Students record the information that they gain about a topic in a chart. For example, if a student is researching rock climbing, he or she may find information in a textbook, informational trade books, or the Internet. The data chart is a place to record this information and make comparisons across data sources as well (Tompkins, 2004). Figure 6.9 shows the beginning of a data chart on rock climbing created by a third-grade student.

Learning Logs. All of the writing activities already described can be placed in a learning log. A *learning log* is a journal or notebook where students record information they are learning. Their entries can take multiple forms, some being teacher-directed and others recorded independently as students explore a topic (Tompkins, 2004). An entry in a learning log may also reflect the knowledge that students have gained after participating in a science experiment, after solving a complex math problem, or after viewing an informational film. Figure 6.10 shows the thinking of Kirby as he described how he figured out how to multiply 27 × 4.

Equipment	Techniques	Mountains	How to learn	Special words
Harness, rope, carabiners (*Rock Climbing*, Joe Ramsey, 2000, p. 8)	Work with a partner (*Rock Climbing*)	El Capitan (*Rock Climbing*)	Gym (From me)	*Carabiner*— metal loops where the rope goes
Shoes and helmet (*Rock Climbing*)	Use ledges (*Rock Climbing*)	Joshua Tree Forest (*www.climbing.com*)	The Internet (*www.allexperts.com*)	Smearing— putting your whole shoe on a rock

FIGURE 6.9. Data chart on rock climbing.

> Solve this problem in two ways—27 x 4. Then write how you did it so that you can share your strategy with another student.
>
> 1. I did this in my head. I found out what was 27 x 2. It was 54. I added 54 plus 54.
> 2. I used groups of 27 to get the answer. I just added 27 + 27 + 27 + 27 = 108.

FIGURE 6.10. Kirby's learning log entry.

Vocabulary

Graves (2000) has documented how the development of vocabulary complements comprehension instruction. Indeed, developing vocabulary is as important to comprehension for readers in the transitional stage and above as developing phonemic awareness is to early reading. He writes:

> The books and other reading materials used by school children include well over 100,000 different words. The average child enters school with a reading vocabulary of only a handful of words but learns reading vocabulary at a rate of 3,000 to 4,000 words a year, accumulating a reading vocabulary of something like 25,000 words by the time he or she is in eighth grade. (p. 117)

Graves has recommended several ways to help students acquire this necessary vocabulary. Following are his recommendations, with further instructional suggestions and examples.

Wide Reading

Wide reading simply means extensive reading of a wide variety of texts. To support wide reading within a classroom, books, magazines, and Internet text need to be available to students, and the time to engage with them needs to be provided as well. To support students in focusing on vocabulary as well as text during independent reading, teachers can provide pieces of paper or bookmarks where students can record interesting or puzzling words. Later, these jottings can serve as the basis for academic conversation centered on vocabulary. Figure 6.11 is an example of a bookmark used by a student as he read *Maniac Magee* (Spinelli, 1990).

Teaching Words

Although it is clear that teachers cannot directly teach the 3,000 to 4,000 words that students need to acquire in a year, they can teach words that are necessary for students to understand text in more teacher-directed reading. Teachers can identify these words by (1) considering words that are critical to understanding; (2) generating words in which their meanings are related to other words (e.g., learning what *sub-* means in *subtract*, and then figuring out other words that include the root *sub-*); and (3) gathering words students will see in other reading experiences.

Maniac Magee—My vocabulary

Confusing   Interesting

p. 16 blundering   p. 18 finsterwallies

p. 44 cast-iron digits   p. 38 cringed

FIGURE 6.11. Bookmark of vocabulary for *Maniac Magee*.

There are many ways for teachers to provide this more structured instruction of words. Lenski and Nierstheimer (2004) suggest a strategy known as *four-square*. To use this strategy (see Figure 6.12), the teacher gives the students an important word—for instance, *evaporate* for the book *Deserts* (Simon, 1990). Students then write what they think, find a dictionary meaning, illustrate, and write words with the opposite meaning.

Another strategy is the *list–group–label* approach developed by Taba (1967). The teacher identifies key words that students will encounter in text. Students work in groups or with the teacher to group words and then label them. Figure 6.13 provides a brief example of this sorting and labeling process. The words can be written on cards, so that students have flexibility in determining where a word may be placed before recording their final decisions.

Teaching Word-Learning Strategies

Rather than just teaching specific words necessary for comprehension, the teacher also models strategies for learning words independently. One way to do this is for the teacher to model through a think-aloud how he or she deals with unknown words.

Word evaporate	What I think I think it has to do with water because I see water boiling and the steam is evaporation I think.
Definition To change liquid into a vapor Illustration 	Opposite appear

FIGURE 6.12. Example of the four-square strategy.

Deserts	Plants in the desert	Important things to know
Gobi	creosote bush	evaporation
Mojave	yucca	rain shadows

FIGURE 6.13. Example of the list–group–label strategy.

For example, the teacher may read the following sentence from *Maniac Magee* to the class: "They bundled themselves and ventured into the silent night" (Spinelli, 1990, p. 112). At this point, the teacher may stop and say the following:

"I am not sure what *ventured* means, but they put on warm clothes, because that is what I think *bundled themselves* means. Then there is that part about the silent night. So I think *ventured* must mean something like go outside, because they put on warm clothes and it talks about the night."

Following the think-aloud, several students can check various dictionaries, including an online or CD-ROM dictionary, and decide whether the teacher's thinking led to an appropriate definition. Teachers want to help students engage in similar metacognitive strategies as they read. One way to support this is to engage in conversation with students about how they figured out a word and comprehended text. Teachers want to help students become aware of the processes they use, and help them develop a repertoire of appropriate ways to deal with confusions encountered while reading.

Word study strategies also help students to learn new and unfamiliar words; these are discussed later in this chapter.

Writing

Tasks for Transitional Writers

The biggest tasks for transitional writers are dealing with the additional complexity (and length) of their writing, revising with an eye to writing traits, and sustaining their writing over several days or weeks. In this section, the focus is on revision by considering writing traits. The increased complexity of writing about reading and learning has been discussed previously in this chapter. The issue of sustaining writing over several days depends on the teacher's organization of his or her classroom: If students know that they will engage in writing on each day of the week for a certain period of time, they feel more comfortable leaving writing unfinished, because they know that they will return to it. Teachers can also help students at the end of a writing period by providing time for each student to summarize what he or she accomplished and what his or her writing goal will be for tomorrow. When these few minutes are provided for reflection and planning, students are prepared to start writing when their writing time recurs the following day.

Writing Traits

There are six traits that children can focus on as they write and revise their writing: (1) ideas (presenting a clear and complete message); (2) organization (putting ideas in a meaningful order); (3) voice (conveying what the writer really thinks or feels); (4) word choice (using words the reader understands); (5) sentence fluency (using multiple structures for sentences—short vs. long, different beginnings); and (6) writing conventions (making conventional use of paragraphs, spelling, punctuation marks, and capitals). Although teachers may feel that working on these traits should be saved for later, more sophisticated writing, they can be noticed and focused upon in children's earliest writing. For example, a young child who writes a string of B's, *BBBBBBBBB*, is emphasizing the sound that a motorcycle makes and is focused on word choice.

While there are a multitude of ways to help students improve their writing, the focus here is on two specific ways to help children incorporate and focus on writing traits: by conferring with them during the revision process, and by letting them see how expert writers include these traits in their own writing.

Revision

Spandel (1996) suggests that teachers might help students focus on the traits during conferences. She has developed questions for each trait to help a student focus on it and revise his or her writing accordingly. Following are her prompt questions for each trait:

- Ideas
  —What is my message?
  —Is my message clear?
  —Do I have enough information?

- Organization
  —How does my paper begin?
  —Did I tell things in order?
  —How does my paper end?

- Voice
  —Does my paper sound like me?
  —How do I want my reader to feel?

- Word choice
  —Can my reader understand my words?
  —Did I use any new words?
  —My favorite words are _____

- Sentence fluency
  —Did I use sentences?
  —How many different ways did I start a sentence?
  —Did I use long and short sentences?

- Conventions
  —Did I leave margins on the sides?
  —Did I use capitals?
  —Did I use periods, question marks, and exclamation marks?
  —Did I spell my words correctly?

Throughout the year, a teacher may want to collect student writing in a portfolio that is scored more formally with a trait checklist. Figure 6.14 shares a student's writing sample that was used in a writing conference to help the student focus on organization in an informational piece of writing. This student's writing has a clear introduction and conclusion. She has provided details and has used a compare–contrast structure. She has also used conventions accurately during her first-draft writing about lizards. Her teacher complimented her on these strengths and then nudged her to move beyond the redundancy of her topic sentence—"Lizards are amazing"—in further writing.

By keeping samples like these over time, a teacher and student can see development in the use of traits. Figure 6.15 is a checklist that can be used to assess writing traits.

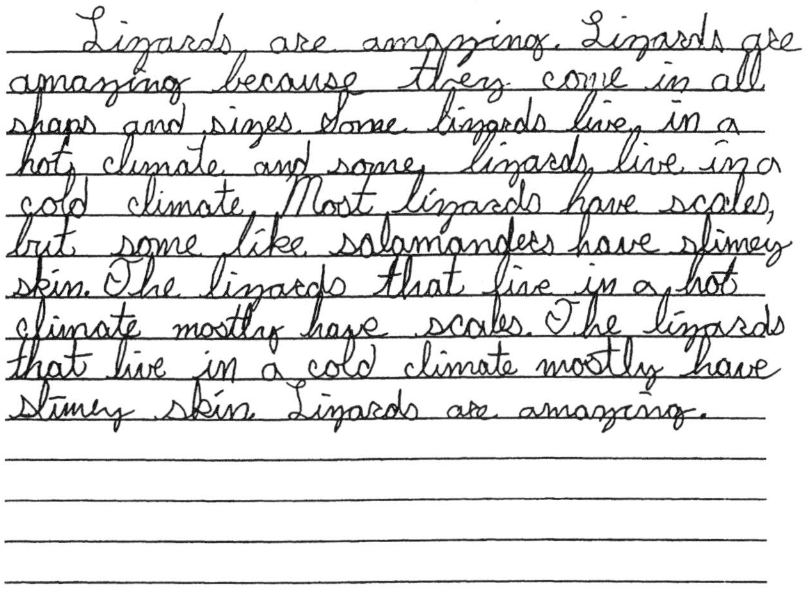
Lizards are amazing. Lizards are amazing because they come in all shaps and sizes. Some lizards live in a hot climate and some lizards live in a cold climate. Most lizards have scales, but some like salamanders have slimey skin. The lizards that live in a hot climate mostly have scales. The lizards that live in a cold climate mostly have slimey skin. Lizards are amazing.

FIGURE 6.14. Writing sample used in a writing conference that focused on traits.

FIGURE 6.15
Writing Trait Checklist for Children

Name _____ Date _____

Ideas

    1. My message is clear.

    2. I have enough information.

Organization

    1. I tell things in order.

Voice

    1. I hear my voice in my paper.

Word choice

    1. My reader will understand the words I chose.

    2. I have used new words: _____.

    3. My favorite words are _____.

Sentence fluency

    1. I have started my sentences with different beginnings.

    2. I have used short and long sentences.

Conventions

    1. I have margins, paragraphs, and sentences.

    2. I have used capitals.

    3. I have used periods, question marks, and exclamation marks.

    4. I have spelled words correctly.

The trait I have used best in my writing:

The trait I want to practice more:

Book Models

One way for students to see the traits in action is by sharing children's books and having teachers point out the masterful use of various traits. All books model all of the traits, but some are particularly good for voice. The *Ramona* books by Beverly Cleary demonstrate voice and give students a clear picture of this trait. Throughout each of the *Ramona* books, Ramona's voice is heard—both internally in her narration, and externally as she interacts with other characters. For example, in *Ramona's World* (Cleary, 1999), Ramona revisits her friendship with Susan from kindergarten to fourth grade. She says, "In first grade, when the class was making owls out of paper bags, Susan copied. . . . The teacher held up Susan's owl to show the class what a splendid owl Susan had made. This was so unfair" (pp. 14–15). Ramona is not alone in sharing who she is; Julian in several books by Ann Cameron is as forthright. In *Julian's Glorious Summer* (Cameron, 1987), he says, "I am a nice person. I practically almost always tell the truth" (p. 5).

These examples from professional writers provide models for students as they develop their own voices in their writing. Students can also explore authors' own websites and web pages to find out how they learned to write, such as *www.pilkey.com*, where Dav Pilkey discusses writing his *Captain Underpants* series. (See Table 7.5 in Chapter 7 for a list of other authors' websites and web pages.) Teachers need to share informational text as well, so that students see it is possible for their voices to be present in informational writing.

To help students with organization, and particularly with how text begins, teachers can facilitate the making of charts that record how several authors begin their books. In Figure 6.16, the first sentences from several informational texts are compared so that students think about how they might bring readers into their own informational texts.

Students may appropriate the structures used by professional writers as they write their own books. Eventually, they will move away from this support as they develop their own ways to begin their writing.

Rock Climbing by Joe Ramsey (2000)	High overhead, Sue seems to float in the air. Her fingers are pressed into a tiny crack.
Our American Flag by Susan McCloskey (2000)	Did you know that the first American flag was very different from the one we see today?
Here Come the Bison! by Elizabeth Savage (2000)	The ground shakes. The air rumbles. The sound of many hooves fills the sky. Here come the bison.

FIGURE 6.16. Beginnings of informational text.

Word Study

Word study for transitional readers and writers is most often centered on long-vowel patterns in single-syllable words. In these words, students learn about the variability of representing long vowels. They also discover homonyms (e.g., *tail* and *tale*) that sound the same but are spelled differently as they explore these patterns.

Assessing Developmental Spelling

A teacher can determine whether a child is ready for the exploration of long-vowel patterns by informally assessing the way he or she represents words in writing. One way to do this is to examine the way the student represents long-vowel patterns in a journal entry. If a child is representing long-vowel words with two letters, even if they are not correct, he or she is ready for this word exploration. Another way to determine whether a child is ready for this exploration is to use a developmental spelling list (Bear & Barone, 1989). Such a list moves from simple consonant–vowel–consonant (CVC) words to multisyllabic words (Ganske, 2000). Figure 6.17 shows Mark's completed spelling inventory. He was asked to spell all of the words on a developmental list (*bed, ship, drive, bump, when, train, closet, chase, float, beaches, preparing, popping, cattle, caught, inspection, puncture, cellar, pleasure, squirrel,* and *for-*

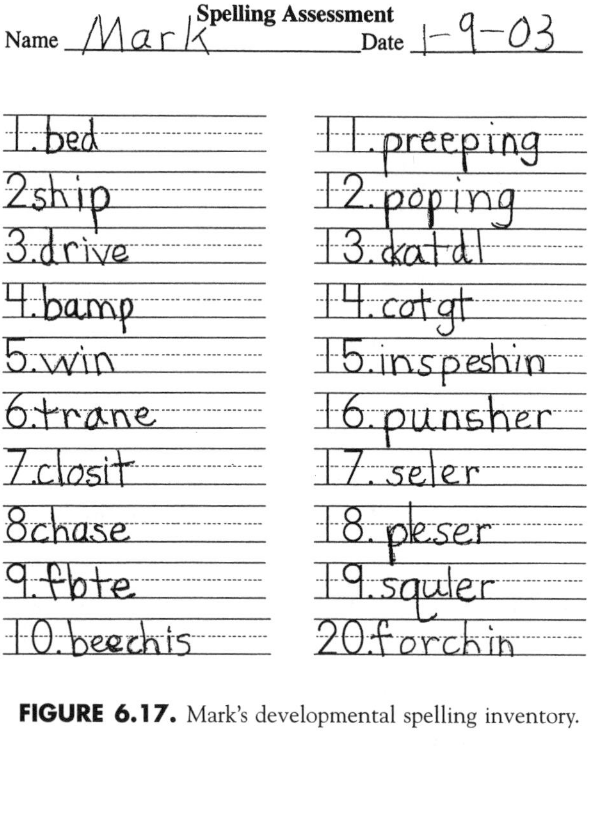

Spelling Assessment

Name __Mark__   Date __1-9-03__

1. bed	11. preeping
2. ship	12. poping
3. drive	13. katdl
4. bamp	14. cotgt
5. win	15. inspeshin
6. trane	16. punsher
7. closit	17. seler
8. chase	18. pleser
9. fote	19. squler
10. beechis	20. forchin

FIGURE 6.17. Mark's developmental spelling inventory.

tunate). When Mark's teacher considered his list, she noted that he became more inventive with his spellings when the words became more difficult. But, most importantly, she noticed that Mark was ready to explore long-vowel patterns, because he was using two letters (e.g., TRANE for *train* and FLOTE for *float*) to represent such patterns. She labeled him as a within-word-pattern speller, and he joined a group of children who were similar in development to explore long-vowel patterns.

Moving beyond the Alphabetic Principle to Pattern Exploration

Students begin the exploration of long-vowel patterns by first considering the differences between short-vowel and long-vowel words. For example, Mary recorded a sort in her notebook that showed the short-*o* and long-*o* words she found in her reading (see Figure 6.18). After exploring this difference, she then considered some of the various ways to record short-*o* and long-*o* patterns. Figure 6.19 shows that Mary was beginning to explore long-*o* patterns; in this first sort, she considered *oa* and *old*. From this beginning, she would refine her knowledge of the various representations of long *o*. Similar word study would occur with each vowel.

In addition to this focused exploration that was recorded in Mary's word study notebook (a spiral notebook where she recorded her sorts), Mary participated in creating word posters and games, among other word study activities. In her classroom, Mary's teacher had posters around the room where students posted words they found in reading that represented patterns. Because the students were focusing on long-vowel patterns, there were five charts with a vowel on each. Periodically, the stu-

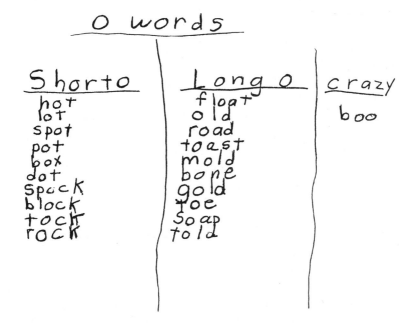

FIGURE 6.18. Mary's first *o* sort.

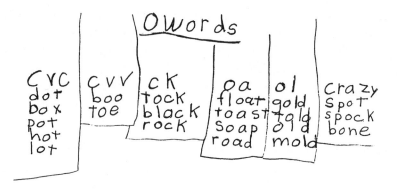

FIGURE 6.19. Mary's second *o* sort, including early consideration of two long-*o* patterns (*oa* and *ol*).

dents pulled the words from a chart for sorting based on the long-vowel patterns. Students also created games like Bingo or racetrack games, using long-vowel words (see Bear et al., 2004, for examples of potential games).

In addition, Mary's teacher used children's books that helped students focus on the patterns in words. One book that she found particularly helpful was Carrier's (1998) *Do Not touch*. On each page of this book, Carrier has a phrase like *quite bright*. The page is set up so that one page folds out; for example, on the quite bright page, the word *right* is highlighted when it is unfolded. With such a book, students begin to look for the words within words and to note their meanings and patterns. Another book that highlights patterns is Viorst's (1994) book *The Alphabet from Z to A with Much Confusion along the Way*. Each letter is represented by several words that have different long-vowel patterns and the same sound. On the Y page, Viorst highlights *you* and *yew*; for V, she notes *vale* and *veil*, and then *vein*, *vain*, and *vane*. Books like this let children participate in word play that accompanies single-syllable long-vowel words. They provide a model for word study and allow children to be flexible when considering words and their patterns.

Word study, where students consider the patterns in words, allows them to use these strategies when they read. By thinking about the pattern in a word and how it is pronounced, they can decipher words in text that previously caused them to stumble and interfered with their reading fluency. They simultaneously learn how to spell these words, and thus their writing fluency is enhanced.

Conclusion: Visiting a Second-Grade Classroom

Lisa Rambur and Amal Singer share a second-grade classroom in a school filled with students from high-poverty backgrounds who often speak languages other than English at home. They decided that they would focus on two major goals throughout the academic year: (1) language and the importance of learning a new language; and (2) content knowledge. These goals were established as they noted that many of their students were fluent in conversational English but not academic English, and they often struggled with the vocabulary in informational books. In addition, Miss Singer had learned English as a second language herself, and she knew how difficult it was to learn in a new language. Shortly after the beginning of their academic year, they indicated that they were very pleased with their students as literacy learners. Miss Singer said, "We have great kids. Only four are not at grade level. I think Reading Recovery in first grade really helped. Now we just have to nudge them to understand informational text."

Organizing for Instruction

These teachers established a routine where students began the day working together and then, following recess, students worked in small groups or with partners. An instructional aide joined the room during the small-group instruction.

Each morning, as children entered the room, one of the teachers greeted them at the door. These simple greetings extended into longer conversations with the students and often their parents as well. Students then proceeded to their desks, where they wrote in journals. As they wrote, both teachers moved among their students and talked to them privately about the content of their journal entries.

Following this writing, the students helped their teachers correct a few sentences that had numerous errors. Miss Rambur and Miss Singer carefully crafted sentences with errors they noticed in their students' writing. They also personalized the sentences by including students' names. Children giggled when they saw their names written in these sentences.

After this beginning, students moved to the front of the room and sat on the carpet. During most days, the students engaged in interactive writing, where they summarized their reading from the basal text. Through this interactive writing, the teachers built on writing skills as they simultaneously focused their students on comprehension. Following this activity, the students read silently from their basal texts and engaged in conversation about the story or informational piece they were reading.

Students then left for a short recess, and when they returned, the organization was quite different. Students worked either with a teacher (each teacher worked with three small, homogeneous reading groups), with the instructional aide, or independently at their desks or a center. When students worked with a teacher, they read leveled text that was usually informational. When they left this guided reading time, they extended their reading by completing charts, reading related books, or exploring more information about their topic in other books or on the Internet. The instructional aide typically worked with students on Readers' Theatre performances and word study activities.

This part of the day was quite busy, as students were engaged in a variety of activities and configurations for almost 2 hours. At the end of this time or right after lunch, one teacher read to the students and engaged them in conversation about the book.

Reflecting

As one of us (Diane Barone) chatted with the teachers at the end of the year, both said, "We don't have enough time to do everything we want." They went on to say, "We have great kids. We love our first year working together as a team. We are fortunate, because we use the same discipline and we have similar teaching philosophies. We believe every child can learn. What happens at home cannot be used as an excuse. We focus on reading. We teach social studies and science through reading. We want all of our kids to read at grade level or above; then they can learn anything.

"We want the children to participate in research. So in a center, we have them research and write about animals or other topics. Then in reading groups, we make sure we have books on their level that deal with animals or whatever topic they are exploring. They learn about the books too, like the words in bold and the table of contents. We were lucky this year, because we had about $3,000 to spend on books for our room. We chose informational books that we thought would be interesting to our students."

Miss Singer also talked about the importance of language. She said, "I learned English growing up, but when I came to the United States, I couldn't read as well as the other kids. I hear teachers say that it's okay for second-language learners not to read as well as other kids. I don't agree. Because of this expectation, they are not reading well. I know these children can do well and will be stronger because they know more than one language. I encourage my students to read in English and Spanish. I want their parents to read to them in Spanish."

As our conversation continued, I asked them whether they would do anything differently in the future, based on this year's experience. They said, "We would focus more on comprehension and vocabulary. We really need to figure out better ways to extend our students' vocabulary knowledge. It hinders them when they read all kinds of books."

Miss Rambur added, "I think we have fluency and guided reading down. We need to figure out ways to get books to our students over the summer, maybe with some comprehension activities. They lose too much during the summer. We can't have them coming in the fall six or seven levels below where they left in the spring. And we have to figure out how not to get so stressed with all the tests. I guess we'll have to work on test-taking skills so the kids won't be so stressed. We are really torn. We hate to use class time to prepare for the tests, but when they see a test, they don't know what to do. So they need to be prepared. This whole testing part is hard, and we know it won't get easier, especially in our school."

As we reflect on the classroom and comments of Miss Rambur and Miss Singer, it is apparent that they must strike a balance among many requirements. Some of these include meeting all the literacy needs of their students (e.g., fluency, comprehension), building their students' vocabulary, and preparing their students for testing expectations.

Chapter 7

TRANSITIONAL LITERACY AND ENGLISH LANGUAGE LEARNERS

In case you were wondering, I'm Maritza Gabriela Morales Mercado. At home, I am Gabi. At school, I'm Maritza Morales. . . .

My walls are covered with posters. Some are of my favorite superheroes. Others are of real-life heroines I read about in a book called *Brave Women in History* that Abuelita, my grandmother, sent me from Puerto Rico. . . .

Mr. Fine walked to the board. He began to write as he spoke. "First, you'll work together to choose one or two animals from each team member's list. Then you'll vote on which animals to use for your project. Finally, you'll present your animals to the class—as a *team*." . . .

Friser is Spanglish for "freezer" or "fridge." Mami hates when I use Spanglish. Spanglish is when you take an English word and add some Spanish to it. Or when you say an English word with a Spanish accent, like *friser*. It sounds like it's really Spanish, but it's not.

—Montes (2003), *Get Ready for Gabi!: A Crazy Mixed-Up Spanglish Day*

Gabi, a Spanish–English bilingual third grader, demonstrates the proficiency in English language skills and in English literacy that characterize an English language learner (ELL) at a transitional stage. She has mastered communicative language in English, although at times she mixes in some Spanish words in oral communication. Gabi is developing her academic language as well, for she reads a book related to social studies that has complex language patterns and content-specific concepts and vocabulary (Corson, 1997; Cummins, 2003; Hernandez, 2003; Peregoy & Boyle, 2001). She also participates in a group project that requires research and discussion with her peers, using content-specific vocabulary and language patterns.

Old and New Challenges for ELLs

ELLs like Gabi exhibit transitional language and literacy behaviors similar to those of their native English-speaking peers as described in Chapter 6. However, they also have unique needs (Peregoy & Boyle, 2004). For example, ELLs continue developing oral language skills as well as academic language, such as producing more complicated sentences with appropriate word choice and grammatically accepted sentence structures (e.g., "I am sorry that I have woken you up. I did not mean to. I thought you had already gotten up").

In Cummins's (1979, 1986, 1989) early work, he categorized language proficiency into communicative language (i.e., basic interpersonal communicative skills [BICS]) and academic language (i.e., cognitive academic language proficiency [CALP]), as described in Chapter 3. Communicative language involves face-to-face, daily communication. This language is contextualized with the support of a speaker's use of gestures, body language, and *realia* (i.e., coins, tools, or other objects used in everyday living). A listener can ask the speaker questions for clarification. Some examples of BICS or communicative language involve asking for directions for cooking, carrying on a playground conversation, and following class routines. It usually takes an ELL child 2–3 years to develop communicative language.

CALP or academic language, on the other hand, is often decontextualized without the support of gestures, body language, or realia. An ELL child needs 5–7 years to develop academic language. For example, in order for an ELL child to understand the concept of *temperature* discussed in a book, the child has to have some prior knowledge of other related concepts, such as *hot, cold, warm,* and *seasons.* In addition to its decontextualized nature, academic language is characterized by content-specific vocabulary words and concepts, and by complex sentence structures that often do not exist in conversational or communicative language (Cummins, 2003). For example, we seldom hear or use the word *asteroid* in daily communication, and we infrequently hear or use a sentence like the following: "Our travelers approached an unexplored asteroid belt, where they encountered an amazing collection of UFBs (Unidentified Flying Bugs)" (Carter, 1997).

In more recent work, Cummins (2003) has described three dimensions of language proficiency that ELLs must master in order to succeed in American schools. The dimensions are conversational fluency (i.e., communicative language), discrete language skills, and academic language. *Discrete language skills* are specific aspects of English linguistic knowledge, such as concepts about print, concepts of alphabet, alphabetic principle, decoding skills, spelling patterns, and grammatical rules. Cummins has pointed out that ELLs acquire some language skills during early stages of their language development (e.g., learning letter names and sounds) and continue to develop these skills throughout their schooling (e.g., learning the past tense of irregular verbs, such as *went* for *go*).

Cummins has further stated that the three dimensions of language proficiency develop simultaneously and are interdependently related to one another throughout ELLs' language and literacy development. He specifically points out the importance of ELLs' mastery of academic language: "Students who developed fluent decoding skills can still experience a sharp drop in reading comprehension scores when the instructional focus changes from learning to read (grades 1–3) to using reading as a tool for learning (grades 4 and up)" (p. 4). He has also criticized isolated phonics instruction by arguing that ELLs who have developed discrete language skills through isolated and intensive phonics instruction demonstrate limited proficiency in comprehending what they are able to decode. Similarly, ELLs who are proficient in conversational skills still need to develop academic language in order to reach grade-level performance.

The focus of this chapter is on helping ELLs at a transitional level develop academic language and continue developing their conversational fluency (i.e., communicative language) and discrete language skills. Many of the strategies and materials described in Chapter 6 can be applied to ELLs with modifications, for ELLs' language and literacy development is similar in many ways to that of native English-speaking children (Fitzgerald, 1995; Krashen, 1985, 1993). This chapter also stresses how classroom teachers can address the unique challenges that ELLs face in acquiring academic language. These challenges include specific sentence and text structures, culture- and content-specific concepts and vocabulary, and prior knowledge. Although the bulk of this chapter consists of three discrete sections—Fluency in Oral and Written Language," "Reading," and "Writing"—again it is important to keep in mind that effective literacy instruction for ELL children addresses all these areas concurrently (Cummins, 2003; Freeman & Freeman, 2003, Hernandez, 2003; Peregoy & Boyle, 2001, 2004). For example, while helping children develop fluency in oral language, a teacher also provides them with opportunities to participate in group discussions. Children's familiarity with the expectations of group discussions allows them to participate actively in a literature circle after reading a book. Word study, instead of being covered in a separate section, is integrated into the discussions of reading and writing to show how word study can be more closely related to ELLs' development in these other areas.

Fluency in Oral and Written Language

Developing fluency continues to be a major task for transitional-level ELLs. Fluency in both oral and written language becomes increasingly important for ELLs as they use English to communicate ideas with their peers and the teacher, and to demonstrate their understandings in concepts and vocabulary in content areas (Cummins, 2003; Faltis, 2001; Peregoy & Boyle, 2001). As Hernandez (2003) has put it, oral communication needs to be embedded in content area learning. Freeman and Freeman (2003) have suggested using stories about content area concepts in conjunction with expository texts to facilitate understanding and conversation. Following are ideas for developing ELLs' fluency in oral and written language.

Show and Tell with a Focus on Content

Teachers do a disservice to transitional-level ELLs if they stop providing opportunities for oral language development. Faltis (2001), Olson (1997), and Hernandez (2003) all indicate that ELLs who have developed conversational language still benefit from activities geared toward furthering their conversational skills as well as supporting content area learning. The materials and strategies for developing fluency can be tied to ELLs' content area learning.

In traditional show and tell, a kindergartner or a first grader talks mainly about the shape, size, color, and sentimental value of an object. In a show and tell with a focus on content, a transitional ELL child focuses his or her talk more on the materials from which an object was made, the place where the object was purchased, and/ or steps to take care of the object. This type of show and tell requires children to use and practice more complex academic language patterns and to integrate content information. For example, when José brings a map of Mexico to show and tell, he shares information related to social studies, such as the shape and size of Mexico, the number of states in Mexico, the population density in each state, the dialects used across Mexico, the people, and so on. José may include in his show-and-tell a brief comparison between the United States and Mexico, which demonstrates his knowledge and provides an opportunity to use compare-and-contrast skills. Figure 7.1 is a form for the teacher to use in evaluating an ELL child's performance on a show-and-tell activity.

Extensive Reading

Cummins (2003), Freeman and Freeman (2003), and Krashen (1993, 1999), among other scholars in the field of second-language acquisition, stress the importance of extensive reading. They point out that extensive reading allows ELLs to strengthen their knowledge of language—and, more importantly, to gain multiple exposures to complex language patterns and content vocabulary that are often absent from communicative language. Extensive reading includes books in various genres on different topics that possess different text structures and language patterns. Students need to understand the differences in sentence structure between an expository text and a narrative text, and between an expository text and a poem. Each day, ELLs require a block of time for extensive reading and the recording of ideas from the books they complete in a reading log (see Figure 7.2). If a teacher notes that a child has only chosen storybooks, the teacher needs to conduct a conference or have an informal chat with the child to nudge him or her to include other genres. If the child's difficulty with informational books is an issue, the teacher may need to have a mini-lesson to scaffold strategies for comprehending this genre. The topics of the mini-lesson might include the structure of an expository text, the differences between a narrative and expository text, or strategies for comprehension.

Books on Tape

More difficult books for transitional-level ELLs often have complicated sentence structures and vocabulary words that they have not often heard and used in their oral communication. Listening to these books on tape enables the children to become relatively familiar with the flow of the sentence structures and the pronunciation of content-specific words (Drucker, 2003). After the students have heard the text and acquired this relative familiarity, this frees up some of their cognitive resources for comprehension. When teachers cannot find books on tape related to curriculum content, they can tape-record the books themselves or ask native

FIGURE 7.1
A Show-and-Tell Evaluation Form

Name:		Date:	
Object:			
Evaluation categories	Often	Sometimes	Never
Integrates content area information (e.g., social studies for an object on a map)			
Uses content-specific vocabulary words (e.g., refers to California as a *state* rather than a *place*)			
Presents ideas in a well-organized way			
Uses appropriate verb tenses			
Uses simple sentences			
Uses compound sentences			
Uses complex sentences			

FIGURE 7.2
Reading Log

Name:	Date:
Book title:	
Genre:	Pages completed:

If the book is informational, circle *all* that apply:

    Social studies   Science   Math

Circle one of the following about the level of the book:

    Too easy   Just right   Too difficult

State why you found it easy, just right, or difficult:

Share one or two important ideas that you discovered in this reading:

English-speaking children in upper grades to tape-record them. Or the teacher can read the book aloud in a small-group setting, so that each child can hear *and* see the text.

Reading Variations of Books or Multiple Books on the Same Topic

ELLs benefit from reading books with variations. After reading one or two versions of a story (e.g., *The Three Little Pigs*), children become familiar with the story plot, vocabulary words, and theme, which later become prior knowledge for other readings of a similar story (Krashen & Terrell, 1983). Prior knowledge helps reduce the difficulty children may encounter while reading a different version of the story with a twist in plot or in characterization. For example, there are different versions of the story about the three little pigs and one bad wolf. Through reading these book variations, ELLs have multiple exposures to a similar set of vocabulary words (e.g., *house, straw, sticks/twigs, bricks, huff, puff, blow down,* and *chimney*) and story elements (e.g., the pigs and wolf as characters). The story elements and vocabulary words thus gradually serve as prior knowledge.

When children are reading other versions of the story with a twist on story elements—say, Scieszka's (1989) *The True Story of the Three Little Pigs*, where the wolf is not a villain—they use their prior knowledge to assist with comprehending the new text and learning about new vocabulary words. For example, in *The True Story of the Three Little Pigs*, the wolf does not huff and puff the house of straw, the house of sticks, and the house of bricks, but his sneeze blows up the first two houses. The plot is therefore different from the traditional story of *The Three Little Pigs*, and it contains new words (e.g., *snuffed, sneezed*). The first section of Table 7.1 lists versions of *Cinderella* from different cultures that can be explored with ELLs.

In a similar manner, children can build up their fluency in reading informational books. Multiple exposures to books on a similar topic help build children's prior knowledge of the content and vocabulary. The books listed in the second section of Table 7.1 on apples share a similar description of the life cycle of apples and vocabulary (e.g., *seed, blossom, fruit, core, Granny Smith, Golden Delicious, apple cider,* and *apple juice*). Because many content words do not frequently occur in daily communication, it is even more important for ELLs to develop full word knowledge of these words through multiple exposures.

Reading

Prior Knowledge of the Structure of Written Text

ELLs at the transitional level begin reading books with many expressions that do not exist in oral communication. For example, no one ever hears the following in oral language:

> "Good morning!" said Trang.
> Trang said, "Good morning!"

TABLE 7.1. Books about Cinderella and Apples

Books about Cinderella

Climo, S. (1989). *The Egyptian Cinderella*. New York: Crowell.
Climo, S. (1996). *The Irish Cinderlad*. New York: HarperCollins.
Climo, S. (1999). *The Persian Cinderella*. New York: HarperCollins.
Coburn, J. R. (1996). *Jouanah: A Hmong Cinderella*. Arcadia, CA: Shen's Books.
Coburn, J. R. (1998). *Angkat: The Cambodian Cinderella*. Arcadia, CA: Shen's Books.
Daly, J. (2000). *Fair, brown and trembling: An Irish Cinderella story*. New York: Farrar, Straus & Giroux.
de la Paz, M. J. (2001). *Abadeha: The Philippine Cinderella*. Auburn, CA: Shen's Books.
Hellee, R. (1993). *The Korean Cinderella*. New York: HarperCollins.
Hickox, R. (1998). *The golden sandal: A Middle Eastern Cinderella story*. New York: Holiday House.
Jaffe, N. (1998). *The way meat loves salt: A Cinderella tale from the Jewish tradition*. New York: Holt.
Marceau-Chenkie, B. (1999). *Naya, the Inuit Cinderella*. Yellowknife, North Territories, Canada: Raven Rock.
Pollock, P. (1996). *The Turkey girl: A Zuni Cinderella story*. Boston: Little, Brown.
Ruffins, R. (2000). *The gift of the crocodile: A Cinderella story*. New York: Simon & Schuster.
San Souci, R. D. (1994). *Sootface: An Ojibwa Cinderella story*. New York: Delacorte Press.
San Souci, R. D. (1998). *Cendrillon: A Caribbean Cinderella*. New York: Simon & Schuster.
San Souci, R. D. (2000). *Little Gold Star: A Spanish American Cinderella tale*. New York: Morrow.
San Souci, R. D. (2000). *Domitila: A Cinderella tale from the Mexican tradition*. Auburn, CA: Shen's Books.
Sneed, B. (1997). *Smoky Mountain Rose: An Appalachian Cinderella*. New York: Dial Books.
Young, E. (1982). *Yeh Shen: A Cinderella story from China*. New York: Philomel Books.

Books about apples

Gibbons, G. (1984). *The seasons of Arnold's apple tree*. San Diego, CA: Harcourt Brace Jovanovich.
Gibbons, G. (1996). *From seed to plant*. Carmel, CA: Hampton-Brown Books.
Gibbons, G. (2000). *Apples*. New York: Holiday House.
Hall, Z. (1996). *The apple pie tree*. New York: Scholastic.
Hutchings, A., & Hutchings, R. (1994). *Picking apples and pumpkins*. New York: Scholastic.
Maestro, B. (1992). *How do apples grow?* New York: HarperCollins.
Micucci, C. (1992). *The life and times of the apple*. New York: Orchard Books.
Royston, A. (1998). *Life cycle of an apple*. Des Plaines, IL: Heinemann Library.
Selsam, M. (1973). *The apple and other fruits*. New York: Morrow.

In addition, more advanced books contain longer sentences, more complicated language patterns, and content- and culture-specific vocabulary. Again, these linguistic features do not appear in children's oral communication. The following excerpt is taken from one of the nonfiction books recommended by the California State Department of Education (*www.cde.ca.gov/ci/literature*) for children in grades K–2, *A Pinky Is a Baby Mouse and Other Baby Animal Names* (Ryan, 1997):

> Baby pigs are piglets wallowing in the pen. Kids are baby goats ramming now and then. Baby pigeons are squabs perched near the windowpane. I am a baby mouse. Tell me, what's my name? Cozy, rosy mouse snuggling in the loft, you are called a pinky because you're pink and soft!

The sentence structure in the first two sentences is similar: A present participle is used to describe the animals' actions. But the second sentence is different from the first one, in that the name of *baby goats—kids—*is the subject of the sentence. In the third sentence, a past participle is used to indicate the state of the animals. The last sentence does not follow a regular subject–verb–object pattern. The first half of the sentence includes a subject (i.e., *mouse*) and adjectives (i.e., *cozy, rosy*) describing it, and a present participle (i.e., *snuggling*) that portrays the subject's action. The second half of the sentence is a complete sentence in itself, with an independent clause (i.e., "you are called a pinky") and a dependent clause (i.e., "because you're pink and soft!"). This excerpt with six short sentences exhibits a great variety of linguistic sentence patterns.

Consider the vocabulary words used in these sentences. ELLs who are familiar with *kids* (i.e., *children*) and *pen* (i.e., a writing utensil) now have to figure out a new layer of meaning for each word within the context of these sentences. *Kids* and *pen* are content-specific words. The word *loft* can be a culture-specific word. If an ELL child has not seen a loft, it would be hard for the child to understand this word. Although the book suggests the meaning of *loft* through the illustration, the child still needs prior experience with the word to understand its meaning.

Prior Knowledge of the Structural Differences between Narrative Text and Expository Text

An additional challenge for ELLs' comprehension is their level of familiarity with narrative and expository text structures. Although an increasing number of teachers introduce nonfiction books to children in kindergarten, the reading of nonfiction books in primary grades continues to be rare (Duke, 2000; Duke, Bennett-Armistead, & Roberts, 2003; Yopp & Yopp, 2000). Therefore, children have less exposure to expository text than to narrative text in school. Their limited familiarity with expository text structures hinders their understanding and consequently their learning in content areas. As Table 7.2 illustrates, an expository text exhibits many characteristics that are absent from a narrative text. To complicate this situa-

TABLE 7.2
Comparison of Characteristics of Narrative Text and Expository Text

Characteristics of narrative text	Characteristics of expository text
Layout of the book	
Book covers, title, author(s), and/or illustrator(s)	Book covers, title, author(s), and/or illustrator(s)
Dedication page	Dedication page (not often)
Title page	Title page
	Table of contents
	Preface, afterword
	Appendices
	Index
	Glossary
	Bibliography/references
	Further readings
	Credits/acknowledgement
	Quiz or activity with answer keys
Structure of the text	
Text and/or pictures	Text (with headings and subheadings); captions for pictures, diagrams, figures, graphs, lists, maps
	Sidebar text
	Footnotes, endnotes
	Websites, other Internet resources
Mainly active voice	A mix of active and passive voice
Varied fonts and typography (not very often)	Varied fonts and typography (e.g., boldface, italics), pronunciation keys
Characters, settings, problems/conflicts and solutions, theme/moral/lesson	Description, comparison and contrast, sequence, cause and effect, problem and solution
Vocabulary	
Many high-frequency words with common and uncommon meanings (e.g., *course* in "of course" vs. "course" in "a three-course dinner")	Many low-frequency words; common words with content-specific meaning (e.g., *table* in a house vs. *table* used for information); content-specific words (e.g., *circuit*); culture-specific words (e.g., *president, democracy*)

From *Teaching Early Literacy: Development, Assessment, and Instruction* by Diane M. Barone, Marla H, Mallette, and Shelley Hong Xu. Copyright 2005 by The Guilford Press. Permission to photocopy this figure is granted to purchasers of this book for personal use only (see copyright page for details).

tion, expository text structures are not necessarily universal, which may present an additional challenge. For example, in any expository text written in Chinese or in Japanese, the feature of an index does not exist.

Even after ELLs become familiar with expository text, their success in comprehending such text depends on how well they select appropriate reading strategies (Chamot, Barnhardt, El-Dinary, & Robbins, 1999). Whereas many reading strategies that a reader uses with narrative text (e.g., predicting, making connections) continue to be useful to the reader when he or she is reading expository text, some reading strategies are unique to comprehension of expository text. For example, the strategy of note taking plays a far more important role in the reading of expository text.

Prior Knowledge on Culture-Specific Content

A large body of research in the fields of reading and second-language acquisition (e.g., Anderson, 1994; Anderson & Pearson, 1984; Carrell, 1984, 1987; Carrell & Eisterhold, 1988; Droop & Verhoeven, 1998; Fitzgerald, 1995) has found that a reader's prior knowledge has an important effect on comprehension. This is true even with a text that is seemingly simple. For example, what does the phrase "0 down till 2005," in an advertisement for a refrigerator mean? Does it mean that the freezer of this refrigerator will work well (i.e., keep food frozen below 0 degrees) till 2005? An ELL student who is reading this advertisement has to have some knowledge of Americans' different ways of paying for commodities.

Consider a short paragraph from Fritz's (1993) *Just a Few Words, Mr. Lincoln*:

> President Lincoln was one busy man. He had two big jobs. He had to free the slaves. And he had to win the war. The Civil War. . . . (p. 5)

In order for ELLs to fully understand this part of the text, they must have prior knowledge of American history, which is very culture-specific. Their prior knowledge must include answers to such questions as these: Who is a President? What does a President do? Why was Lincoln busy? Why did he have to free the slaves? Who were the slaves? Why did he have to win the Civil War? In order for ELL children to have a successful experience with comprehending this book, the teacher needs to build background knowledge about American history during that particular period of time.

Facilitating ELLs' comprehension

To enhance ELLs' comprehension of various texts, teachers need to consider using instructional strategies as well as adapting appropriate instructional materials. Many of the instructional strategies described in Chapter 6 can be applied with ELLs. Two additional strategies—a KWL chart for a story, and outlining—can be used with ELLs. These strategies activate ELLs' prior knowledge, provide adequate scaffolding, and engage children in actively constructing meaning from text.

A KWL Chart for a Story

As described in Chapter 6, a KWL chart (Ogle, 1986) has been traditionally used to activate students' prior knowledge about a subject in a content area and to provide students with a purpose for reading an expository text. However, it can also be used with a narrative text. It then becomes a strategy to engage students in sharing what they know about the book, based on the book's cover and title, about the book (i.e., "what we know"); in predicting what they think is going to happen in the book (i.e., "what we want to find out"); and in summarizing what they have learned from the book (i.e., "what we have learned"). Figure 7.3 is an example of a KWL chart for the story "The Wolf Who Cried Boy" (Hartman, 2002). The unanswered questions in the W column, after children have completed the L column, may motivate children to write a sequel to the book that tries to answer these questions.

A Partially Completed Outline

Echevarria, Vogt, and Short (2004) suggested using an outline as a way to scaffold ELLs' comprehension process. Specifically, the teacher includes major concepts from the book that children will be reading, and children complete the rest of the outline with other information from the book. The teacher may vary the ways to include major concepts. For example, in Figure 7.4, the teacher-completed portion of the outline for the book *All about Owls* (Arnosky, 1995) includes sentences

K	W	L
What we know	**What we want to know**	**What we have learned**
—A wolf and a boy are the characters in the story.	—Why is the wolf screaming?	—The wolf lives with his mother and father.
—The wolf is a baby wolf because he only has four teeth.	—From whom is the wolf running away?	—The wolf hates the meals his mother cooks.
—The wolf is screaming.	—Will the wolf eat the boy?	—The wolf wants to eat boys.
—The wolf looks scared.	—Will the wolf and the boy become friends?	—The wolf tricks his mother and father.
—The wolf is running.	—Will the wolf's parents believe him?	—The wolf sees a lot of boys, and they are Boy Scouts.
—There may be other wolves in the story.	—Will this be the same story as The Boy Who Cried Wolf?	—One of the boys does visit the wolf's home.
—There may be another human in the story.		—Wolf's parents do not believe that there is a boy in their home.
		—The wolf has to eat whatever his mother prepares for him.

FIGURE 7.3. A KWL chart for a story.

The text:

Owls are birds of prey, which means they hunt, kill, and eat small animals. Eagles and hawks are also birds of prey. But they are daytime birds. Owls are creatures of the night. After sleeping all day, they awaken at dusk and hunt until dawn.

The outline:

1. Owls are birds of prey.
    A. _____ small animals.
    B. _____ are daytime birds.
    C. _____ from dusk to dawn.

FIGURE 7.4. An outline for *All about Owls.*

directly from the text, except for the last sentence ("After sleeping all day . . . "). These sentences guide ELLs in locating specific information and in completing the sentences under the heading "Owls are birds of prey" on the outline.

After children become familiar with a partially completed outline, the teacher includes only key concepts and vocabulary from the book. The phrases (or sentences) are not exactly the same as those in the text. Figure 7.5 illustrates an outline variation in which key concepts, such as *poisonous, species, scales, movement,* and *senses,* are recorded from the book *All about Rattlesnakes* (Arnosky, 1997).

The text (the first sentence from the text on each page):

Rattlesnakes are poisonous reptiles. . . .
There are 31 species of rattlesnakes. . . .
Depending on the species, snakes have either keeled scales or smooth scales. . . .
Snakes move by contracting and expanding powerful muscles under their skin to inch them forward. . . .
A rattlesnake's eyesight is very good. . . .

The outline:

1. Rattlesnakes—poisonous reptiles
    A. _____
    B. _____
    C. _____

2. 31 species of rattlesnakes
    A. _____
    B. _____
    C. _____

FIGURE 7.5. A partial outline for *All about Rattlesnakes.*

Providing Textual Scaffolding

Brown (2000) has talked about *textual scaffolding* for beginning readers, in which a teacher matches a book with a child's reading level. Specifically, the child begins with simple, predictable books; moves on to transitional and decodable books; and then reads books with more complex storylines and linguistic patterns. Brown's concept of textual scaffolding can be extended to teaching ELLs at a transitional level. Following are ways for teachers to provide textual scaffolding.

Hybrid Texts with Features of Narrative and Expository Text

Like their native English-speaking counterparts, ELLs may not have much exposure to informational books. Therefore, it is important that teachers first introduce books with mixed characteristics of narrative and expository text and gradually move to include more expository texts. Some book series, such as the *Magic Tree House* (*www.randomhouse.com/kids/magictreehouse*) and *The Magic School Bus* (*www.scholastic.com/magicschoolbus*) series, are written in a narrative format, but focus on specific content. The *Magic Tree House* series covers topics in social studies and science, and *The Magic School Bus* series contains information about various areas of science. *The Wild Thornberrys* series, based on a popular TV show on the Nickelodeon channel in which a family travels around the world to film documentaries on various creatures and cultures, address topics in social studies and science.

After finishing reading hybrid texts, children can complete a learning log (see Figure 7.13, below) where they record content information, content-specific vocabulary, or organization. For example, after reading *The Magic School Bus: In the Time of the Dinosaurs* (Cole, 1994), children may note the features of sidebar texts, pictures with captions, and timelines, all of which are common characteristics of an informational book.

Book Sets of Informational Books and Storybooks

Another way to provide textual scaffolding is for teachers to use book sets on specific content topics that include both storybooks and informational books (Camp, 2000; Vacca & Vacca, 2001). Such a text set makes teaching content less challenging for teachers and learning about content information less difficult for ELLs. Table 7.3 provides a book set on colors. *Autumn Leaves* and *Color* are the only two books that are written in an expository format. Most books with a storyline describe concepts related to colors such as primary colors, secondary colors, the color wheel, or opposite colors (e.g., *White Rabbit's Color Book* and *Hello, Red Fox*). Some books expand the concept of color to include its associations. In Dr. Seuss's *My Many Colored Days*, children learn about feelings associated with colors (e.g., "On bright red days how good it feels to be a horse and kick my heels!"). Hamanaka's *All the Colors of the Earth* celebrates the diversity among human beings (e.g., "Children come in all the colors of the earth—the roaring browns of bears and soaring eagles . . ."). This book set helps children learn about the concept of color in science, and also different layers of meaning associated with color (e.g., diversity).

TABLE 7.3. A Book Set on Colors

Baker, A. (1994). *White rabbit's color book.* New York: Kingfisher Books.
Brown, M. W. (1986). *Color kittens.* New York: Golden Books.
Cabrera, J. (1997). *Cat's colors.* New York: Dial Books.
Carle, E. (1998). *Hello, red fox.* New York: Simon & Schuster.
DeRolf, S. (1996). *The crayon box that talked.* New York: Random House.
Ehlert, L. (1991). *Red leaf, yellow leaf.* San Diego, CA: Harcourt Brace
    Jovanovich.
Hamanaka, S. (1994). *All the colors of the earth.* New York: Morrow.
Heller, R. (1995). *Color.* New York: Grosset & Dunlap.
Jonas, A. (1989). *Color dance.* New York: Morrow.
Lionni, L. (1959). *Little blue and little yellow.* New York: McDowell, Obolensky.
Robbins, K. (1998). *Autumn leaves.* New York: Scholastic.
Seuss, Dr. (1996). *My many colored days.* New York: Knopf.
Walsh E. S. (1989). *Mouse paint.* San Diego, CA: Harcourt Brace Jovanovich.

Multimedia Texts Related to Content Areas

ELLs bring their experiences of interacting with multimedia texts, such as TV shows and videotapes, to school. Some of these texts are specifically related to content. Table 7.4 provides some examples. Teachers can capitalize on children's experiences with multimedia texts. For example, the teacher may include a multimedia text in a book set for a specific content area. Children can go to the appropriate web resource to learn about the content area. The web resource often has text accompanied by other visual and audio aids, such as pictures, animation, and sounds. These aids help

TABLE 7.4. Multimedia Texts Related to Content

PBS Kids TV shows

Liberty's Kids (social studies): *pbskids.org/libertyskids*
The show focuses on events that happened during the period 1773–1789 in American history.

Reading Rainbow (social studies, math, science): *pbskids.org/readingrainbow*
Each episode of the show features a book set on a content area, and includes book reviews by children who have read the book.

Zoboomafoo (science, social studies): *pbskids.org/zoboo*
The show features different animals and their habitats, and talks about protecting endangered species and their environment.

ZOOM (social studies, math, science): *pbskids.org/zoom/index.html*
The show, hosted by students in upper grades, features activities, games, experiments, interviews, and so on that are related to all content areas children are learning in school.

Nickelodeon TV show

The Wild Thornberrys (social studies, science): *www.nick.com/all_nick/tv_supersites/thornberrys/flash_index.jhtml*
The show features a family that travels around the world to film documentaries on creatures and cultures.

contextualize the information presented in the text and reduce the difficulty of reading the text.

Informational Picture Books with Labels

Some informational books focus on a topic in one content area not only through the text, but also through labels in the illustrations. For example, in Gail Gibbons's (1984) *Fire! Fire!*, labels are used in the pictures of part of the fire station, different parts of the fire engine, and tools that firefighters use. Jerry Pallotta's math books (e.g., *The Hershey's Milk Chocolate Multiplication Book* [2002b], *Apple Fractions* [2002a]) also have labels for math equations (e.g., $5 \times 4 = 20$, three-thirds = $3/3$). The *Scholastic Visual Dictionary* (Corbeil & Archambault, 2000) includes 5,000 labels in 350 illustrations of topics ranging from the solar system to human body. Often a visual label for an object (or a living thing) can enhance ELLs' understanding of the descriptive text about it. Visual labels facilitate children's understanding of relationships between an object and other objects (e.g., the distance between the Earth and Mars), between a living thing and other living things (e.g., a food chain among carnivores, herbivores, insectivores, and omnivores), and between concepts (e.g., condensation, precipitation, and evaporation).

Enhancing Vocabulary Development

At the transitional level, ELLs expand their vocabulary, continue to learn about familiar words with unfamiliar meanings (e.g., *note* in "a musical note," whose meaning is different from *note* in "I wrote you a note"), and learn about new words in content areas. Vocabulary development can be more challenging to ELLs than to native English-speaking children for two reasons. First, as noted earlier, there is a huge difference between the vocabulary used for communication and that for academic language (Corson, 1997; Cummins, 2003). Corson and Cummins have both pointed out that the vocabulary used for daily communication consists primarily of high-frequency words, one or two syllables in length, from the Anglo-Saxon lexicon. By contrast, many words used in academic language are low-frequency words, three or four syllables in length, derived from Greek and Latin. As Corson (1997) further confirms, Greco-Latin words mainly appear in books. The nature of Graeco-Latin words makes it relatively difficult for people to learn them unless they have read books of various genres and topics. Corson suggests that "Words are only fully learned when they are available for active use" (1997, p. 699). Transitional-level ELLs have developed fluency in oral language, and are developing fluency in reading and writing. But they may have had limited exposure to texts in content areas and to highly literary texts with sophisticated vocabulary. In addition, ELLs are continuing to catch up with their native English-speaking peers, who do not stop to wait for ELLs while developing their own academic language proficiency (Collier & Thomas, 1999; Cummins, 2003).

Another reason why vocabulary development, particularly in content areas, may be difficult for ELLs is the complex process of word knowledge development. Nagy and Scott (2000) have identified five characteristics of word knowledge development: incrementality, polysemy, multimensionality, interrelatedness, and heterogeneity. *Incrementality* means that children develop full knowledge about a word over time and through multiple exposures. An ELL child's initial understanding of the word *van* can be applied to any big vehicle in a rectangular shape, including a sport utility vehicle. The child later learns to differentiate between a van and a sport utility vehicle. Many words in English possess *polysemy*—that is, multiple meanings. High-frequency words tend to have multiple meanings. Consider the word *run*. The most common meaning is "to go by moving the legs rapidly, faster than in walking." Its other meanings include *manage*, as in "run a company"; *participate in an election*, as in "run for president"; *use up something*, as in "run out of gas"; *continue*, as in "the show runs through the week"; and *operate*, as in "run a program on a computer."

When a child's knowledge of a word is characterized by *multimensionality*, the child has mastered many aspects of this word. That is, if a child knows the word *educate*, the child (1) knows how to say the word; (2) can use it appropriately within the context (i.e., in a grammatically and semantically correct manner); (3) knows other words associated with it, such as synonyms (e.g., *teach, instruct, train*), antonyms (e.g., *learn*), and derived words (e.g., *education, educator, educated, ill-educated*, and *educating*); and (4) knows the morphemic structure of the word (i.e., *-ate* is a suffix indicating that the word is a verb). *Interrelatedness* refers to the connection between a child's knowledge of one word and that of other related words. For example, the phrase *a laptop computer* will be familiar to a child who already knows words like *computer, hardware*, and *software*. The last characteristic of word knowledge, *heterogeneity*, related to the other characteristics, means that "to know a word depends on what kind of word one is talking about. For example, knowing function words such as *the* or *if* is quite different from knowing terms such as *hypotenuse* or *ion*" (Nagy & Scott, 2000, p. 273).

The complex process of word knowledge development that Nagy and Scott (2000) have described indicates again the importance of extensive reading and multiple exposures to a wide range of vocabulary. In addition, Cummins (2003) has advocated that "as learners read more in their second language, repeated exposure to unfamiliar words will exert an incremental effect on vocabulary learning" (p. 26). Following are a few specific activities that can be used with ELLs to develop vocabulary.

A Reversed Word Cluster

Peregoy and Boyle (2001) describe a new way to a use word cluster that they learned from a classroom teacher, Stephanie Marion. In a conventional word cluster, the teacher places a target word in a center circle, and asks children to come up with words associated in meaning or in concept with the target word. Ms. Marion used a word cluster in a reversed way. She first presented a text in which a target word was omitted. She next asked her students to think about a list of possible words that might fit the sentence. Then she provided the students with the target word. Peregoy and Boyle comment that this is a great way to encourage students to participate in discussion of a word, share their word knowledge, and use context clues. In Figure 7.6 the word *protest* from the text *A Picture Book of Martin Luther King, Jr.* (Alder, 1989), has been omitted.

Collecting Big Words

Cunningham (2000) suggests that students should collect big words that they have encountered in their reading and study them. Big words, often with multiple syllables, may present difficulty in decoding. They also contain meanings important to the text in which they appear. This is especially true of big words related to content areas. For example, from Gibbons's (1984) book *Fire! Fire!*, students can jot down these big words: *apartment, bulldozer, chemicals, damaged, discharge, dispatcher, electrical, emergency, equipment, explosion, farmhouse, fire dispatch, firefighters, forest rangers, hydrants, nozzles, parachute, poisonous, pressure, prevention, propeller, standpipe,* and *volunteer.* However, just having children list big words is not going to be effective in helping them learn these words. Rather, children should explore the words, including their meanings and structural elements (i.e., syllables, affixes, and the effects of affixes on base words) (Bear, Invernizzi, Templeton, & Johnston, 2004). This exploration is a way to activate children's prior knowledge about the words. One way to explore these words is to list those that are specifically related to fires and firefighters, and also to ask children to provide other big words related to fires and firefighters (see Figure 7.7). A second way for children to learn more about these words is to give them a chance to explore the meanings of the words. Each child can provide contexts and meanings for the words as shown in Figure 7.8, and then the children can compare their responses.

Collecting Interesting Words

Cunningham (2000) also recommended that teachers encourage students to collect interesting words, especially those from their outside-school literacy experiences. These collected words provide children with a sense of ownership, which may motivate them to study the meaning and spelling. In Figure 7.9, a student included two

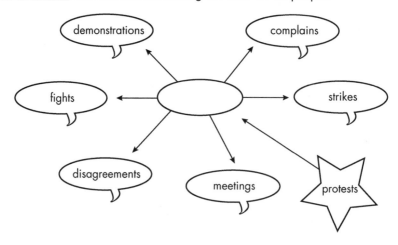

Martin Luther King, Jr. was one of America's great leaders. He was a powerful speaker, and he spoke out against the law which kept black people out of many schools and jobs. He led _____ and marches demanding fair laws for all people.

FIGURE 7.6. A reversed word cluster on *protest.*

A–E	F—J	L–O	P–T	V–Z
bulldozer chemicals damaged discharge dispatcher electrical emergency equipment explosion	fire dispatch firefighters forest rangers hydrants	nozzles	parachute poisonous pressure prevention propeller standpipe	volunteer

Other big words we know

ambulance	helicopter
apparatus	hospital
compressed-air	self-contained
cylinder	waterproof
extinguisher	fireproof
fireproof	

FIGURE 7.7. Big words related to fires and firefighters.

The word	The context	Meanings
discharge	Pumps in the fire trucks control the water pressure and push the water up through the discharge hoses.	sending, pouring
extinguisher	The fireman used hoses and a fire extinguisher to put out the fire.	equipment/device container that has foam or liquid that is sprayed on a fire

FIGURE 7.8. What I know about these big words.

Word	Meaning
mystic	magical, spiritual
mystical	supernatural

Other related words:

mystery
mysterious

FIGURE 7.9. Interesting words: *mystic* and *mystical*.

words from his Yu-Gi-Oh trading cards: *mystic* on a magic card titled *Mystic Plasma Zone*, and *mystical* on a monster card titled *La Jinn, the Mystical Genie of the Lamp*. One way for the student to explore these two words is to study the meanings of these words and to think about other derivational words. Figure 7.10 illustrates some examples of interesting words whose meanings are not commonly known, from Farshtey's (2003) book *The Official Guide to Bionicle*.

Word Storm

In the word storm activity (Klemp, 1994), the teacher chooses a word related to a content area. Then each student completes a seven-part worksheet (see Figure 7.11 for a completed worksheet for the word *environment*). The student does the following:

1. Writes down the target word.
2. Includes the sentence where the word appears.
3. Writes down words the student can think of when hearing the target word.
4. Jots down derivational words.
5. Identifies people who would use these words.
6. Identifies other words that may have a similar meaning.
7. Uses the word in a new sentence.

After each student has completed the worksheet, the teacher presents a transparency of the worksheet and guides the class members to share what they have written. Interesting discussions can be generated through the sharing process. The sharing is also another way for the teacher to assess students' level of word knowledge related to the target word.

Exploring Prefixes and Suffixes

The English language contains many derivational words, each of which is formed through a prefix and/or a suffix attached to a base word. Some examples of base words and derivational words are *happy—happily, happiness, unhappy; expect—expected, unexpected*. Studying word structural elements (i.e., prefixes, suffixes, and base words) helps children to make the connections between known base words and

Word	Context	New meanings	Common meanings
check	His temper is as legendary as his powers, but he tries hard to keep it in check.	control	payment, make sure things are okay, √
rash	Lewa Nuva is rash, bold, and often plunges into situations without considering the danger.	quick, fast	red spots on the skin

FIGURE 7.10. Common words with new meanings.

Word storm

Student's name _____

To understand a word, it is sometimes better to know more than just the dictionary definition. A word map lets you write down different types of information to help you understand what a word means and the many ways in which the word can be used.

What is the word? *environment*

Write the sentence from the text in which the word is used (use the space below):
All living things need an environment that is right for their needs.

What are some words that you think of when you hear this word?
homes, city, habitat

What are some different forms of the word? *environments, environmental,*
environmentalist, environmentally

Name three people who would be most likely to use the word besides teachers:
1. *scientists*   2. *environmentalists*   3. *Biologist*

What are some other ways of saying the same thing? *habitat, home, surroundings,*
neighborhood

Make up a sentence using this word. Let your sentence tell what the word means.
My neighborhood is an environment and very noisy but safe.

FIGURE 7.11. A completed word storm worksheet.

unfamiliar derivational words (Bear et al., 2004). Another reason for exploring prefixes and suffixes is that some nonalphabetic languages (e.g., Chinese and Japanese) do not have affixes as in English that indicate a particular part of speech (e.g., *-tion* in *education* indicates that the word is a noun) or a particular meaning (e.g., *unhappy* is the opposite of *happy*). Children whose native language is a nonalphabetic language may find it confusing to use different prefixes—say, for negation, such as *un-* for *unhappy* and *in-* for *incorrect*. ELLs whose native language shares some Latin or Greek roots with English may also find that some affixes are confusing. For example, in Spanish, the suffix *-ion* (as in *education*) indicating that the word is a noun is different from the suffix *-tion* (as in *education* in English).

Teachers can lead a discussion on different types of prefixes with a similar meaning (e.g., *un-*, *im-*, and *in-* all mean negation) and suffixes with the same grammatical function (e.g., *-tion* and *-ment* signify that a word with such a suffix is a noun). For example, the teacher can ask children to come up with words that contain a prefix meaning negation. For example, the prefix *de-* can mean negation (as in *devalue*) and taking away (as in *defrost*). Figure 7.12 lists words that contain a prefix meaning negation. This list of words can also be displayed on the word wall, so that children can add more words under each prefix.

FIGURE 7.12
A List of Prefixes with the Meaning of Negation

Prefixes	Words
a-	atypical
ab-	abnormal
anti-	antisocial
de-	devalue
il-	illegal
im-	improper, impolite
in-	incorrect, inappropriate, inexpensive
ir-	irregular
mis-	mistrust
non-	nonfiction
un-	unhappy, untrue, unimportant, unsatisfactory

Writing

The writing strategies described in Chapter 6 can be effectively used with ELLs (Ada, 2004; Peregoy & Boyle, 2001). However, teachers of ELLs need to integrate continued support for developing ELLs' knowledge of English linguistic structures in general and knowledge of linguistic patterns for academic language writing in particular. Word study on different spelling patterns can be part of the editing process, in which various mechanical errors (including spelling errors) are addressed. This section describes several specific strategies to support ELLs' writing.

Learning Logs

Often learning logs are used after children have read books. Logs can also be used to help ELLs organize information learned for later writing of a paper or report on a content topic. Figure 7.13 is a form that allows each student to document what he or she has learned about the content, to define vocabulary words, and to list information he or she is interested in learning more about. As the form indicates, each student can use a list format to complete the categories of "What I have learned about the content," "What I still want to know about the content," and "New features of an expository text that I have noted." Gradually, however, the teacher requires each student to complete information in a paragraph format. This way of scaffolding supports the student by making it easier to transfer the information from the log to a paper or a report that he or she may later write.

Reading–Writing Connections

Another way to make writing more authentic and relatively less challenging for ELLs is to ask them to write something based on what they have read. They can rewrite a book with a different ending or with characters playing different roles. Or children can write a new story based on different stories they have read. Some children's books can serve as models for this type of reading–writing connection. For example, Jon Scieszka's (1992) *The Stinky Cheese Man and Other Fairly Stupid Tales* is a collection of rewritten fairytales, such as *The Ugly Duckling*, *Red Riding Hood*, and *Chicken Little*. Palatini (1995) has nicely blended the song "Old McDonald Had a Farm" and the tale *The Three Little Pigs* into the book *Piggie Pie*, in which pigs outsmart the witch who tries to make piggie pie out of them. Eugene Trivizas's (1993) *The Three Little Wolves and the Big Bad Pig*, and Jon Scieszka's (1989) *The True Story of the Three Little Pigs*, are two examples of the tale of *The Three Little Pigs* with twists in plot and in characterization. After children have read one of the books described above, the teacher may ask them to think about ways to rewrite a familiar story. The teacher and children may rewrite the story as a class before children do this independently.

FIGURE 7.13
A Learning Log

Name:	
Book title:	
Pages completed:	Date:
Circle *all* that apply: Social studies Science Math	

What I have learned about the content:
1.
2.
3.
4.
5.

New vocabulary words (Please define each in your own words):
1.
2.
3.
4.
5.

Vocabulary words with new meanings (Please define each in your own words):
1.
2.
3.
4.
5.

What I still want to know about the content:
1.
2.
3.
4.
5.

New features of an expository text that I have noted:
1.
2.
3.
4.
5.

Topics for a mini-lesson or an individual conference (for the teacher to complete):

Learning about Authors

It is important for ELLs to explore how professional writers choose topics, conduct research, and present information. Table 7.5 lists the websites and web pages of some authors of children's literature. After visiting an author's site or page, children can jot down information about the author, the titles of books, and questions that they may want to ask the author. Information about the author becomes handy when children are doing an author study. Children can also develop an outline on how an author organizes informational books. The outline helps children learn the art of writing information. Even if two books have a compare-and-contrast text structure, two authors can come up with different ways to present the comparison (Vukelich, Evans, & Albertson, 2003).

Collecting Different Types of Sentences

It is imperative for ELLs to become familiar with and start using more complex sentence structures (i.e., compound sentences, complex sentences, and compound–complex sentences) in their academic writing. Here are some examples of different types of sentences from Jim Arnosky's (2002) *All about Frogs*:

- A simple sentence has a subject and predicate: "Frogs, toads, and salamanders are amphibians."
- A compound sentence contains two or more independent sentences (or

TABLE 7.5. Websites and Web Pages
of Children's Authors

Ada, Alma Flor: *www.almaflorada.com*
Arnosky, Jim: *www.jimarnosky.com*
Brett, Jan: *www.janbrett.com*
Carle, Eric: *www.eric-carle.com*
Cleary, Beverly: *www.beverlycleary.com*
dePaola, Tomie: *www.tomie.com*
Gibbons, Gail: *www.gailgibbons.com*
Hoberman, Mary Ann: *www.maryannhoberman.com*
Martin, Bill, Jr.: *www.billmartinjr.com*
Mayer, Mercer: *www.littlecritter.com*
Montes, Marisa: *www.marisamontes.com*
Munsch, Robert: *www.robertmunsch.com*
Pallotta, Jerry: *www.alphabetman.com*
Park, Barbara: *www.randomhouse.com/kids/junieb*
Pilkey, Dav: *www.pilkey.com*
Polacco, Patricia: *www.patriciapolacco.com*
Ryan, Pam Muñoz: *www.pammunozryan.com*
Say, Allen: *www.eduplace.com/author/say*
Soto, Gary: *www.garysoto.com*
Wood, Audrey: *www.audreywood.com*
Yolen, Jane: *www.janeyolen.com*

clauses) joined by such words as *and, but,* or *then,* or a semicolon: "This bull-frog is not facing you, but it can see you."

- A complex sentence includes two sentences (or clauses); one is independent and the other is dependent: "When a frog leaps, it always touches down on its hands."
- A compound–complex sentence includes at least two independent sentences and one or more dependent sentences: "Few predators eat toads because when a toad is threatened its skin excretes moisture that irritates the eyes, mouth, and nasal membranes of many animals, including humans."

Tompkins (2002) has suggested that children collect examples of these four different types of sentences from their books. Then the class and teacher share the structure of each sentence. These sentences become authentic and meaningful instructional materials for the teacher to use not only to assess children's comprehension, but also to help children see the effective use of sentences. Gradually, each child can collect different types of sentences from his or her own writing. For example, Figure 7.14 presents an ELL student's writing on her experience of Halloween. Although it is a relatively short story, the text includes many sophisticated linguistic patterns. These collected sentences become assessment data for both the teacher and the child. If the teacher has noted that the sentence patterns in the child's writing do not vary much, the teacher may want to conduct a mini-lesson.

The text:

October 1, 2003

It was a dark Halloween night while I was going to trick or treat when a spooky witch grabbed me by the foot. She took me to her house and tied me up. She left the room and slammed the door and giggled. She went back and gave me some food and left again. When I was done eating, she took me and put me in a room filled with black cats. I started to pet the cat, then I saw a girl with one eye. Then I said, "Hi!, but I ran away and screamed. She caught me, and . . . The End

Sentence type	Example
Simple sentence	She went back and gave me some food and left again.
Compound sentence	I started to pet the cat, then I saw a girl with one eye.
Complex sentence	When I was done eating, she took me and put me in a room filled with black cats.
Compound–complex sentence	It was a dark Halloween night while I was going to trick or treat when a spooky witch grabbed me by the foot.

Self-reflection:

I used compound and complex sentences in my Halloween story.

FIGURE 7.14. A collection of effective sentences.

TABLE 7.6. Sentence-Manipulating Activities

Activity	Definition	Example[a]
Sentence unscrambling	1. The teacher selects a rather complex sentence from a reading book, and divides it into phrases. 2. Children put the phrases into a sentence. 3. Children compare the new sentence with the original one from the text to see whether the meaning of the new sentence is consistent with the one by the author.	Original sentence: "Tree frogs are small, slender frogs with large, sticky toe pads for climbing on branches and leaves." Phrases: • Tree frogs are small, slender frogs • with large, sticky toe pads • for climbing on branches and leaves
Sentence combining	1. The teacher selects a complicated sentence from a book, and breaks it into several short sentences. 2. Children combine the short sentences into one sentence. 3. Children compare the new sentence with the original one from the text to see whether the meaning of the new sentence is consistent with the one by the author.	Original sentence: "Some, like the spring peeper tree frogs, are so small that you cannot find them even when you follow the sound of their call!" Sentences and phrases: • Some are so small • like the spring peeper tree frogs • you cannot find them • you follow the sound of their call
Sentence expanding	1. The teacher selects a beginning from a sentence from a book. 2. Children complete the sentence, reflecting the author's meaning. 3. Children compare the new sentence with the original one from the text to see whether the meaning of the new sentence is consistent with the one by the author.	Original sentence: "Tree frogs living in tropical places are more brilliant in color and have bolder markings than tree frogs living anywhere else." A beginning of the sentence: *Tree frogs living in tropical places* . . .

[a]All examples are from Arnosky (2002).

Exploring Sentence Structures

Several sentence-manipulating activities recommended by Tompkins (2002) enhance ELLs' abilities to use more complicated sentence patterns in their narrative and expository writing. These activities are sentence unscrambling, sentence combining, and sentence expanding (see Table 7.6). Initially, the teacher picks sentences from children's books; gradually, the teacher chooses sentences from children's writing that can be combined and/or expanded.

Conclusion: Visiting a Third-Grade Class

Maryvel Cárdenas's third-grade class with 25 students consists of Latinos, Filipinos, Cambodians, and African Americans. Of these 25 students, 5 are ELLs at the intermediate or early advanced level. Most of the other 20 students who were ELLs and have reached the English proficiency levels are considered as English-only speakers.

Mrs. Cárdenas's class is full of instructional materials of varied genres and interests. Besides the required Open Court Reading series, the students have access to a wide range of texts in the classroom, such as realistic or historical fiction, poetry, informational books, chapter books, newspapers, and Internet texts. The students also have access to the school library with a very large selection of materials; in addition, they use the school computer lab (weekly) and the class computers (daily) to read, research, and collect information on topics. Mrs. Cárdenas describes how she provides scaffolding for her ELLs to continually develop their English language literacy and to master vocabulary and concepts in subject areas:

"I strongly believe that an ELL student is capable of performing exceptionally in all academics. Every morning, I provide my students with clear objectives that are written on the board for them to read. For example, in one of the lessons for the unit on Halloween and *Los Días de los Muertos* (the Days of the Dead), I wrote, 'Today we will learn to compare and contrast cultures of Mexico with those of the United States by creating a double-bubble map [Venn Diagram graphic organizer].' Making objectives clear and visible to the students helps them develop a sense of the goals for each day's learning. The daily activities or lessons I provide are meaningful and with integrated opportunities for my students to speak, write, read, and listen. We do daily journal writing for 20–30 minutes, which is used to connect prior knowledge to a concept we are studying, or I use it as a motivational tool to stimulate the students to express their thoughts about themselves in writing. We do daily silent sustained reading of and book discussions on Open Court and children's literature books. For listening, we have partner readings and sharing of writing assignments. During math time, students share their problem-solving strategies with one another and later with the class.

"I do a lot of read-alouds for teaching content areas, such as science and social studies. For example, *The Magic School Bus* series is great for science! I used *The Magic School Bus: Lost in the Solar System* [Cole, 1990] to introduce our solar system unit. I read to my class constantly, and it is from the read-alouds that I pull the content and create lessons and activities like the unit on *Los Días de los Muertos* and Halloween. The books that I used for this unit were *Beto and the Bone Dance* [Freschet, 2001], *The Spirit of Tío Fernando* [Levy, 1995], *The Vigil of the Little Angels* [Andrade, 2001], and *Maria Molina and the Days of the Dead* [Krull, 1994]. I always try to link the concepts that are being taught to the prior knowledge of the students, like comparing Halloween to *Los Días de los Muertos*. Halloween is not celebrated in Mexico. However, November 1 and November 2 are important days: Mexicans celebrate All Saints' Day on November 1 and All Souls' Day on November 2. All Saints' Day is the day when the souls of the little departed children return to their homes. All Souls' Day is a national holiday when adults' souls return to their homes. Many Mexican people believe that on these days the spirits of the dead return to earth to be fed. All over Mexico, families expect visits from the spirits of their dead ones and receive them as honored guests. After reading books on *Los Días de los Muertos*, each student did a concept map of *Los Días de los Muertos* [see Figure 7.15] and then wrote about *Los Días de los Muertos* [see Figure 7.16].

FIGURE 7.15. A concept map on *Los Días de los Muertos*.

"I routinely use several strategies to support my ELLs and those who are now considered English-only speakers, but still need my support. One form of support focuses on the text. My students are reading at or above the third-grade level, so some of the materials that I provide for them are appropriate for their grade level, and at times at a bit higher level. I adapt the content being taught to all levels of student proficiency. For those who have trouble comprehending a text on a subject area, I provide a summary or notes of what we will be reading, and also discuss the text with the students.

"Another way for me to support my students is to constantly explain and review vocabulary words for the students and to often engage them in using these words. For example, I do a daily word storm [Klemp, 1994], which introduces content area vocabulary words. In completing a word storm, the students define a new word, explore its word forms (e.g., one of the word forms for the word *explore* is *exploration*), write up synonyms for the word, and use the word in a sentence [see Figure 7.11 in this chapter].

"A third way of scaffolding my students' learning is my constant modeling of reading strategies by thinking aloud. Thinking aloud, I believe, is very effective, because the students get to see and hear how I think in order to understand the text. During reading of a text on a content area, for example, I create a graphic organizer. After I have read aloud a page or a paragraph that contains an important fact or idea, I sum up what I read and write it on the organizer. Not only do I sum up aloud, but also I write it down on paper as a visual support for my students. The modeling process also helps my students learn how to focus on important ideas, organize them, and present them in a graphic organizer.

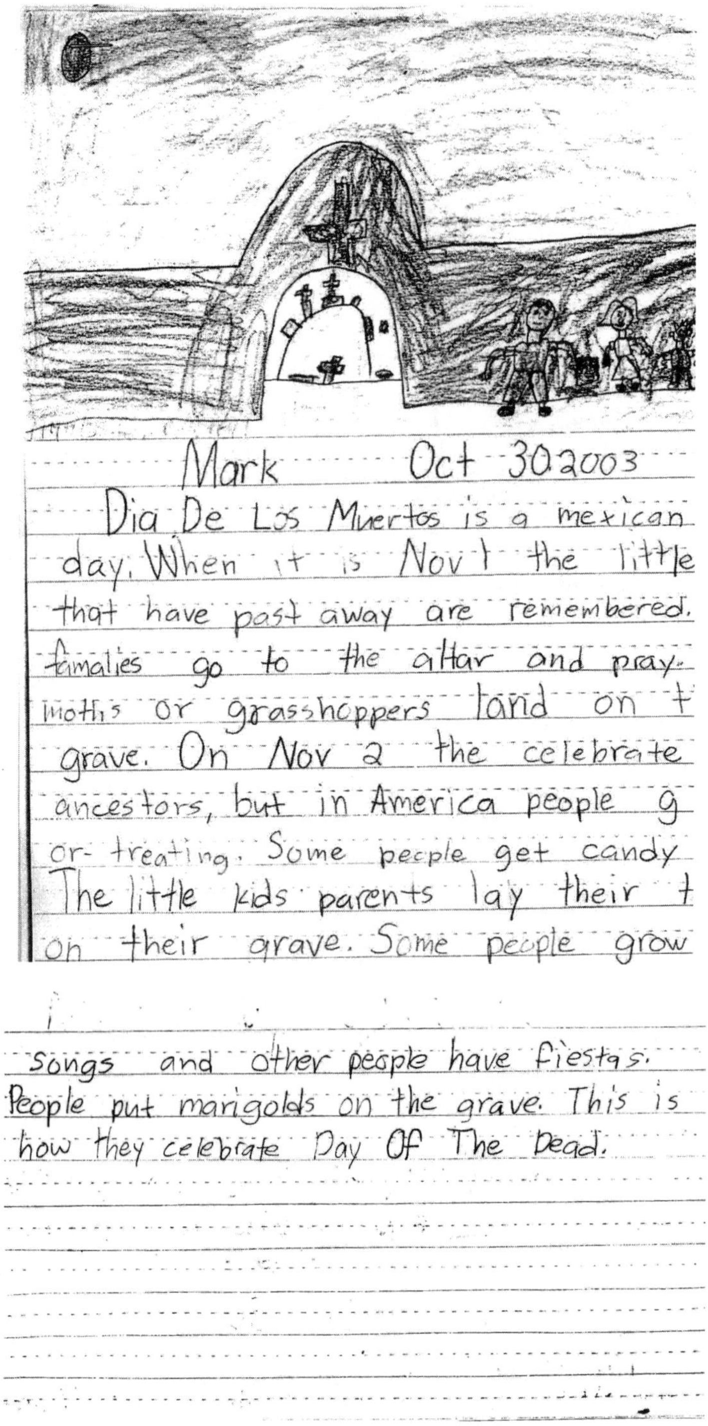

> Mark   Oct 30 2003
> Dia De Los Muertos is a mexican
> day. When it is Nov 1 the little
> that have past away are remembered.
> fimalies go to the altar and pray.
> moths or grasshoppers land on †
> grave. On Nov 2 the celebrate
> ancestors, but in America people g
> or-treating. Some people get candy
> The little kids parents lay their †
> on their grave. Some people grow
>
> songs and other people have fiestas.
> People put marigolds on the grave. This is
> how they celebrate Day Of The Dead.

FIGURE 7.16. A journal entry on *Los Días de los Muertos*.

"A last way of scaffolding is to gradually withdraw my support and to engage my students in taking charge of their own learning. For example, for each writing assignment on an expository topic (e.g., *Los Días de los Muertos*) and a narrative topic (e.g., a field trip to the aquarium), we create a scoring guide to follow. I guide my students in brainstorming the characteristics of a good piece of writing (which will earn a score of 4 on the state standardized test). I ask my students, 'What makes a writing piece earn a score of 4?' Here were some characteristics that my students came up with:

- 'It makes sense to the reader.'
- 'You stay on the topic.'
- 'Your sentences and paragraphs are detailed and complete.'
- 'You have very few spelling or grammar errors like periods or capitals.'
- 'Your handwriting is very neat.'

"I believe that my students are very bright. Through my modeling the behaviors of a scholar (professionalism, exercising the mind by reading, setting goals, etc.), by giving time for them to think and respond to what we are studying, and by providing opportunities to discuss and share with classmates, I have created a positive and challenging learning environment. This environment is crucial for my ELL students to become fluent readers, writers, speakers, listeners, and thinkers."

Chapter 8

ENGAGING FAMILIES

Tell me a story, Mama, about when you were little.
What kind of story, baby?
Just any old story. . . . Remember the time when you were little and you found that
puppy with no tail by the side of the road?
Poor little thing. . . .
You kept it hidden in your sweater, huh, Mama?
We had three dogs already. . . .
I like it when you tell me stories, Mama. Tell me more tomorrow.
Okay, okay. More stories tomorrow.

—JOHNSON (1989), *Tell Me a Story, Mama*

The African American girl in this book likes listening to Mama tell stories about Mama's childhood. The characters in these stories often include Mama, grandparents, relatives, and neighbors, and the settings are situated in Mama's community. *Tell Me a Story, Mama* reflects, through an African American girl's experiences with bedtime stories told by her mother, the oral tradition of literacy in African American communities (Gee, 1996; Heath, 1983). Although Mama does not seem to engage the girl in activities that are traditionally considered school-related (e.g., reading aloud a story and asking comprehension questions), Mama's stories do provide the girl with an opportunity to learn about what a story is—that is, *story grammar*, to use a literary term.

Tell Me a Story, Mama stimulates teachers to think more fully about family involvement and about children's home literacy experiences. This chapter describes ways of engaging families to support children in their literacy development. It also encourages teachers to examine their own beliefs for any misconceptions they may have about families' and children's home literacy experiences. The chapter begins with the evolving concept of family involvement and possible misconceptions about family involvement. It also discusses children's literacy experiences in which their families participate. Finally, it focuses on various ways classroom teachers can engage families.

Family Structures

Family structures have changed dramatically in the last century, and many families in the United States today do not have a standard structure with a father and a mother. Many children live with one parent; with one parent and grandparent(s); with grandparent(s); with relatives (e.g., aunts, uncles, and/or cousins); with many members of an extended family (e.g., grandparent[s], aunts, uncles, and cousins); with stepparents; or with foster or adoptive parents (Wasik, Dobbins, & Herrmann, 2001). English is no longer the only language used in U.S. homes, and for many children, a native language or an English dialect is the medium of communication and learning. Many families maintain their native cultures and languages, and these may have some impact on children's literacy experiences, which may be different from those of children living in the mainstream culture (Delgado-Gaitan, 2002; Xu, 1999).

These changes in family structures are often not reflected on the form that a school asks each family to complete at the beginning of a school year. Instead, the form requires the educational backgrounds and employers of a child's father and mother only. Figure 8.1 can be used to learn much more about the family structures of students. Classroom teachers can obtain the information through a teacher–family conference and through more informal interactions with families, such as a brief chat with a family member who drops off and/or picks up a child at school. The information about each student's family structure will give a classroom teacher a better understanding of who plays an important role in the student's literacy experiences outside school. Throughout the school year, the teacher will know who in the student's family should be contacted to discuss literacy development. For example, the information on the school form may indicate only that a student does not live with his or her parents. But if the teacher knows about the student's family structure, and is aware that the student lives with very supportive grandparents, the teacher can make efforts to communicate with the grandparents—instead of focusing on the fact that the student does not have a father and a mother, and lamenting that he or she will probably never get any parental support.

While gathering information about students' family structures, teachers explain to the families why they want this knowledge and how school learning is enhanced through an understanding of students' home literacy. Some families may not be comfortable sharing details about their family structure, and it is important to respect a family members' wish to keep their family structures private. But teachers can ask such a family for a contact person to discuss a student's literacy development. Given the changes in family structures, the terms *family/families*, *family members*, or *caregivers* instead of *parents*, and *family involvement* instead of *parental involvement*, are used throughout this chapter.

Appreciating Families' Ways with Words

Examining Possible Misconceptions about Family Involvement

Before teachers make efforts to engage families, it is important for teachers to examine their own possible misconceptions about family involvement in children's literacy development. Research has indicated that many teachers today do not share the lin-

FIGURE 8.1
Family Interview

Child's name _____ Date _____

In the spaces below, list all family members who reside in the home with the child. Circle or highlight the name of the contact person for the family. In the "Relationship to child" column, the following abbreviations may be used: M, mother; F, father; B, brother; S, sister; GM, grandmother; GF, grandfather; A, aunt; U, uncle; C, cousin; N, niece; Ne, nephew; SM, stepmother; SF, stepfather; FM, foster mother; FF, foster father; AM, adoptive mother; AF, adoptive father.

Name of family member	Relationship to child	Languages spoken

Are there family members or friends who are not residents in the home with the child, but with whom the child maintains a close relationship? If so, list them below. The abbreviations given above may be used in the "Relationship to child" column, as well as the following: CG, caregiver; GodM, godmother; GodF, godfather; Fr, friend.

Name of family member	Relationship to child	Languages spoken

Questions a teacher may ask to obtain further information on family structure:

1. Who takes care of the child at home? _____
   _____

2. Who helps the child with homework? _____
   _____

3. Who reads to/with the child? _____
   _____

4. Who plays with the child? _____
   _____

5. Who watches TV or plays games with the child? _____
   _____

6. Who talks to/with the child? _____
   _____

Other questions:

guistic and cultural backgrounds of their students, and that many do not live in the same community as their students (Ladson-Billings, 2000; Nieto, 2000). For many such teachers, the media may have become a main source of information about students' cultures, languages, and communities. This source of information can be stereotypical, inaccurate, and at times demeaning, thus reinforcing misconceptions that teachers may hold (Lewis, 2001; Sleeter, 2001). As Taylor and Dorsey-Gaines (1988) put it, "If we are to teach, we must first examine our own assumptions about families and children and we must be alert to the negative images in the literature" (p. 203).

A large body of research has shown that evidence of family involvement in children's literacy development varies among families of different cultural, linguistic, and socioeconomic backgrounds (e.g., Delgado-Gaitan, 2001; Heath, 1983; Rodriguez-Brown, 2003; Taylor, 1983; Taylor & Dorsey-Gaines, 1988). Such variations may lead teachers to develop misconceptions about the involvement of families from culturally and linguistically diverse backgrounds and of low-income families. These families' backgrounds are often unfamiliar to teachers from the mainstream culture. Many such teachers tend to misinterpret limited participation in school activities and support for children's learning from these families as families' not valuing and showing interest in children's education (Rodriguez-Brown, 2003; Perez, 2001). To the contrary, numerous studies (e.g., Paratore, 1999, 2001, 2003; Perez, 2001; Reese, Balzano, Gallimore, & Goldenberg, 1995, Rodriguez-Brown, 2003) have shown that Latino families, for example, do consider themselves as teachers for their children, but in a way different from what teachers in school may define. The family members focus their role as teachers for their children on educating their children to develop morals, values, and high standards, and to become good people. The families leave academic subjects to teachers. Moreover, family members who speak limited English often feel incompetent in teaching academic subjects to their children.

Likewise, research has challenged misconceptions about low-income families' not supporting their children's learning. In an ethnographic study of five low-income families with children who were successful at school, Taylor and Dorsey-Gaines (1988) found that the parents provided their children with various types of support, ranging from reading to children to modeling reading and writing. Similarly, Purcell-Gates's (1996) study of 20 low-income families showed that parents did engage their children in literacy practices at home, though the types and frequencies of these literacy practices varied. She further indicated that parents in the study began or increased their support for children's literacy learning after the children started formal schooling. In support of the findings by Taylor and Dorsey-Gaines and by Purcell-Gates, Barone's (1999) longitudinal study of 26 children from poverty described how family members provided safe and supportive home environments for the children and how family members played different roles in promoting children's literacy learning (e.g., the roles of a parent, a religious leader, and a teacher). Furthermore, Barone identified several factors limiting family members' participation in children's learning. These factors included family members' limited educational level, a scarcity of funds for purchasing literacy-related materials, and a lack of transportation for traveling a long distance from home to school.

Redefining Students' Home Literacy Experiences

Similar to misconceptions about family involvement, teachers may consider only school-related and print-based literacy activities (e.g., reading books and writing stories) in which students participate as valuable literacy experiences. Again, this is especially true for teachers from the mainstream culture whose students are from nonmainstream, limited-English, and low-income backgrounds. Such teachers are more likely to have limited knowledge of how literacy is valued and used in communities with different cultures and languages. According to a sociocultural perspective on literacy, literacy practices will vary with culture and language, and students construct literacy knowledge through daily living (Delgado-Gaitan, 2001; Gee, 1996, 2001; Heath, 1983; Purcell-Gates, 1996; Street, 1984).

In her seminal ethnographic work on the use of language and literacy by children in an African American working-class community, a European American working-class community, and an unspecified middle-class community, Heath (1983) observed that there were differences in how each community valued language and literacy, and in how children in each community practiced literacy. Some literacy practices (e.g., reading bedtime stories) in one community gave its children a better chance to be successful at school than other literacy practices (e.g., "two or more story-tellers collaborate on story," p. 295) that occurred in another community.

In their work in Latino communities, Moll and his colleagues (Moll, 1997, 1998; Moll & Gonzalez, 1997; Moll, Amanti, Neff, & Gonzalez, 1992) identified rich funds of knowledge about language and literacy that the children and their communities possessed. These funds of knowledge included cultivating plants, providing first aid, fixing cars, and applying for welfare benefits. Although such funds of knowledge may not seem to be school-related, they did allow children in the communities to experience the conventional and social uses of language and literacy. In support of the observations by Moll and his colleagues, Paratore, Melzi, and Krol-Sinclair (2003) found a range of literacy practices in Latino/Latina families. These practices included "literacy for the sake of teaching/learning literacy" (e.g., a parent read to a child), "daily literacy" (e.g., a parent wrote a letter to a teacher), and "literacy in leisure activities" (e.g., a mother read a book) (p. 105).

In addition to literacy practices involving varied ways with words, families also engage their children in using nonprint text. During the last decade, the field of *new literacy studies* has offered a unique lens for examining literacies and literacy practices. Through this lens, literacies and literacy practices are perceived as being local, situated, embedded, dynamic, and social; moreover, literacy practices are viewed as related not only to printed words, but also to symbols (e.g., images, music notes) (Barton & Hamilton, 1998; Gee, 1996, 2000, 2001, 2003; Hull & Schultz, 2002; Luke & Freebody, 1997; New London Group, 1996; Street, 1984, 1995). One area of literacy practices in students' communities that has drawn increasing attention is students' experience with popular culture texts. Young children learn about the functions and conventions of language and literacy through such nonprint texts as movies, songs, and computer games (Buckingham, 1993; Dyson, 1997, 2003a; Gee,

2003; Marsh, 1999; Marsh & Millard, 2000). Teachers of kindergartners may be familiar with this scenario: Five-year-olds can retell what they have seen on a TV episode of *Pokemon* or explain how they have solved a mystery by finding all the clues that Blue gave in *Blue's Clues*. These kindergartners are often unable to read the books based on *Pokemon* and *Blue's Clues*, but they have developed through interacting with popular culture texts some implicit understandings about characters, settings, plot, problems, problem solutions, and theme.

Learning about Students' Home Literacy Experiences

Because students engage in a wide range of literacy practices outside school that are not always necessarily associated with print-based texts, it is important for teachers to learn about students' home literacy experiences, even before engaging families to support students' literacy learning. The following are some ways that teachers can learn.

Visiting Students' Communities

Many teachers do not live in the same community as their students; therefore, they may not be familiar with literacy practices unique to their community. Teachers can walk through students' neighborhoods with a community member as a guide if they don't feel comfortable exploring on their own. During the walk, they need to pay attention to facilities (e.g., a supermarket, a library, a church) and to print and nonprint texts in the environment (e.g., road signs, store names, graffiti). They should also observe how people in the community use language and literacy. For example, a teacher who drives to work may not have experience in reading a bus schedule and waiting for the right bus, which is identified by words, numbers, or signs on the bus. But for people who rely on public transportation, the acts of reading a bus schedule and identifying the correct bus become significant literacy practices that are related to survival in this particular community.

While visiting students' communities, a teacher can invite his or her students to be navigators (Orellana & Hernandez, 1999). This visit can be part of a classroom field trip. During the walk, students tell about environmental print in English and in other languages, and explain how they are able to read this print. Teachers can also ask students to explain some of the details in their everyday lives. Table 8.1 lists some sample questions that the teacher may ask students while visiting a grocery store, a supermarket, or an open-air market. The interactive walk in students' neighborhoods gives students an opportunity to share their funds of knowledge about their neighborhood and their literacy knowledge; it also provides the teacher with information about students' communities.

A teacher who visits students' communities or takes an interactive walk with students can be supportive of students' literacy learning in several ways. For example, knowing the importance of reading a bus schedule allows the teacher to describe functional uses of language and literacy outside school during instruction. The teacher can explain that reading a bus schedule is very similar to reading a book, in that the rules of reading from left to right and from top to bottom apply to

TABLE 8.1. Sample Questions for an Interactive Walk in a Grocery Store

1. Where does your family get food? Is it here? Is it somewhere else? (Do not assume that everyone goes to a supermarket to get food.)
2. How do you know which food is on sale?
3. What is this food?
4. What does its label say?
5. Can you tell me more about how to cook and eat this food?
6. What does it taste like?
7. Do you eat this food very often or only on a special holiday?

Note. Other questions can be asked, depending on the circumstances. For example, in an open-air market, some prices may be negotiable; if so, ask how prices are determined.

both. The teacher can also guide students to compare identifying the right bus to predicting an event in a book by using multiple textual clues. The teacher can explain: One uses phrases, words, and a number written on the upper front of the bus, and the colors and logo of the bus, to identify the right bus; in a similar way, one needs pictures and sentences on the pages as clues to predict what is going to happen on the next pages.

After an interactive walk, the teacher can engage the students in a language experience activity where the teacher dictates what the students have described about the walk. The text becomes authentic and meaningful, in that it comes from the students and is about their lives. Later in the day, the teacher types up the dictation and provides each student with a copy. The students read and reread the text during their independent work or during center time. The teacher walks around to ask individual students to read the text with/to him or her, and to identify words the students know.

Visiting Students' Homes

Information that teachers have obtained from visits to students' communities may not be representative of each student's family, and literacy practices in individual students' families may vary. A visit to a student's home thus helps the teacher identify patterns of literacy practices unique to this particular student's family; it also provides an opportunity to establish a relationship with the student's family. A teacher is expected to walk into each student's home with an open mind and willingness to learn from the family. He or she makes an effort to pay such visits early in the school year. A home visit that occurs when the teacher needs to discuss problems related to learning or behavior does not yield the same benefits as one where the teacher wants to learn about the family, its life, and its literacy practices. During the visit, the teacher engages family members in causal conversation and learns about the family's literacy practices. Figure 8.2 is a home visit guide that lists some areas for observation and for interactions with family members. A good practice is for the teacher to send a thank-you note to the family the day after the home visit. This note helps establish and strengthen the teacher's relationship with the family.

FIGURE 8.2
Home Visit Guide

Family _____ Date _____

Literacy environment
List observed print materials, in English and/or a native language (e.g., books, TV schedule, papers for writing, ads, Bible or other religious text, bills, student's work, etc.):

List observed nonprint materials, in English and/or in a native language (e.g., PlayStation, Game Boy, TV, VCR, DVD player, computer, etc.):

(*Note:* For both print and nonprint materials, ask family members about things that you have not observed. For example, you may not see a computer in a living room, but this does not necessarily mean that the family does not own a computer.)

School-related literacy practices
Reading, in English and/or in a native language (e.g., an assigned book):

Writing, in English and/or in a native language (e.g., an assigned essay):

Word study, in English and/or in a native language (e.g., studying spelling words):

Non-school-related literacy practices
Functional and survival, in English and/or in a native language (e.g., reading ads to identify items on sale):

Spiritual, in English and/or in a native language (e.g., reading Bible or other religious text):

Entertainment, in English and/or in a native language (e.g., reading a TV schedule, watching a TV show):

Information about students' non-school-related literacy practices provides the teacher with a point of reference during literacy instruction. For example, when a student has been read the Bible or another religious text (e.g., the Koran), and the family members have discussed lessons from this text, the student may have developed skills of inferring a theme from the read text. If the teacher knows about this non-school-related literacy practice, the teacher can refer to the student's experience while helping him or her make inferences from a school text to understand the theme of the story.

Asking Families to Take Anecdotal Notes

During a home visit, teachers may not obtain all of the relevant information under each category in Figure 8.2. Teachers can ask families to jot down anecdotal notes about their children as readers and writers (Austin, 1994). The notes can be taken during a 2-week or even longer period of time. The two examples given in Figure 8.3 include the date and setting that a literacy event occurred and a brief description of the event. (Figure 8.4 is a blank form for recording such notes that a teacher can give to a family member.) At times, families may have a narrow view of what is considered a literacy practice. It is important that teachers explain to families a wide range of literacy practices.

Anecdotal notes taken by family members provide information about a child's literacy abilities outside of school to share with the teacher during a teacher–family conference. The way that teaching is conducted at school may produce fewer opportunities for some students to demonstrate their literacy knowledge. In-class assignments and formal and informal assessments do not always provide evidence of students being good readers and writers. For example, in Xu's (1999) study, a bilingual Chinese boy was not considered by his teacher as a good reader and writer, whereas at home the boy read different genres of books and understood his favorite TV shows. The boy was not accustomed to completing worksheets, which constituted the major form of daily literacy instruction in his classroom.

Rethinking Students' Home Literacy Experiences

After teachers have done community and/or home visits, it is time to record the discoveries about students' outside-school literacy practices and to note similarities and differences in literacy practices (see Figure 8.5 for a filled-in version, and Figure 8.6 for a blank version). The information from the comparison is a tool for teachers to challenge any misconceptions they may have about students, their families, and their communities, and to develop a view that appreciates, values, and supports students' prior experiences of ways with words and symbols.

Inviting Families to the Classroom Community

A school can be an institution that is unfamiliar to many families, especially when the families are from another cultural and linguistic background (Edwards,

Child's name Dylan Smith   Family member's name Jan Smith (mother)

My child is a reader!		
Date	Setting	Example
01/02/2002	In the living room	Dylan read the instructions for the Bionicles (Lego toys).

My child is a writer!		
Date	Setting	Example
01/10/2002	At the kitchen table	Dylan copied from an ad pizza and eggs and gave it to me. He said, "I want pizza and eggs."

FIGURE 8.3. A family's guide for anecdotal notes (filled-in, abbreviated version).

Pleasants, & Franklin, 1999). Many families are not sure whether they can be part of the classroom learning community, or whether they really can do something to help classroom teachers. Many family members work, and some may have more than one job; coming to the classroom to help is virtually impossible in such cases. Teachers need to seek innovative ways to involve families.

Soliciting Family Members' Funds of Knowledge

At the open house, teachers can provide families with a list of literacy projects students will be doing during the school year, such as writing a book, *My Family and Me*. Two or three weeks prior to the project of writing the book, a note is sent home asking each family for artifacts to be included in the book (e.g., photos, postcards, notes, etc.). At the conclusion of the project, when each student shares his or her completed book, the teacher can invite members of each family to be the audience and to share additional information about the family. If no one from a family can attend the event, it can be videotaped so that the family can watch at home.

In the beginning of the school year, teachers can ask families to list things they might share with students (e.g., cooking, building things, singing, calligraphy, etc.). This information becomes handy when teachers consider the learning activities they have planned for their students. In an example described by Xu (2001), during a third graders' unit on popular culture music, Sherry Mead asked Latino parents to teach the students how to do the *La Cumbia* dance. The dance was performed by a Mexican band, *Los Kumbia Kings*, whose music the students were studying. Learning this dance would have been impossible without the Latino/Latina parents' participation.

FIGURE 8.4
A Family's Guide for Anecdotal Notes

Child's name _____ Family member's name _____

My child is a reader!		
Date	Setting	Example
My child is a writer!		
Date	Setting	Example

Literacy practice	Frequency among students in class	Occurs in students' community (or communities)?	Occurs in teacher's community?
Reading books	7/20	Yes	Yes
Reading graffiti	15/20	Yes	No
Reading a bus schedule	14/20	Yes	No

FIGURE 8.5. Ways with words and symbols in students' community (or communities) and in a teacher's community (filled-in version).

Informing Families about School Learning

Another way to invite families into a classroom community is to familiarize them with children's school learning. Wollman-Bonilla (2000) suggests having each child write about school experiences in a family message journal and take the journal home to share. Family members can respond to what is written. In a similar way, a school–home journal provides a two-way communication opportunity between the teacher and families (Hanhan, 2003). In a school–home journal, the teacher writes about a student's learning at school and sends it home. Then the family responds to the teacher's comments and describes the student's learning at home. Both the family message journal and the school–home journal are good avenues for teacher–family communication, but they can be time- and energy-consuming. A variation might be to focus on some students who seem to be making slower progress in literacy and to send journals to these children's homes more often. Teachers can also ask families questions that may help explain why these students are not making satisfactory progress. The journal communication allows everyone to work together to help the students achieve, even if family members find it difficult to visit the school.

Involving Families in Class Projects

A third way to include families in the classroom community is to ask each family to help a child complete a project. For example, one child read a mini-book created by the teacher, *Fall Leaves* (e.g., "The leaves turn yellow. The leaves turn red"), to his family and his neighbors. Then the family members and neighbors signed the "Reader's Response Page" of his book and wrote about their favorite color of leaves (see Figure 8.7). Figure 8.8 shows how the family members supported the child in putting together a book, *My Senses*. The family provided the child with pictures related to the content on each page. Then the family members helped the child copy or spell the label for each picture. Sending books home to be read or written can be a year-round project for families to do with their children.

FIGURE 8.6
Ways with Words and Symbols in Students' Community (or Communities) and in a Teacher's Community

Literacy practice	Frequency among students in class	Occurs in students' community (or communities)?	Occurs in teacher's community?
Reading books			
Reading graffiti			
Reading a bus schedule			

A variation of this practice was developed by Cohen (1997), who has created a book backpack program in her kindergarten classes. Each backpack contains five to seven high-quality children's books on a theme, written by the same author, of a similar genre, or related to student interests. Each book pack includes a letter to the family, explaining the purpose of the family's reading books with the child. The teacher can also include a description of what the child is learning at school, to inform the family.

Helping Families Become Teachers of Their Children

During children's early language development, families play an important role. During children's schooling years, it is still crucial for family members to continue to be their children's teachers of language and literacy; this is especially critical, considering that children only go to school for half a year. When families engage their children in literacy practices in various outside-school settings, children have additional opportunities to strengthen, expand, and extend their literacy skills. This section discusses a list of activities (see Figure 8.9) that families can do to engage their children in literacy learning and exploring. Teachers can share these activities with families during an open house, through newsletters, and through school or district workshops for families.

A: Alphabet Books

Alphabet books vary in their content and difficulty levels, and they serve different purposes for children at different stages of literacy development. Some alphabet

Reader's Response Page

After I have read my book, *Fall Leaves*, to you, please sign your name below. Also, please tell me which color of fall leaves is your favorite.

1. _Erwin Stipp_

My favorite color of leaves is _red_.

2. _Mike Castillo_

My favorite color of leaves is _Orange_

3. _Shelly Xu_

My favorite color of leaves is _Red_.

4. _Shelley Xu_

My favorite color of leaves is _Golden_

FIGURE 8.7. Reader's Response Page in a child's mini-book, *Fall Leaves*.

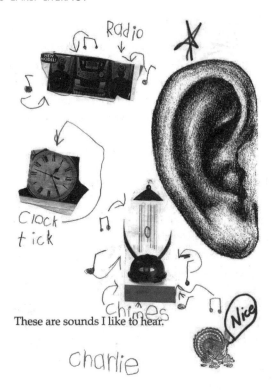

FIGURE 8.8. A page from *My Senses*, a book put together by a child and his family.

books are appropriate for young children to develop their alphabetic knowledge. These books often include a one-to-one correspondence between the picture on the page and the labeling word or words starting with a target letter. For example, in *On Market Street* (Lobel, 1981), *Apples* is the label for the apples that a child uses to decorate herself.

Another type of alphabet book centers on a theme or a subject and is supportive of children who are at the transitional phase of literacy development. This type of book provides a rich source of content information. For example, in Pallotta's (1988) *The Flower Alphabet Book*, each page has a flower whose name starts with an alphabet letter and a description of the flower: "B is for *Buttercup*. Buttercups have petals that are yellow and shiny. People say, if you put one under your chin and it reflects yellow light onto your skin, it means you like to eat butter." Families may need some support when engaging their children with these more complicated alphabet books. A teacher can send home a KWL chart to help.

B: Books of Various Genres

While selecting books to read to/with children, families need to expose children to books of different genres (e.g., alphabet books, storybooks, informational books, poetry books, fantasy, biography, etc.). It may take a child a while to become com-

FIGURE 8.9
ABC Literacy Activities for Families

A: Alphabet books

B: Books of various genres

C: Comic strips

D: Discussions of text

E: Environmental print

F: Family modeling

G: Graphic organizers

H: Homemade books

I: Internet resources

J: Journaling

K: Kidwatching

L: Library visits

M: Message boards

N: Newspapers

O: Oral reading

P: Predictable books

Q: Quotes from a text

R: Read-alouds

S: Spelling words

T: Thematic exploration

U: Uninterrupted sustained silent reading

V: Visual literacy

W: Words, words, words

X: Xmas gifts of literacy materials

Y: Year-round reading and writing

Z: Zone of proximal development

fortable reading books of a less familiar genre. For example, a kindergartner who has been read alphabet books, storybooks, and books with rhythm and rhyme may find it difficult to understand an informational book. A family member needs to begin reading a simple informational book with the child and help him or her learn about a unique feature of an informational book: telling facts about something. Gradually, the family member can move on to a more complex informational book that is about the same topic as the simple one, but explores the topic in depth. For example, *Growing Colors* (McMillan, 1988) is a simple book on colors. It has a color word on a left page (e.g., *red*) describing the color of a fruit or a vegetable on the right page (e.g., *raspberries*). Walsh's (1989) *Mouse Paint* introduces the primary colors and secondary colors, and explains how mixing two primary colors to make a secondary color. This informational book is written in a story format. After the child has heard this book, he or she is ready for a book on colors with more depth, like Heller's (1995) *Color*. It explores the topic of colors in depth, with descriptions of basic concepts of colors and of how colors affect nature and people.

C: Comic Strips

Some comic strips that are popular among children can be used to support their literacy learning. Comic strips such as *Classic Peanuts* by the late Charles Schultz, *Garfield* by Jim Davis (*www.garfield.com*), *Dennis the Menace* by the late Hank Ketcham, and *The Family Circus* by Bil Keane (*www.familycircus.com*) describe situations that many children also encounter in their daily life. Family members can read the captions to children, discuss the situation, and ask why one particular piece is funny. Many comic strips contain vocabulary associated with new concepts and technologies. In one piece in *The Family Circus*, Billy's dad does not know where to make a turn at an interaction. Billy comments, "See, Daddy? That's why we should have a global positioning receiver." After reading the strip, a family member can talk with a child about the words *global* and *positioning receiver*, and ask the child how Billy's dad can figure out which way to turn. Another way of using comic strips is to download an online comic strip, wipe out the captions, and discuss possible captions for the pictures. This activity supports children in developing their ability to make meaning.

D: Discussions of Text

It is not enough for a family member just to read a text (e.g., a book or other print material) to a child. It is even more important to spend time discussing it. A discussion of a text involves more than a family member's asking the child questions related to characters, setting, plot, solution, and theme. Rather, during a discussion, a family member shares his or her response to the text, talks about his or her thinking process (e.g., why he or she predicted this part), describes his or her favorite part of the text, and expresses puzzlement about certain parts of the text. This part of the discussion models for the child how another literate person understands the text.

Another aspect of a discussion is persuading the child to show what he or she knows or can find out. When the child is asking a question about the text, the family member tries not to give the answer to the question too quickly. Instead, the family member may ask, "Where do you think you may find the answer? Let's find that page together. Did the author say anything about . . . ?" By referring the child back to the text, the family member shows the child how to make use of contextual clues and repeated reading to enhance comprehension.

E: Environmental Print

Environmental print is "print and other graphic symbols, in addition to books, that are found in the physical environment, [such] as street signs, billboards, television commercials, building signs" (Harris & Hodges, 1995, p. 73). (See Xu & Rutledge, 2003, for details on different types of environmental print.) This is a valuable and very cheap source of print material for families and children to explore different aspects of written language. Here are a few activities:

1. *An environmental print alphabet book.* A child can cut out from environmental print pictures whose labels begin with a target letter. For example, the child can glue a picture of apples and an apple pie on the page for the letter *a*. A family member can encourage the child to write or copy down the label for each picture.

2. *A word sort activity.* A child can copy from environmental print words on cards that he or she already knows. A family member and the child then collaboratively sort the words according to the sounds (i.e., a beginning sound, a middle sound, and an ending sound), spelling pattern or word family (e.g., long-*a* pattern, short-*a* pattern), or content (e.g., store names, fruit) (Bear, Invernizzi, Templeton, & Johnston, 2004). It is helpful if the child is encouraged to verbalize how he or she has put certain words in one group. The family member can further ask the child to provide additional words that belong to the group.

3. *Label everything in the house.* A family member and a child start with a set of five labels for the first week. The labels are introduced and placed on Monday, then reviewed on Tuesday and Wednesday. On Thursday, Friday, and Saturday, the family member places each label on a wrong entity (e.g., puts the label of *bed* on a wall) and asks the child to put the label back where it belongs. On Sunday, all five labels are reviewed. During the second week, the family member introduces another set of five labels, and the same steps used for the first week are repeated. The family member continues adding new sets of words during the following weeks (Xu & Rutledge, 2003).

F: Family Modeling

Nothing is more powerful for a child to understand the importance of being able to read and write than family members' daily modeling of reading and writing in various social settings (Neuman, Copple, & Bredekamp, 2000). A teacher can ask a child to observe a family member's acts of reading and writing, such as writing a check or reading a TV schedule.

G: Graphic Organizers

Graphic organizers help children organize information in a visual format to enhance their understanding of the interrelationships among parts in a concept. Graphic organizers include webs (or semantic and concept mapping), flow charts, and tree charts. When families use graphic organizers to assist children in organizing information they encounter in their lives, they are also reinforcing children's skills in using such organizers. A family member and a child, for example, may do a web to organize the facilities available in a new neighborhood playground. With the word *playground* in the center circle, the family member and the child put down labels for different facilities in the playground, such as *play equipment* (e.g., *swing, see-saw*), *sports facilities* (e.g., *baseball field, soccer field*), and *picnic area.*

H: Homemade Books

Families can involve children in writing their own books based on their experiences (e.g., a trip, a camp-out, getting a new book). The Bare Books company (*www.barebooks.com*) supplies blank hardcover books of various sizes and with different themes on the covers. Oglan and Elcombe (2000) suggested that family members can take down stories from children's dictation and allow children to design and illustrate the books. Homemade books help children develop a sense of accomplishment at being authors and illustrators.

I: Internet Resources

The Internet offers families a multitude of resources on different topics that children are learning at school and in which they are personally interested. By visiting these resources, children can obtain updated information and also practice reading print and nonprint texts. Families without computers and Internet access can find Internet resources in public libraries. The following are examples of useful resources:

1. The search engine *Google* (*www.google.com*) can be used to find websites and web pages on any chosen topic.
2. Amazon.com (*www.amazon.com*) can be used to find books on a theme or topic.
3. The *Family Fun* website (*www.familyfun.go.com*) can be used to find information on literacy-related activities (e.g., cooking a dish based on a recipe).
4. For family members, the *National Parent Information Network* site (*www.npin.org*) provides discussions of such topics as "What Does 'No Child Left Behind' Mean for Parents?" and "Educational Technology: Preparing Students and Parents for the Digital Age."

J: Journaling

A family member can give a child a notebook (or loose papers stapled together to make a book) and a pencil or pen so that he or she can write every day. There is no better way for a child to learn to write and to sharpen writing skills than practicing writing every day. When the child runs out of writing topics, family members can try out some of the following ideas:

1. Ask the child to write captions for a picture he or she has chosen.
2. Ask the child to rewrite a folktale or fairytale (e.g., *Little Red Riding Hood* or *Cinderella*) or another familiar story by adding some twists.
3. Ask the child to write a different ending to a familiar story.
4. Ask the child to write a recipe for his or her favorite food.
5. Ask the child to write a description of a person in his or her class, family, or neighborhood. The family members then guess who that person is, based on the description.
6. Ask the child to write a grocery list or to draw a group of pictures representing the groceries.

K: Kidwatching

Children in American public schools spend half a year in an outside school setting. Family members thus have as many opportunities as children's teachers to "kidwatch" how children learn about language and literacy, and to carry out literacy practices (Goodman, 1985). They can use Figure 8.3 to focus on reading and writing behaviors to be observed. For preschoolers and kindergartners, family members can also observe how children use oral language in various settings.

L: Library Visits

Not all families can afford to buy books for their children. A school library should be available to children and their families, so that they can select books to read in the library or to check out. In an open house, teachers can inform families of the simple steps to apply for a public library card. For families who may lack transportation to a public library, teachers can provide information on which bus to take. Teachers may work with social services staff on campus to think of other ways for families to get to a library (e.g., carpooling).

M: Message Boards

Each family can designate one place (e.g., on a refrigerator door) for a message board. Each member can leave a message for the others. Writing notes, though brief, gives children a chance to experience functional uses of writing. Reading notes helps children practice reading skills. Young children can start with pictures and phrases in the notes and gradually move on to sentences.

N: Newspapers

Newspapers are another rich source of learning materials for families and children. When some families do not subscribe to a newspaper, due to economic hardship and/or the limited literacy skills of some family members, teachers can give their classroom newspapers to children. Families can also go to a public library with children to do some activities with newspapers. Teachers need to inform families of different activities that they can do with newspapers. Here are some ideas for family members:

1. Discuss with the child, and help the child come up with, captions for a picture in a newspaper; then compare the captions in the paper with what the child has created.
2. Read aloud a newspaper article on a topic of the child's interest, and then ask the child to retell what he or she has heard and identify some known words.
3. Discuss new words in the same article.
4. Complete a graphic organizer for an article on a topic of the child's interest.

O: Oral Reading

It is as important for a young child to read aloud as for a family member to read aloud to a child. While orally reading, a child demonstrates his or her ability to decode words and to read with expression, and this helps develop a sense of pride. While listening to a child's oral reading, a family member can pay attention to the child's unexpected errors, which are different from the words in the original text, and also note how often the child self-corrects the errors previously made. The family member can use Figure 8.10 to document a child's oral reading errors. Some children may shy away from oral reading at school, but like to read aloud at home. The information from Figure 8.10 can be especially valuable for the family and teacher to know about the child's reading process and strategies the child used during oral reading of a text.

P: Predictable Books

Use of predictable books makes reading aloud an interactive experience for children, because children join in reading after becoming familiar with the sentence patterns. For example, after listening to these linguistic patterns in Bill Martin's (1967) *Brown Bear, Brown Bear, What Do You See?*—

> Brown bear, brown Bear, What do you see?
> I see a red bird looking at me.
> Red bird, red bird, what do you see?
> I see a yellow duck looking at me.

FIGURE 8.10
A Guide to Document Oral Reading Errors

Title of the book _____   Date _____

Word in the text (e.g., *house*)	Substitution (e.g., *home* for *house*)	Omission (e.g., *house* was omitted)	Repetition (e.g., *house* was repeated)	Insertion (e.g., *big* was inserted before *house*)	Self-correction (e.g., the child said *home* first and then said *house*)	Family member assistance (e.g., the child was told the word, *house*)

—the child may join in reading "Yellow duck, yellow duck, what do you see?" Similarly, predictable books with rhythm and rhyme (Tompkins, 2003) provide a child with an opportunity to guess a rhyming word on a next page. For example, in *Bright Eyes, Brown Skin* (Hudson & Ford, 1990), a family member can ask a child to guess a word that rhymes with the word *skin* in "Bright Eyes, Brown Skin . . . " on the following page. Families can also use predictable books to engage children in predicting. For example, while reading *If You Give a Moose a Muffin* (Numeroff, 1991) from Numeroff's *If You . . .* series, a family member can ask the child to predict what might happen if a moose gets a muffin and what the moose might ask for next.

Q: Quotes from a Text

A family member and a child get a notebook apiece and vertically fold each page in half to make two columns for each page. The family member and the child each select their favorite quotes from a read text and write these in the left column in the notebook (see the discussion of the double-entry draft in Chapter 6). In the right column, the family member and the child write their own responses to the selected quotes. Then the family member and the child share each other's quotes and responses. This activity helps the child learn to respond to a book and to appreciate other perspectives in responses.

R: Read-Alouds

Children should not go to bed without the experience of being read to; even older children enjoy being read to. The benefits of reading aloud to children are evidenced in many studies (e.g., Clark, 1976; Bus, van IJzendoorn, & Pellegrini, 1995; Purcell-Gates, 2000). The materials for a read-aloud do not always have to be books. Reading materials can include an advertisement in a paper from a local store, a cereal box, an newspaper article, or a label on a T-shirt. While reading aloud, the family member should encourage the child to join in reading; to identify known words; to share his or her understanding of the text; and to make text-to-self, text-to-text, and text-to-world connections.

S: Spelling Words

When a child brings home a list of spelling words for the weekly spelling test, family members can use the following approach to help the child study the words and use them:

1. Ask the child to identify the patterns that he or she has noted from the list of words (e.g., *thing* and *king* are from the *-ing* family). Then two words on the list virtually become one word for the child to remember.
2. Ask the child to identify known words not on the list that look and/or sound

similar to a word on the list (e.g., *sand* shares *-and* family membership with a known word, *hand*). The word *sand* on the list then becomes a familiar word.

3. Ask the child to use each word on the list in a sentence, to ensure that he or she understands its meaning.

Teachers can encourage families to develop a family list of words. Each family member chooses important words to put on the list for the whole family to learn.

T: Thematic Exploration

One way for families to integrate children's literacy experiences is through thematic exploration. For example, family members can read, write, draw, and talk about anything related to summer, including weather, trips, food, sports activities, camp-outs, family get-togethers, and so on. Because the content of the thematic exploration is part of the child's life, he or she may begin to see literacy experiences as more related to him or her.

U: Uninterrupted Sustained Silent Reading

Each day, a child needs some quiet time to read independently, during which he or she can apply comprehension, metacognitive, and word identification strategies. Teachers need to suggest to family members that they set up a time and place for this, and make uninterrupted sustained silent reading a ritual for the whole family.

V: Visual Literacy

Visual literacy is a complex concept; it encompasses such elements as developing abilities to appreciate artistic representation (e.g., to enjoy a painting), creating a text with images and print (e.g., designing a cover for *People* magazine), exploring techniques of media production (e.g., computer-designed image of a flying superhero), and viewing media text with a critical eye (e.g., noting the gender stereotypes in a movie) (Pailliotet, 2002). Following are a few ways families can promote their children's critical viewing of media texts.

1. At least one family member should spend some time watching a movie or a TV show with the child.

2. After the viewing, the family member and the child share each other's response to the media text. It is always interesting to note that an adult and a child may see the same text from very different perspectives.

3. The family member asks the child questions to guide the child to think critically about the text. For example, such questions may nudge the child to pay attention to gender issues: "I have seen that there are mostly boy [or men] superheroes.

Can girls [or women] also be superheroes? Why do you think that there aren't many girl [or women] superheroes?" The family member can also further the child's understandings of superheroes through asking, "What else do superheroes do besides flying and beating up the bad guys?"

W: Words, Words, Words

Children learn and master a large body of vocabulary through *extensive* reading and writing (Beck & McKeown, 1991; Nagy & Scott, 2000). Families need to make word learning fun, exciting, and related to children's interests. In addition to encouraging children to read and write every day, another way to promote children's vocabulary development is playing family word games such as Scrabble or Boggle. Family members can also collect interesting and unusual words that they have encountered. For example, *family* in English has the same root as *familia* in Spanish. The word *spaghetti* has *gh* that does not follow either the rule of being silent (as in *light*) or the rule of the /f/ sound (as in *rough*).

X: Xmas Gifts of Literacy Materials

Family members can give a child Christmas (or other year-end holiday) gifts and birthday gifts of literacy materials (e.g., books, writing utensils, talking-book software, and word games). The child is also encouraged to write on cards and gift tags for friends and relatives, and to send self-written or homemade books as gifts to relatives and friends.

Y: Year-Round Reading and Writing

Family involvement with a child's literacy development should be continuous throughout a year. Year-round reading and writing will have cumulative effects on the child's growth in literacy knowledge and skills.

Z: Zone of Proximal Development

The ABC Literacy activities for families end with a concept that is crucial to children's continued literacy development. As noted in Chapter 1, the *zone of proximal development* (ZPD) is the distance in a child's ability between what the child can do with a more capable person's support and what the child can do without that support (Vygotsky, 1978). ZPD is an important concept for teachers to communicate to families. Families need to support their children as much as possible, but also need to withdraw that support gradually so that children can become independent readers and writers.

As Snow (1999) and Edwards et al. (1999) have suggested, engaging families in children's literacy development is not an easy task. But many practical ideas presented in this chapter at least equip teachers with some tools. Teachers need to view literacy practices through a new lens—as being sociocultural, local, and dynamic. Only through this lens is it possible for teachers to learn about students' communities and families, and about literacy practices in these settings. Such a lens further makes it possible for teachers to invite families to be part of a classroom community, and to acknowledge that family members can continue to be teachers of their own children throughout the children's schooling.

Chapter 9

ISSUES IN EARLY LITERACY

Once upon a time there was a town that was having a serious health problem. Approximately 30 percent of the children in the town were coming down with typhoid and other diseases because of contaminated drinking water. The town council allocated millions to medical care for the typhoid victims, yet some of them died or were permanently disabled. One day, an engineer proposed to the town council that they install a water treatment plant, which would prevent virtually all cases of the disease. "Ridiculous!" fumed the mayor. "We can't afford it!" The engineer pointed out that they were already paying millions for treatment of a preventable disease. "But if we bought a water treatment plant," the mayor responded, "how could we afford to treat the children who already have the disease?" "Besides," added a councilman, "most of our children don't get the disease. The money we spend now is targeted to exactly the children who need it!" After a brief debate, the town council rejected the engineer's suggestion.

—SLAVIN (1994, p. 206)

The parable told by Slavin is, of course, inconceivable. It seems probably equally inconceivable that intervention for struggling readers could ever have paralleled this tale. However, historically, remedial reading was approached very much as a corrective intervention (Allington, 2002b). In many instances, the intervention (i.e., remediation) did not begin until the third or fourth grade (Shanahan & Neuman, 1997). This was based on several assumptions: (1) A child might catch up to his or her peers; and (2) in order to be considered a remedial reader, the child needed to be two grade levels behind in reading. The most unfortunate circumstance resulting from corrective instruction was letting a child experience failure for several years before intervening. Fortunately, the field of literacy took a different turn from the Slavin tale: A shift from a medical model to a wellness model occurred (see, e.g., Clay, 1993b). Rather than waiting for the "disease" to occur, and then diagnosing and treating it, literacy professionals began focusing more on prevention—the prevention of difficulty in those readers most likely to experience difficulty. This chapter examines approaches to early intervention, and then discusses the political influences on early literacy instruction and intervention.

Understanding and Helping At-Risk Readers:
Four Approaches

The conception of early intervention is grounded in the construct of *at-riskness*. The term, though, often has a very negative connotation. For example, Hixson and Tinzmann (1990) suggest, "Historically, 'at-risk' students were primarily those whose language, culture, values, communities, and family structures did not match those of the dominant white culture that schools were designed to support" (pp. 1–2). Clearly, then, in this historical definition, the risk of failure for these children was seen as a deficiency within the children. However, blaming children and applying negative labels to them have decreased significantly. Rather, there has been a more introspective examination of how to characterize who is at risk—and more importantly, of how to help those students designated as at risk to experience success in school.

Hixson and Tinzmann describe four approaches to understanding the construct of *at-riskness*. In the following sections, each of their approaches is discussed, along with programs that have been implemented within these theoretical models.

Predictive Approach

The predictive approach, quite similar to the medical model previously described, looks at children in terms of deficits. Children are characterized as being *at risk* if they have a number of risk conditions—for example, poverty, a single-parent family, and limited English proficiency. The more factors a child possesses, the more at risk the child is considered to be. Clearly, this model has limitations, in that it is essentially a checklist approach to understanding school successes and failures. It is derived from correlational data on the characteristics of students who did not succeed in school; researchers predict from these data who will be most likely to fail.

Programs that are grounded in this approach are often funded by the states and the federal government. For example, Head Start and public school prekindergarten programs are probably the most visible and notable examples. Children qualify for these programs on the basis of the previously mentioned risk factors. There has been some success in these types of interventions, yet very little research reports any sustained effects (McGill-Franzen & Goatley, 2001). Perhaps—although this is not a research-based assumption—the limited view of at-riskness undermines the true capabilities of these programs. That is, if the view is based on a deficit in the child, then the solution is to *fix* that deficit with early intervention. Yet this is a rather narrow conceptualization. In other words, Head Start and prekindergarten programs are not inherently flawed, but their limited view of at-riskness may undermine their potential for success.

Descriptive Approach

The descriptive approach is one in which students are selected for special services after they have demonstrated some failure in a regular reading program (Hixson & Tinzmann, 1990). This approach has changed dramatically over the past 20 years, in relation to the amount of reading failure children experience. Reading Recovery is one program that exemplifies a more contemporary interpretation of this approach. Students do indeed experience some failure; however, intervention happens very early. That is, the students chosen to participate in Reading Recovery are those who are performing at the lowest level in first grade, as determined at the school site.

Reading Recovery, based on the work of Marie Clay (e.g., 1993b), is an intensive one-on-one tutoring program that attempts to accelerate the learning of struggling readers. Children are tutored for approximately 30 minutes each day for 20 weeks. The tutoring consists of reading new books at the children's level, rereading familiar books, and writing. Reading Recovery teachers prompt children with many different strategies that are based on the children's knowledge. The research on the success of Reading Recovery has been quite compelling and has shown that the professional development Reading Recovery teachers receive is vital to the success of the program (Pinnell, Lyons, DeFord, Bryk, & Seltzer, 1994).

However, Reading Recovery is not without its share of criticism, especially in regard to the cost of implementing the program (Shanahan & Barr, 1995). Again, perhaps this criticism is fundamental to the model in which it operates. Specifically, within the notion of the descriptive model, teachers can only serve a limited number of students. Even more problematic for Reading Recovery is that due to the one-on-one nature of the intensive tutoring, the number of students being served is quite small in relation to the number of students who would truly benefit from more intensive reading instruction. More generally, the descriptive approach to identifying and serving at-risk students creates the possibility for cognitive dissonance: Students are taught certain strategies in their classroom, and then may learn very different strategies in their intervention program (Allington, 1983).

Unilateral Approach

From a unilateral perspective, all children are viewed as being at risk in some way, and therefore all qualify for special programs (Hixson & Tinzmann, 1990). Although this is certainly a fair approach to instruction, equity is not the same as equality. Some students need more special services than others. In many ways, Success for All (Slavin, 1991) is framed within this approach. In Success for All, students are grouped for reading instruction by ability in grades 1–3. Reading aides are typically hired, to work with small groups of students and to reduce class size. The lessons in Success for All are based on a particular scope and sequence, and while cooperative learning groups are stressed, the teachers' manual is highly scripted.

This program has met with some success, but equally as much criticism (Venezky, 1998). The problem with a unilateral approach such as this one may be situated in the approach itself—a predetermined curriculum for all children. From this perspective, teaching in many ways becomes a nonvariable; the assumption is that if this method is used correctly, all children will become successful readers. However, it does raise this question: If the children were not successful with this type of reading instruction in heterogeneous grade levels, why would they be successful in homogeneous groups?

Ecological Approach

In an ecological approach, at-riskness is a characteristic of a student, a school, a community, and the interaction of the three. Therefore, a successful intervention program will need to take all these factors into consideration. It seems that as we expand the construct of at-riskness, it becomes necessary to rethink intervention. However, equally important to a broader definition of at-riskness and to the development of a successful intervention program are the strengths of the programs previously described. Head Start, Reading Recovery, and Success for All have all provided important steps in understanding at-riskness and in helping to prevent reading problems. And it is with this foundation that early intervention can continue to move forward in helping children experience success in reading.

Much as Chapters 2–7 have done, the following discussion presents an overview of a successful program that is framed within this broad, ecological approach to at-riskness. However, instead of a visit to a classroom, we present an overview of the reading room at a primary grade school.

The Anna Plan

The Anna Plan (Miles, Stegle, Hubbs, Henk, & Mallette, in press) is a program that has been recognized by the International Reading Association (IRA) as one of its Exemplary Reading Programs. The Anna Plan was developed as a school-wide literacy reform effort at Lincoln Elementary School in Anna, Illinois. Theoretically, the plan is grounded in the ecological model—one that incorporates the strengths of the other models. The student population is currently at a 64% poverty rate, and thus one of the characteristics of the predictive approach is acknowledged. When the reform began, only 50% of the students were meeting the state standards in reading; this was an important issue from a more descriptive perspective. The school factors involved in at-riskness (another important issue, though not discussed earlier because of the lack of intervention programs grounded in this approach) were essential in the development of this program, because the impetus for change was grounded in the shortcomings of reading instruction. Finally, the unilateral approach is visible in the notion that all children need services; however, it is kept in mind that not all children need the same services. Thus the melding of the four major perspectives (with the inclusion of additional factors) provides the theoretical underpinnings of this successful intervention program, and the most important perspective is the broad, ecological view of at-riskness.

Building on the ecological theory of at-riskness (Hixson & Tinzmann, 1990), the Anna Plan is also based on research on best practices in literacy instruction. That is, once conceptualized, the practical applications of this intervention needed to be theoretically sound as well.

The program was spearheaded by the three reading specialists in the school, Pam Miles, Kathy Stegle, and Karen Hubbs. They, along with the entire school community, were not satisfied with their literacy program. Although all three teachers were trained in Reading Recovery, the disadvantages of that program were being felt. The reading teachers recognized that they were unable to provide services to all the students, as well as to support those who completed the program. A caveat here is to acknowledge that they were quite pleased with the progress the students made while in the Reading Recovery program.

Rather than unilaterally making decisions on the reading curriculum, the three reading specialists asked all the classroom teachers to collaborate in this reform effort. They visited other programs, read many journal articles, and attended conferences. Based on these experiences, they developed the seven tenets of their program:

- Focus on research-based best practices.
- Allow for common professional development.
- Include all children.
- Provide for continuity within and between grade levels.
- Permit time each week for collaboration among teachers.
- Provide scaffolding that permits each child to work at his or her instructional reading level.
- Maintain a team orientation.

Once the reading teachers developed these tenets, they began to examine curriculum through attending various types of staff development as a team, together with the classroom teachers and the administrator. They remained committed to the important principles of Reading Recovery, as well as considering the more current approach of using these principles in small groups. They also attended workshops on Four Blocks (see, e.g., Cunningham, Hall, & Sigmon, 2001). Then they pulled together what they thought to be research-based best practices, and the Anna Plan was conceived.

The Anna Plan provides students in grades K–2 with additional reading support each day. During the first half of the year, students in first and second grades are in the program. Then, during the second half of the year, students in kindergarten and first grade are in the program. The reading teachers have designed the schedule this way so that they can still provide Reading Recovery to students in the afternoon. The students, along with their classroom teachers, go to the reading room. The reading room is partitioned into four mini-classrooms. That is, the students are divided into four groups, and each group works with one of the four teachers (i.e., one classroom teacher and the three reading teachers) for 25 minutes. The children are grouped by ability, but these groups are very flexible. The teachers periodically rotate the groups with which they work.

Figure 9.1 presents an overview of a 5-day plan, which includes many examples of the types of activities and lessons that are planned.

Each week the same structure is followed; however, the activities vary. The first 2 days of the week, which include introducing and extending a new book, clearly draw on aspects of Reading Recovery. On the first day, the students are taught strat-

Day 1	Day 2	Day 3	Day 4	Day 5
Introduction of new book Prior knowledge Book concepts/ language structure Making predictions and locating unfamiliar words Strategy instruction First reading of book Strategy reinforcement Review of problem solving and predictions	**Discussion of new book** Story connections Comprehension instruction Language mini- lesson Rereading of new book for fluency Running records	**Word work** Solving words while reading for meaning Making words Guessing the covered word Onsets and rimes Word wall work Practice with white boards	**Journal writing** Modeled mini- lesson Language experiences Familiar words Invented spelling Linking written and oral language	**Planning** *Team decisions about:* Grouping Individual progress Book choices Word wall words Comprehension strategies Focus of mini- lessons Scheduling

FIGURE 9.1. Overview of a 5-day plan.

egies, and they read a new book. They reread the same (now more familiar) book on the second day, and running records are taken. However, to extend the process, there is also an important focus on comprehension. The third day focuses on text at the word level. The activities are primarily drawn from Four Blocks. Day 4 provides opportunities for students to make connections between reading and writing, while building literacy knowledge. The 4 days in total represent a broad view of literacy, and truly build on the strengths of many approaches to literacy instruction. In addition, the small-group setting allows children to work at their own reading levels and receive individual attention.

The fifth day truly represents the heart of this successful program. This day is reserved strictly for planning. During the scheduled reading time, two of the reading teachers meet with the classroom teacher to debrief, reflecting on the week and planning for the following week. The third reading teacher goes into the classroom. Again, the reading teachers continually shift their roles. This shared planning time allows for the discussion of individual students and their progress. Group placements are often made at these sessions, as the premise of the small groups is flexibility.

Figure 9.2 shares an example of a week's plan for a second-grade class. This plan is also used at the end of first grade. The plan is based on the reading levels of the students, and this particular group is at Reading Recovery level 8. Due to space constraints, each activity is explained in greater detail below. (However, when creating these charts, the teachers leave ample room for details.) Here are Mrs. Belcher's extended notes on her week's plan:

Classroom teacher: <u>Mrs. Belcher</u>   Week: <u>16</u>   Date: <u>11/17–21</u>   Team: <u>2</u>

Book title: <u>A Friend for Little White Rabbit</u>   # of words: <u>113</u>   Book level: <u>8</u>

Word wall words	Day 1	Day 2	Day 3	Day 4	Day 5
1. <u>friend</u> 2. <u>best</u> 3. <u>an</u> 4. <u>did</u> 5. <u>play</u>	Book intro./ prior knowledge Concepts/lang. structure Words to locate First reading of book Strategy reinforcer	Discussion of new book Language mini-lesson from new book Second reading of book Running records Familiar rereading	Comprehension strategy work Phrasing/ <u>fluency</u> (select one) Connections Retelling Visualizing Questioning Other: Partner read— practice strategy	Word work	Planning day Notes:
Students:					
1. Karen					
2. Kathy					
3. Pam					
4. Mike					
5. Larry					
6. Ron					

FIGURE 9.2. Mrs. Belcher's weekly plan.

Day 1

Prior knowledge. (students do not have books in hand)
- "Who has ever seen a real rabbit?"
- "What animals do you think rabbits might play with, and why?"

Concepts
- Rabbit versus bunny

Language structure
- Have students repeat the phrase "Oh, who will play with me?"

Words to locate
- *Oh, rabbit, who*

Strategy reminder
- Have students get their mouths ready to say the first sound of the tricky word

First reading of book
- Take notes/monitor students' reading of the book

Strategy reinforcer
- For the last 2–3 minutes of class time, have the students tell how they used the new strategy to "fix" a tricky word

Day 2

Discussion of new book
- Students give a retelling of the book, which includes:
  - Characters
  - Setting
  - What happens first
  - What happens next (sequence of events)
  - What is the problem?
  - How does the story end?
  - Favorite part (if there is one)

Language mini-lesson: Commas
- Talk to the students about the use of commas and what they should do when they come to one in their reading

Second reading of the book
- Take running record while students read

Day 3

Comprehension strategy
- Phrasing/fluency—model fluent reading, stressing punctuation marks (i.e., period, comma, exclamation mark)

Phrasing/fluency
- Select one from list on chart

Partner read—practice strategy

Day 4

Word work—use white boards to transfer word wall words
- Tell students, "Write the word *best*. Now say the word *best*, but don't say the *b* sound. Now, on your white board, make it say *rest*."
- Repeat the procedure to change the onset and make *west, test, crest, test*
- Use the same procedure for:
  - *an—tan, man, fan, plan*
  - *did—hid, bid, rid, ride, hide*
  - *play—day, way, say, tray*

The section on day 5 is reserved for notes during the week, so the teacher can reflect on the students' progress. In addition, each teacher takes note of the actual activities, in order to modify and strengthen them for future use.

Figure 9.3 shows a different example, from the first week of kindergarten (which is the first week of school after winter break).

Classroom teacher: <u>Mrs. James</u>   Week: <u>1</u>   Date: <u>1/5–9</u>   Team: <u>1-4</u>
Book title: <u>Poem "Humpty Dumpty"</u>   # of words: <u>36</u>   Book Level: <u>Early emergent</u>

Sight words	Day 1	Day 2	Day 3	Day 4	Day 5
1. the 2. on Color word: red	Introduction Use pointer to model Students point under words Practice saying in different voices Concepts about print	Shared writing Predictable sentence on chart tablet: _____ sat on the _____. Students point and read to group	Student page for class book Each student has a page to complete and illustrate Students practice reading their page, pointing	Class book Student pages are put together to make book "Reader's Chair": Students sit in a special chair and read the class book	Planning day Notes: New popcorn words: Poem for next week:
Students:					
1. Sam					
2. Alice					
3. Kelsey					
4. Brian					

FIGURE 9.3. Mrs. James's weekly plan.

The way the Anna Plan operates at Lincoln School allows the Reading Recovery teachers to continue providing Reading Recovery services to the lowest-achieving first-grade students. As Vellutino and Scanlon (2001) have pointed out, some struggling readers need individualized instruction; however, others can make equally significant gains with small-group instruction.

The Anna Plan began in 1996, and (as mentioned previously) at its inception, only 50% of the students were meeting the state standards. Since then, the number of children who experience success in literacy has grown dramatically. Consider the following:

Nearly 90% of our children consistently met the standards on statewide assessments. Similarly, some 85% of our children come to first grade operating in the Early Emergent stage and the remainder in the Emergent stage (Wright Group, 1996). By the end of the most recent year, however, none of our children could be classified at these lower levels. Rather, 4% had ascended to the Early Fluency stage, but more impressively, some 96% of them reached the most advanced Fluency milestone. In fact, over the past six years, 75% of our children have obtained the Fluency stage. (Miles et al., in press)

These results provide concrete support for the success of this intervention program. The Anna Plan is an exemplary model of early intervention. The program is grounded in best practices of literacy instruction, allows for collaboration and communication between reading teachers and classroom teachers, provides time for extra support (i.e., recognizes equity), and continues to grow. The teachers at this school are proud of the work they are doing; yet, at the same time, they always strive to do more and improve their reading instruction. It seems clear that the Anna Plan has successfully pulled together the necessary components from other early interventions. And it is clear that this work provided the foundation. For example, the Reading Recovery backgrounds that the reading teachers bring to this program are truly essential. They have an excellent command of reading processes—and, arguably, an intervention program of this caliber cannot be successful without reading teachers who are truly knowledgeable.

Views of the best way to provide intervention to struggling readers have certainly evolved in recent years. To return to Slavin's parable at the beginning of this chapter, we need the water treatment plan; however, we need it to operate in a thoughtful and equitable way.

It seems, though, that a thoughtful and equitable way has lately been called into question with the new No Child Left Behind (NCLB) legislation. In fact, the nature of early intervention has seemingly transplanted early reading instruction. The remainder of this chapter examines the NCLB legislation (U.S. Department of Education, 2001) and its influence on early reading instruction and intervention.

The NCLB Act and Its Influence

The Elementary and Secondary Education Act (ESEA) of 1965 was the largest source of federal aid to public schools. President Lyndon B. Johnson established this act as part of his war on poverty. Since its inception, the ESEA has been expanded, amended, and revised eight times. The act has provided resources to support Title I services in schools. And, as previously discussed, the grades at which the services have been deployed have shifted over time, with the current emphasis on the primary grades.

On January 8, 2002, President George W. Bush signed into legislation the NCLB Act. This piece of legislation represented the most sweeping change since the original 1965 ESEA. The NCLB Act reauthorized and increased federal support to public schools. However, along with these sweeping monetary changes, NCLB also set many new provisions for schools. The goal of the NCLB legislation is that by the year 2014 *all* students will meet their state standards in all subjects and at all grade levels. It is believed that this will be accomplished though increased accountability by schools, highly qualified teachers, and the use of scientifically based reading research in instruction.

Each of these notions has tremendous implications for schools. The accountability issue requires that students be tested annually in grades 3 through 8. Each state may choose the assessment that is aligned with its standards. Each year, a greater percentage of students must meet or exceed the state standards. Schools that fail to make adequate yearly progress (AYP) are subject to corrective actions. In addition, if schools fail to meet the AYP requirements, these schools must use their Title I funds to pay for the students to go to another school (i.e., school vouchers will be put into effect). The premise of highly qualified teachers is also interpreted at the state level. For example, in Illinois a teacher can be deemed highly qualified by (1) obtaining a Master's degree in reading, (2) meeting the state's requirements for a reading endorsement, (3) passing a content test, or (4) becoming nationally board-certified in reading. Schools are required to inform parents of the numbers of teachers who are and are not highly qualified. By the end of the 2005–2006 school year, all teachers must meet the requirements for being highly qualified in order to keep their teaching positions. (However, recently this expectation has been relaxed for teachers in rural settings.) More information can be found at the NCLB section of the U.S. Department of Education website (*www.ed.gov.nclb*), which also has links to information on how this act is interpreted and applied in each state.

The reality of NCLB is very problematic, and its influence on early literacy instruction is cause for concern. The first two notions discussed above certainly are important; however, the premise of scientifically based research is one of pivotal importance to early literacy. Much of what is deemed scientifically-based reading research is derived from the findings of the National Reading Panel (NRP, 2000). However, these findings are fraught with complications, and thus we must pause to consider the entire construct of scientifically-based reading research.

A Task Too Large

The NRP was charged by U.S. Congress to "assess the status of research-based knowledge, including the effectiveness of various approaches to teaching children to read" (Yatvin, 2000, p. 1). The initial problem the NRP's members faced was that the task before them was daunting. In order to attempt to make sense of this charge, they first had to make some assumptions about how to define reading. As Yatvin (2000) has explained in her minority report, the philosophical orientations and research interests of the majority of the panel members dictated an extremely narrow view of reading. Their original definition broke reading down into three areas: (1) alphabetics, (2) fluency, and (3) comprehension.

This narrowness of the NRP's definition set the stage for a final report that omitted much of the research in other areas relevant to the understanding of early literacy learning, such as oral language. Even though some researchers who have criticized the report (see, e.g., Pressley, Dolezal, Roehrig, Hilden, 2002) don't necessarily dispute the findings, they express great reservations about the constrained lens through which reading was defined. In relation to understanding early intervention, these omissions are paramount. That is, it seems inconceivable that such topics as concepts about print, language, children's home literacy experiences, and text were not included. This is especially troubling, as the NRP report provided the basis for the political manifesto about what counts in early literacy learning, when indeed the interventions cited in the chapter provide compelling evidence of the importance of these and many other areas of early literacy learning.

The NCLB legislation grounds scientifically based reading research in this narrow construct. Furthermore, monies available for schools to improve early literacy instruction are acquired through Reading First grants that closely adhere to the NRP's definition of reading and research-based findings. Table 9.1 reprinted from another section of the U.S. Department of Education website (*www.ed.gov/programs/readingfirst/guidance.doc*), provides an overview of scientifically based research in reading instruction as the federal government defines it.

Schools that obtain monies to support their reading programs through Reading First grants given to states for early reading materials and instruction and professional development in grades K–3 (and for special education in grades K–2) must use these findings as the cornerstone of their reading instruction. In addition, any reading program adopted in a Reading First school must be based on the scientific evidence from the NRP report. For example, schools and states have been busy analyzing reading programs to determine how well they support phonics in each grade, and how instruction builds from grade to grade.

A worry that develops from the expectation that such programs should be the guides for all reading instruction is that these programs will be followed in a linear way; in other words, all children will experience exactly the same instruction. If this happens, then teachers and schools will fail to consider children from an ecological perspective. That is, there will be no consideration of families and individual differences; rather, at-risk students will be considered those in failing schools, within a more unilateral view of at-riskness. In this context, this view suggests that with a certain type of instruction, all students will be able to succeed. However, it ignores much of the research on successful early intervention, as well as the need to match instruction to individual students' strengths.

This is a critical time for teachers, it appears that the new mandates of NCLB have narrowed the conceptualization of reading for students considered at risk. Whereas comprehensive literacy instructional plans have been recommended for such children by knowledgeable researchers (e.g., Allington, 2002b), the current view is focused on a narrower understanding and unilateral perspective of literacy learning and instruction.

In taking the three main tenets of NCLB together and situating them in the discussion just presented, there is almost a sense of irony. The way in which scientifically based research is being interpreted narrows the construct of literacy, as teachers and schools focus only on phonemic awareness, phonics, comprehension, fluency, and vocabulary. Many teachers no longer find time to read to children, have children independently read, or provide extensive time for writing. Ordinarily, the expectation would be that reliance on the current scientific base to guide reading instruction would enlarge the literacy curriculum and offer teachers a wide array of exemplary practices to use with students. Although this can still be the case, many teachers and schools are taking a safer approach and only focusing on the research shared in NRP report.

TABLE 9.1. Key Findings from Scientifically Based Research on the Essential Components of Reading Instruction

Component of reading instruction	Definition	Key findings
1. Phonemic awareness	The ability to hear, identify, and manipulate the individual sounds, or phonemes, in spoken words.	• Phonemic awareness can be taught and learned. • Phonemic awareness instruction helps children learn to read. • Phonemic awareness instruction helps children learn to spell. • Phonemic awareness instruction is most effective when children are taught to manipulate phonemes by using the letters of the alphabet. • Phonemic awareness instruction is most effective when it focuses on only one or two types of phoneme manipulation, rather than several types.
2. Phonics	The understanding that there is a predictable relationship between phonemes, the sounds of spoken language, and graphemes, the letters and spelling that represent those sounds in written language.	• Systematic and explicit phonics instruction is more effective than nonsystematic or no phonics instruction. • Systematic and explicit phonics instruction significantly improves kindergarten and first-grade children's word recognition and spelling. • Systematic and explicit phonics instruction significantly improves children's reading comprehension. • Systematic and explicit phonics instruction is effective for children from various social and economic levels. • Systematic and explicit phonics instruction is particularly beneficial for children who are having difficulty learning to read and who are at risk for developing future reading problems. • Systematic and explicit phonics instruction is most effective when introduced early. • Phonics instruction is not an entire reading program for beginning readers.

3. Vocabulary development	Development of stored information about the meanings and pronunciation of words necessary for communication. There are four types of vocabulary:
	
	  a. listening vocabulary—the words needed to understand what is heard
	  b. speaking vocabulary—the words used when speaking
	  c. reading vocabulary—the words needed to understand what is read
	  d. writing vocabulary—the words used in writing
		• Children learn the meanings of most words indirectly, through everyday experiences with oral and written language.
		• Some vocabulary must be taught directly.

(cont.)

TABLE 9.1. (*cont.*)

Component of reading instruction	Definition	Key findings
4. Reading fluency	The ability to read text accurately and quickly	• Repeated and monitored oral reading improves reading fluency and overall reading achievement. • No research evidence is available currently to confirm that instructional time spent on silent, independent reading with minimal guidance and feedback improves reading fluency and overall reading achievement.
5. Reading comprehension strategies	Strategies for understanding, remembering, and communicating with others about what has been read.	• Text comprehension can be improved by instruction that helps readers use specific comprehension strategies. • Students can be taught to use comprehension strategies.

In addition to the focus on scientifically based research practices, there is the AYP issue. Each school and each state must disaggregate its test results so that each group of students (e.g., African American students, Latino/Latina students) is reported separately. It is not sufficient for a school to do well on tests; each group of students within the school must also do well. The federal government chose to have schools disaggregate test results in the hope of reducing the achievement gap between European American students and minority students. (Recently, the government has modified the testing expectations for English language learners.)

The AYP requirements have placed great stress on schools and teachers: How will they systematically raise test scores each year for all of their students? An unfortunate consequence of this expectation is that in many schools the curriculum is beginning to mirror what will be assessed. That is, the tests students need to pass are closely aligned to the reading curriculum; ergo, reading instruction is driven by tests and narrow definitions.

The third expectation of NCLB is that teachers will be highly qualified. Teachers need to meet the expectations for this requirement as determined by their state. It is ironic that at the time the federal government is demanding that teachers be extremely knowledgeable about literacy, it is limiting them at the same time. A cynical view would be that teachers are not being asked to use this knowledge, merely to possess it. However, another way to consider this expectation is that the writers of the NCLB legislation understood that knowledgeable teachers know their content and can effectively teach it to students. Although there is criticism of the way teachers meet the highly qualified status, the reality is that teachers do make a difference in the personal and academic lives of their students.

A fitting way to end this chapter is to return to the Anna Plan. The Anna Plan is grounded in the scientifically based reading research offered by the NRP report. However, its success comes from using that research base as a foundation to build upon. This foundation is extended by considering research that is focused on families, oral language, second-language acquisition, and other important areas not considered in the NRP report. Moreover, the teachers have explored research that has been published since the NRP report appeared. At the heart of this successful model, or of any intervention model are knowledgeable teachers who know how to apply research-based best practices to instruction for children on an individual basis. Perhaps most importantly, successful early intervention in literacy occurs when the driving force behind the effort is a community of instructors dedicated to the success of their students—teachers who intelligently use not only the findings of the NRP, but the knowledge that has been generated from the research the NRP didn't examine as well.

Chapter 10

GETTING PRACTICAL

The goal of the first part of this chapter is to provide numerous web resources that can support the work of teachers and parents in helping children develop literacy. These resources are grouped for ease of use, but many overlap. So for instance, a site that provides research may also include related instructional activities.

We believe that many educational websites and web pages can support teachers as they search for the research base for an activity they want to implement. They also provide support for instruction, in that teachers can find content knowledge and suggestions for how to teach that knowledge to students. Teachers can identify web resources for parents so that parents can help their children with literacy. For example, parents may benefit from exploring either the Reading Rockets website in English or its companion Spanish website. Parents can find answers to questions that they may have about how children learn to read, or they can find books to support their child. And many web resources, such as Yahooligans, support students directly as they try to find answers to their important questions.

Throughout this book, we have provided examples of ways for teachers to bring technology into their classrooms. As readers explore the web resources in this chapter, they may want to refer back to Chapter 5 in particular, where numerous suggestions are offered to bring technology into young children's classrooms.

A caution needs to be stated here, however: Websites and web pages sometimes disappear from the Internet. As this book went to press, all of the resources presented in this chapter were functional. Teachers should not despair if one of these resources is not currently available. Numerous sites and pages are available to teachers, and new ones are always being developed. In addition, as teachers explore these resources, they will note redundancy among several of them. This assures that no one resource is irreplaceable. Moreover, websites like those of the International Reading Association (IRA) and many other literacy organizations will continue to be present and will constantly be improved in format and content.

The second part of this chapter lists all of the reproducible materials that have been provided in chapters throughout the book. All may be photocopied for use by teachers.

Web Resources

Evaluating Web Resources

1. Evaluating Web Resources
   www.valpo.edu/library/evaluation.html#topl
   This page features guidelines for evaluating websites and web pages.

Search Engines for Students

1. Ask Jeeves for Kids
   www.ajkids.com
   This site allows students to ask questions, and the site finds the answers. There are other resources available, such as dictionaries, content texts, clip art, and so on.

2. Yahooligans
   www.yahooligans.com
   This site is similar to Ask Jeeves for Kids. Students can ask questions, and there are numerous support materials for in-class learning.

3. Ask Earl
   www.yahooligans.com/content/ask_earl
   This section of the Yahooligans site allows students to ask questions and get answers. It also posts most frequently asked questions, as well as questions and answers pertinent to a time of year or an event, like Christmas.

Creating Websites and Web Pages

1. My School Online
   www.myschoolonline.com
   This site provides teachers with tools to create their own websites or web pages. It includes templates that can be used for newsletters and homework assignments.

Research Laboratories with Information about Literacy and Urban Students

1. Appalachia Educational Laboratory in Charleston, WV
   www.ael.org

2. Mid-continent Regional Educational Laboratory in Aurora, CO
   www.mcrel.org

3. North Central Regional Educational Laboratory in Oak Brook, IL
   www.ncrel.org

4. Northwest Regional Educational Laboratory in Portland, OR
   www.nwrel.org

5. SouthEastern Regional Vision for Education at the University of North Carolina at Greensboro
   www.serve.org

6. Southwest Educational Development Laboratory in Austin, TX
   www.sedl.org

7. WestEd Laboratory for Educational Research and Development in San Francisco, CA
   www.wested.org

8. Pacific Resources for Education and Learning in Honolulu, HI
   www.prel.org

Literacy Organizations

1. Center for Research on Education, Diversity, and Excellence
   www.crede.org
   This website is centered on research and instruction that target students whose ability to reach their potential is challenged by language or cultural barriers, race, geographic location, or poverty.

2. International Reading Association (IRA)
   www.reading.org
   The IRA's website is centered on literacy research and instruction. It contains an online journal, *Reading Online*, as well as other articles, position statements, and instructional lessons.

3. Center for the Improvement of Early Reading Achievement (CIERA)
   www.ciera.org
   CIERA's website provides reports of its work. Its task goes beyond finding answers to persistent problems in reading through research, to disseminating those solutions to people who can have an impact on children's early reading achievement: teachers, teacher educators, parents, policy makers, and others.

4. National Council of Teachers of English (NCTE)
   www.ncte.org
   This website shares information about research and instruction in literacy. The site has areas for elementary, middle, and secondary teachers.

5. National Reading Conference
   www.nrconline.org
   This website provides policy papers and articles focused on literacy research, as well as issues like high-stakes testing.

6. National Association for the Education of Young Children (NAEYC)
www.naeyc.org
The NAEYC's website shares information about research and instruction centered on young children. It is focused on all research and instructional content areas, including literacy.

7. Reading Recovery Council
www.readingrecovery.org
This website shares information about Reading Recovery.

8. Success for All
www.successforall.net
This website has information about the Success for All intervention.

General Teacher Resources Focused on Literacy

1. IRA, NCTE, and the Marco Polo Education Foundation
www.readwritethink.org
This site offers numerous lessons focused on phonemic awareness, phonics, comprehension, vocabulary, motivation, and other topics. Teachers can select a grade level and the topic they wish to teach. Multiple lesson choices will appear with all the pertinent instructional resources. There is also a research article to support each lesson.

2. IRA's Miss Rumphius Award
www.reading.org/awards/rumphius.html
This section of the IRA website offers the best teacher web resources focused on literacy, as determined by *The Reading Teacher*.

3. University of Connecticut
www.literacy.uconn.edu
This resource provides current research and topics in literacy. There are sections focused on classroom instruction, where a teacher can identify a grade level and appropriate strategies are provided. There is also a section focused on research, where numerous resources are provided.

4. Reading A–Z
www.readinga-z.com
This site must be subscribed to, but there are materials that are free. Teachers can find leveled books that can be printed for students, and there are accompanying lesson plans.

5. Reading Rockets: Launching Young Readers
www.readingrockets.org
This site is focused on providing information about teaching children to read and helping struggling readers. There is a section that responds to frequently asked questions, such as "How does a child learn to read?" There is also a section with research articles. Other sections include news articles and responses,

and teachers can ask questions and get answers. In addition, there are recommended books and video interviews with famous children's authors and illustrators.

6. Reading Rockets: Launching Young Readers (Spanish version)
   www.colorincolorado.org
   This is the same as the Reading Rockets website described above; however, it is in Spanish.

7. Starfall
   www.starfall.com
   This site has simple books for children to read. They also provide writing journals and books at a low cost. Children can listen and read along with animated text.

8. The Teacher's Corner
   www.theteacherscorner.net
   This site includes lesson plans, thematic units, information about telecommunication projects, and book reviews.

9. Teachers.net
   www.teachers.net
   This site has a gazette with issues about teaching. There are numerous lessons grouped by the ages of students. Although there are lessons in all content areas, there are numerous lessons provided for literacy.

10. Sites for Teachers
    www.sitesforteachers.com
    This site is a compilation of many websites for teachers. Many of these offer teachers printable teaching resources and learning activities they can do with children.

11. Enchanted Learning
    www.enchantedlearning.com
    This site has many areas to explore. Some are focused on early literacy topics (e.g., nursery rhymes), and others on social studies or science topics. There are activities provided for each month, and simple crafts for children to do.

12. The Virtual Vine
    www.thevirtualvine.com
    The Virtual Vine is a resource for early childhood teachers, preschool through second grade. There are ideas and activities for themes and units, displays, literacy connections, and math connections. There are teacher inspirations and tips, website help, and Mississippi state benchmarks, as well as links galore.

13. School Days—Kinderkorner
    www.kinderkorner.com
    This site has information about classes such as Balanced Literacy Workshops around the country. It provides thematic units, author studies, calendars, and professional reading recommendations.

14. The Perpetual Preschool
    www.perpetualpreschool.com
    This website offers numerous activities for holidays and seasonal themes. They also offer learning center ideas and teaching tips.

15. The Global Schoolhouse
    www.gsn.org
    This section of the Global SchoolNet Foundation site provides online opportunities for teachers to collaborate, communicate, and celebrate shared learning experiences.

16. Crayola
    www.crayola.com
    The site offers ideas and activities for teachers, children, and parents. The site has a place for children to design their own cards for special occasions and holidays; publish their poems, stories, and book reviews; and learn about how Crayola crayons are made. Teachers can find lesson plans and arts-and-crafts activities. Parents can find arts-and-craft activities for the whole family to enjoy.

17. The Learning Leap
    www.thelearningleap.com
    This website offers books and thematic units with print material for kindergarten students.

18. Schoolhouse Printables
    www.schoolhouseprintable.tripod.com
    This site offers teachers links to numerous websites. It also allows teachers to create materials for students.

19. Beginning Reading
    www.beginningreading.com
    This site offers numerous decodable book sets for beginning reading.

Reading Aloud

1. Literacy Connections: Reading Aloud
   www.literacyconnections.com/ReadingAloud.html
   This section of the Literacy Connections site includes read-aloud strategies. It has information for parents on the importance of reading aloud. It also has lists of books recommended for reading aloud to children.

2. The Read Aloud Registry
   www.geocities.com/aletain
   This resource has recommended books to read aloud to children. These are grouped by grade level.

Children's Literature

1. Carol Hurst's Children's Literature Site
   www.carolhurst.com
   This is a collection of reviews of great books for kids, ideas of ways to use them in the classroom and collections of books and activities about particular subjects, curriculum areas, themes, and professional topics.

2. Children's Storybooks Online
   www.magickeys.com/books
   This resource contains books for young children, some of which are animated. Some books have such activities as coloring, riddles, and mazes. There are books that can be read on screen and printed for further reading.

3. Childrenstory.com
   www.childrenstory.com
   This site features fairytales, nursery rhymes, interactive stories, and holiday stories. Some stories are written and illustrated by children, and others can be read to children while they are reading along. This site will read the story to children.

4. The Amazing Adventure Series
   www.amazingadventure.com
   This site has stories that children can read and listen to, as well as family fun activities related to the stories (e.g., making an adventure hat by following directions).

5. The Kids' Storytelling Club
   www.storycraft.com/files/ptl.htm
   This resource contains information on how to create stories for storytelling and how to make and use props during storytelling.

6. Monster Exchange Project
   www.monsterexchange.org
   This site features a telecommunication project in which children display their monsters, which are created according to the descriptions written by other children.

Books Focused on Poetry, Rhymes, or Sounds

1. Grandpa Tucker's Rhymes and Tales
   www.night.net/tucker
   This resource features funny, silly stories, poems, and songs for children and their families.

2. The Mother Goose Pages
   www-personal.umich.edu/~pfa/dreamhouse/nursery/rhymes.html
   These pages contain a list of nursery rhymes, suggestions on how to read nursery rhymes to children, and books written about nursery rhymes.

3. Sounds of the Day
   www.readmeabook.com/sounds/sotd.htm
   This resource introduces two sounds per day for children to practice. It also features books related to the sounds.

4. ABC Teach
   www.abcteach.com
   This site offers activities centered around the alphabet. There are research reports, as well as many activities related to reading comprehension or thematic units that teachers might use.

Newbery and Caldecott Medal Winners

1. Newbery Medal Home Page
   www.ala.org/alsc/newbery.html
   This section of the American Library Association (ALA) site gives descriptions of the books that have won the Newbery Medal, along with honor books.

2. Caldecott Medal Home Page
   www.ala.org/alsc/caldecott.html
   This section of the ALA site provides descriptions of the books that have won the Caldecott Medal, along with honor books.

Information about Internet Resources Using Children's Literature

1. Internet Resources Related to Books for Children and Young Adults
   www.ucalgary.ca/~dkbrown
   This resource provides numerous links to children's authors and illustrators, to storytellers, to resources for parents, to Readers' Theatre resources, and more.

2. Kids Domain
   www.kidsdomain.com
   This site includes reviews of children's favorite books, movies, and video games; fun activities that children and their families can do together; and arts-and-crafts projects for children.

Information about Authors and Illustrators

1. Welcome to Berenstain Bears Country
   www.berenstainbears.com
   The site includes interactive Berenstain Bears books, a description of the characters, and a post office where children can send letters to the characters. Children can also watch video clips of the Berenstain Bears stories.

2. Arthur
   www.pbskids.org/arthur
   This section of the PBS Kids site includes many games and activities related to Marc Brown's popular book series and TV show, *Arthur*.

Books for English Language Learners

1. Welcome to the World of Merpy.com
   www.merpy.com
   This site contains animated stories written in English and Spanish.

2. Dave's ESL Café
   www.pacificnet.net/~sperling/eslcafe.html
   This resource features linguistic information about the English language that may be difficult for English language learners (ELLs). It has a list of idioms and phrasal verbs and their illustrative examples. Teachers can also ask questions about teaching ELLs and about the English language.

Puzzles and Activities Related to Books

1. Discovery School's Puzzle Maker
   puzzlemaker.school.discovery.com
   This resource helps teachers make puzzles in all subject areas. The types of puzzles range from letter titles to criss-cross puzzles to word search.

2. All 4 Kids Greeting Cards
   www.marlo.com/all4kids.htm
   This resource contains cards (and some are animated) for many occasions that children can write on and send to friends and family members.

3. Global SchoolNet Foundation
   www.gsn.org
   This site provides information on more than 900 telecommunication projects for children around the world.

Information about Readers' Theatre Scripts

1. Aaron Shepard's RT Page
   www.aaronshep.com/rt
   This resource includes many readers' theater scripts that are ready to print and use with students. There are also resources for storytelling, student writing, and parent literacy activities.

Reproducible Material for Use by Teachers

Chapter 1. The Intersection of Literacy Learning and Instruction

TABLE 1.1. Benchmarks of Literacy Development (p. 8).

Chapter 2. Exploring Early Literacy

FIGURE 2.5. Assessment of Name Writing (p. 19).
FIGURE 2.6. Assessment of Oral Language (p. 23).
FIGURE 2.9. Assessment of Story Structure Retelling (p. 30).
FIGURE 2.10. Assessment of Early Literacy Story Retelling (p. 31).
FIGURE 2.11. Assessment of Concept of Book (p. 32).
FIGURE 2.17. Assessment of Writing (p. 39).
FIGURE 2.20. Assessment of Word Knowledge (p. 43).

Chapter 3. Early Literacy and English Language Learners

FIGURE 3.1. Beginning Stages of Language Development (p. 49).
FIGURE 3.2. ELL Parent Survey (p. 50).
FIGURE 3.3. Learning about Chinese (p. 52).
FIGURE 3.5. Book Selection Guide for ELL Children (p. 62).
FIGURE 3.6. Assessment of ELL Children's Oral Language (p. 67).

Chapter 4. Beginning Literacy

FIGURE 4.2. Guided Reading Prompts (p. 88).
FIGURE 4.3. Checklist for Oral Reading Development (p. 89).
FIGURE 4.4. Writing Checklist for Children (p. 91).

Chapter 5. Early Literacy and Technology

No reproducible materials.

Chapter 6. Transitional Technology

FIGURE 6.1. Charts for Rereadings: Words per Minute and Miscues (p. 116).
FIGURE 6.2. Fluency Rubric (p. 118).
FIGURE 6.5. Self-Assessment Rubric for Children (p. 122).
FIGURE 6.15. Writing Trait Checklist for Children (p. 132).

Chapter 7. Transitional Literacy and English Language Learners

FIGURE 7.1. A Show-and-Tell Evaluation Form (p. 143).
FIGURE 7.2. Reading Log (p. 144).

TABLE 7.2. Comparison of Characteristics of Narrative Text and Expository Text (p. 148).

FIGURE 7.12. A List of Prefixes with the Meaning of Negation (p. 160).

FIGURE 7.13. A Learning Log (p. 162).

Chapter 8. Engaging Families

FIGURE 8.1. Family Interview (p. 172).

FIGURE 8.2. Home Visit Guide (p. 177).

FIGURE 8.4. A Family's Guide for Anecdotal Notes (p. 180).

FIGURE 8.6. Ways with Words and Symbols in Students' Community (or Communities) and in a Teacher's Community (p. 182).

FIGURE 8.9. ABC Literacy Activities for Families (p. 185).

FIGURE 8.10. A Guide to Document Oral Reading Errors (p. 191).

Chapter 9. Issues in Early Literacy

No reproducible materials.

CHILDREN'S BOOKS CITED

Adler, D. A. (1989). *A picture book of Martin Luther King, Jr.* New York: Holiday House.

Amery, H., & Cartwright, S. (1995). *The Usborne first thousand words in Japanese.* New York: Usborne.

Andrade, M. (2001). *The vigil of the little angels: Day of the dead in Mexico.* San Jose, CA: La Oferta Review.

Arnosky, J. (1995). *All about owls.* New York: Scholastic.

Arnosky, J. (1997). *All about rattlesnakes.* New York: Scholastic.

Arnosky, J. (2002). *All about frogs.* New York: Scholastic.

Cameron, A. (1987). *Julian's glorious summer.* New York: Random House.

Canizares, S., & Reid, M. (1998). *Nests, nests, nests.* New York: Scholastic.

Carle, E. (1967). *The very hungry caterpillar.* New York: Philomel Books.

Carle, E. (1971). *Do you want to be my friend?* New York: HarperCollins.

Carlson, N. (1997). *ABC, I like me!* New York: Viking.

Carrier, L. (1988). *Do not touch.* Saxonville, MA: Picture Book Studio.

Carter, D. A. (1997). *Bugs in space.* New York: Simon & Schuster.

Cleary, B. (1999). *Ramona's world.* New York: Morrow.

Cohen, M. (1967). *Will I have a friend?* New York: Collier Books.

Cole, J. (1990). *The magic school bus: Lost in the solar system.* New York: Scholastic.

Cole, J. (1994). *The magic school bus: In the time of the dinosaurs.* New York: Scholastic.

Corbeil, J., & Archambault, A. (2000). *Scholastic visual dictionary.* New York: Scholastic, Inc.

Dahl, R. (1988). *Matilda.* New York: Puffin Books.

De Zutter, H. (1993). *Who says a dog goes bow-wow?* New York: Doubleday.

Dodds, D. A. (1994). *The shapes of things.* Cambridge, MA: Candlewick Press.

Ehlert, L. (1989). *Eating the alphabet: Fruits and vegetables from A to Z.* San Diego, CA: Harcourt Brace Jovanovich.

Farshtey, G. (2003). *The official guide to Bionicle.* New York: Scholastic.

Feder, J. (1995). *Table, chair, bear: A book in many languages.* New York: Ticknor & Fields.

Freschet, G. (2001). *Beto and the bone dance.* New York: Farrar, Straus & Giroux.

Fritz, J. (1993). *Just a few words, Mr. Lincoln.* New York: Grosset & Dunlap.

Galdone, P. (1968). *Henny Penny.* New York: Scholastic.

Galdone, P. (1970). *The three little pigs.* New York: Crowell.

Garza, C. L. (1996). *In my family/En mi familia*. Danbury, CT: Children's Press.

Gibbons, G. (1984). *Fire! Fire!* New York: HarperCollins.

Goldstein, P. (1995). *Hu is a tiger: An introduction to Chinese writing*. Austin, TX: Coming of Age Press.

Harper, C., & Randall, B. (1997). *Goldfish*. Crystal Lake, IL: Rigby.

Hartman, B. (2002). *The wolf who cried boy*. New York: Putnam.

Haseley, D. (2002). *A story for Bear*. San Diego, CA: Silver Whistle.

Heller, R. (1995). *Color*. New York: Grosset & Dunlap.

Hill, E. (1981). *Spot's first walk*. New York: Putnam.

Hoban, T. (1986). *Shapes, shapes, shapes*. New York: Morrow.

Hudson, C. W., & Ford, B. G. (1990). *Bright eyes, brown skin*. Orange, NJ: Just Us Books.

Johnson, A. (1989). *Tell me a story, Mama*. New York: Orchard Books.

Kalan, R. (1978). *Rains*. New York: Greenwillow Books.

Krull, K. (1994). *Maria Molina and the days of the dead*. New York: Macmillan.

Levine, E. (1989). *I hate English!* New York: Scholastic.

Levy, J. (1995). *The spirit of Tío Fernando: A day of the dead story*. Morton Grove, IL: Whitman.

Lionni, L. (1963). *Swimmy*. New York: Scholastic.

Lobel, A. (1981). *On Market Street*. New York: Greenwillow Books.

London, J. (1996). *Froggy goes to school*. New York: Viking.

Lowell, S. (1992). *The three little javelinas*. Flagstaff, AZ: Northland.

Maccarone, G. (1995). *Cars! Cars! Cars!* New York: Scholastic.

Marchetti, V. (2001). *Orangutans*. Bothell, WA: Wright Group.

Martin, B., Jr. (1967). *Brown bear, brown bear, what do you see?* New York: Holt, Rinehart & Winston.

Martin, B., Jr. (1991). *Polar bear, polar bear, what do you hear?* New York: Holt.

Martin, B., Jr., & Archambault, J. (1989). *Chicka chicka boom boom*. New York: Simon & Schuster.

McCloskey, S. (2000). *Our American flag*. Bothell, WA: Wright Group.

McDonnell, F. (1997). *Flora McDonnell's ABC*. Cambridge, MA: Candlewick Press.

McMillan, B. (1988). *Growing colors*. New York: Lothrop, Lee & Shepard Books.

McPhail, D. (1989). *Animals A to Z*. New York: Scholastic.

Montes, M. (2003). *Get ready for Gabi!: A crazy mixed-up Spanglish day*. New York: Scholastic.

Numeroff, L. (1985). *If you give a mouse a cookie*. New York: Harper & Row.

Numeroff, L. (1991). *If you give a moose a muffin*. New York: HarperCollins.

Numeroff, L. (1998a). *If you give a pig a pancake*. New York: HarperCollins.

Numeroff, L. (1998b) *What mommies do best; what daddies do best*. New York: Simon & Schuster.

Numeroff, L. (2000a). *If you take a mouse to the movies*. New York: HarperCollins.

Numeroff, L. (2000b). *What grandmas do best; what grandpas do best*. New York: Simon & Schuster.

Numeroff, L. (2002). *If you take a mouse to school*. New York: HarperCollins.

Palatini, M. (1995). *Piggie pie*. New York: Clarion Books.

Pallotta, J. (1988). *The flower alphabet book*. Watertown, MA: Charlesbridge.

Pallotta, J. (2002a). *Apple fractions*. New York: Scholastic, Inc.

Pallotta, J. (2002b). *The Hershey's milk chocolate multiplication book*. New York: Scholastic.

Park, B. (2001). *Junie B., first grader (at last!)*. New York: Random House.

Ramsey, J. (2000). *Rock climbing*. Bothell, WA: Wright Group.

Riley, L. (1997). *The mouse mess*. New York: Blue Sky Press.

Ryan, P. M. (1997). *A pinky is a baby mouse and other baby animal names*. New York: Hyperion Books.

Savage, E. (2000). *Here come the bison!* Bothell, WA: The Wright Group.

Scieszka, J. (1989). *The true story of the three little pigs*. New York: Viking.

Scieszka, J. (1992). *The stinky cheese man and other fairly stupid tales*. New York: Viking.

Shannon, G. (1995). *Tomorrow's alphabet*. New York: Greenwillow Books.

Shaw, N. (1991). *Sheep in a shop*. Boston: Houghton Mifflin.

Shaw, N. (1992). *Sheep out to eat*. Boston: Houghton Mifflin.

Shaw, N. (1997). *Sheep trick or treat*. Boston: Houghton Mifflin.

Simon, S. (1990). *Deserts*. New York: Morrow Junior Books.

Slate, J. (1996). *Miss Bindergarten gets ready for kindergarten*. New York: Dutton.

Slate, J. (2000). *Miss Bindergarten stays home from kindergarten*. New York: Dutton.

Snyder, Z. K. (1967). *The Egypt game*. New York: Dell.

Spinelli, J. (1990). *Maniac Magee*. Boston: Little, Brown.

Sturges, P. (1999). *I love trucks!* New York: HarperCollins.

Taback, S. (1997). *There was an old lady who swallowed a fly*. New York: Viking.

Trivizas, E. (1993). *The three little wolves and the big bad pig*. New York: Macmillan.

Viorst, J. (1994). *The alphabet from Z to A with much confusion along the way*. New York: Atheneum.

Walsh, E. S. (1989). *Mouse paint*. San Diego, CA: Harcourt Brace Jovanovich.

Wood, D., & Wood, A. (1984). *The little mouse, the red ripe strawberry, and the big hungry bear*. Auburn, ME: Child's Play.

Young, E. (1989). *Lon Po Po: A real Red Riding Hood story from China*. New York: Philomel Books.

REFERENCES

Ada, A. F. (2004). *Authors in the classroom: A transformative education process.* Boston: Allyn & Bacon.

Adams, M. (1990). *Beginning to read: Thinking and learning about print.* Cambridge, MA: MIT Press.

Allington, R. L. (1983). The reading instruction provided to readers of differing abilities. *Elementary School Journal, 83,* 584–559.

Allington, R. L. (2001). *What really matters for struggling readers: Designing research-based programs.* New York: Longman.

Allington, R. L. (2002a). *Big Brother and the national reading curriculum: How ideology trumped evidence.* Portsmouth, NH: Heinemann.

Allington, R. L. (2002b). Research on reading/learning disability interventions. In A. E. Farstrup & S. J. Samuels (Eds.), *What research has to say about reading instruction* (3rd ed., pp. 261–290). Newark, DE: International Reading Association.

Anderson, R. C. (1994). Role of readers' schemata in comprehension, learning, and memory. In R. B. Ruddell, M. R. Ruddell, & H. Singer (Eds.), *Theoretical models and process of reading* (4th ed., pp. 469–482). Newark, DE: International Reading Association.

Anderson, R. C., & Pearson, P. D. (1984). A schema-theoretic view of basic processes in reading comprehension, In P. D. Pearson, R. Barr, M. L. Kamil, & P. Mosenthal (Eds.), *Handbook of reading research* (Vol. 1, pp. 255–291). New York: Longman.

Ashworth, M., & Wakefield, H. P. (1994). *Teaching the world's children: ESL for ages three to seven.* Markham, Ontario, Canada: Pippin.

Au, K. H. (2002). Multicultural factors and the effective instruction of students of diverse backgrounds. In A. E. Farstrup & S. J. Samuels (Eds.), *What research has to say about reading instruction* (3rd ed., pp. 392–413). Newark, DE: International Reading Association.

Austin, T. (1994). *Changing the view: Student-led parent conferences.* Portsmouth, NH: Heinemann.

Barone, D. M. (1990). The written responses of young children: Beyond comprehension to story understanding. *The New Advocate, 3,* 49–56.

Barone, D. M. (1992). "That reminds me of": Using dialogue journals with young children. In C. Temple & P. Collins (Eds.), *Stories and readers: New perspectives on literature in the elementary classroom* (pp. 85–191). Norwood, MA: Christopher Gordon.

Barone, D. M. (1996). Whose language?: Learning from bilingual learners in a developmental first grade classroom. In D. Leu, C. Kinzer, & K. Hinchman (Eds.), *Literacies for the 21st century: Research and practice. 45th yearbook of the National Reading Conference* (pp. 170–182). Chicago: National Reading Conference.

Barone, D. M. (1999). *Resilient children: Stories of poverty, drug exposure, and literacy development.* Newark, DE: International Reading Association/Chicago: National Reading Conference.

Barone, D. M., & Lovell, J. (1990). Michael the show-and-tell magician. *Language Arts, 67,* 134–143.

Barton, D., & Hamilton, M. (1998). *Local literacies: Reading and writing in one community.* New York: Routledge.

Bear, D. R., & Barone, D. M. (1989). Using children's spellings to group for word study and directed reading in the primary classroom. *Reading Psychology, 10,* 275–292.

Bear, D. R., & Barone, D. M. (1998). *Developing literacy.* Boston: Houghton Mifflin.

Bear, D. R., Invernizzi, M., Templeton, S., & Johnston, F. (2004). *Words their way: Word study for phonics, vocabulary, and spelling instruction* (3rd ed.). Upper Saddle River, NJ: Prentice-Hall.

Bear, D. R., & Templeton, S. (1998). Explorations in developmental spelling: Foundations for learning and teaching phonics, spelling, and vocabulary. *The Reading Teacher, 52,* 222–242.

Beck, I. L., & McKeown, M. G. (1991). Conditions of vocabulary acquisition. In R. Barr, M. Kamil, P. Mosenthal, & P. D. Pearson (Eds.), *Handbook of reading research* (Vol. 2, pp. 789–814). White Plains, NY: Longman.

Beck, I. L., McKeown, M. G., & Kucan, L. (2002). *Bringing words to life: Robust vocabulary development.* New York: Guilford Press.

Block, C. C., & Mangieri, J. N. (2003). *Exemplary literacy teachers: Promoting success for all children in grades K–5.* New York: Guilford Press.

Bloodgood, J. (1999). What's in a name?: Children's name writing and name acquisition. *Reading Research Quarterly, 34,* 342–367.

Bond, G., & Dykstra, R. (1967). The cooperative research program in first-grade reading instruction. *Reading Research Quarterly, 2,* 1–142.

Bromley, K. (1996). *Webbing with literature: Creating story maps with children's books.* Boston: Allyn & Bacon.

Brown, K. J. (2000). What kind of text—for whom and when?: Textual scaffolding for beginning readers. *The Reading Teacher, 53,* 292–307.

Buckingham, D. (Ed.). (1993). *Reading audiences.* Manchester, UK: Manchester University Press/New York: St. Martin's Press.

Bus, A. G., van IJzendoorn, M. H., & Pellegrini, A. D. (1995). Joint book reading makes for success in learning to read: A meta-analysis on intergenerational transmission of literacy. *Review of Educational Research, 65*(1), 1–21.

Calkins, L. (1986). *The art of teaching writing.* Portsmouth, NH: Heinemann.

Calkins, L. (1994). *The art of teaching writing* (2nd ed.). Portsmouth, NH: Heinemann.

Camp, D. (2000). It takes two: Teaching with twin texts of fact and fiction. *The Reading Teacher, 53,* 400–408.

Carrell, P. (1984). Schema theory and ESL reading: Classroom implications and applications. *Modern Language Journal, 68,* 332–343.

Carrell, P. (1987). Content and formal schemata in ESL reading. *TESOL Quarterly, 21,* 461–481.

Carrell, P., & Eisterhold, J. (1988). Schema theory and ESL reading pedagogy. In P. Carrell,

J. Devine, & D. Eskey (Eds.), *Interactive approaches to second language reading* (pp. 256–386). Cambridge, UK: Cambridge University Press.

Carver, R. (1990). *Reading rate: A review of research and theory.* San Diego, CA: Academic Press.

Cary, S. (2000). *Working with second language learners: Answers to teachers' top ten questions.* Portsmouth, NH: Heinemann.

Chall, J. (1967). *Learning to read: The great debate.* New York: McGraw-Hill.

Chall, J. (1983). *Stages of reading development.* New York: McGraw-Hill.

Chall, J. (1996). *Stages of reading development.* Orlando, FL. Harcourt Brace.

Chamot, A. U., Barnhardt, S., El-Dinary, P. B., & Robbins, J. (1999). *The learning strategies handbook.* New York: Longman.

Christie, J., & Enz, B. (2003, May). *Using a continuum of environmental print manipulatives to meet the needs of individual children, pre-K to grade 1.* Paper presented at the annual convention of the International Reading Association, Orlando, FL.

Clark, M. M. (1976). *Young fluent readers: What can they teach us?* London: Heinemann.

Clay, M. M. (1972). *Concepts about Print Test: Sand and stones.* Exeter, NH: Heinemann.

Clay, M. M. (1975). *What did I write?* Auckland, NZ: Heinemann.

Clay, M. M. (1979). *The early detection of reading difficulties.* Auckland, NZ: Heinemann.

Clay, M. M. (1982). *Observing young readers.* Exeter, NH: Heinemann.

Clay, M. M. (1993a). *An observation survey of early literacy achievement.* Portsmouth, NH: Heinemann.

Clay, M. M. (1993b). *Reading Recovery: A guidebook for teachers in training.* Portsmouth, NH: Heinemann.

Clymer, T. (1996). The utility of phonics generalizations in the primary grades: RT classic. *The Reading Teacher, 50,* 182–187. (Original work published 1963)

Cohen, L. A. (1997). How I developed my kindergarten book backpack program. *Young Children, 52*(2), 69–71.

Collier, V. P., & Thomas, W. P. (1999). Making U.S. schools effective for English language learners, Part I. *TESOL Matters, 9*(4), 1–6.

Commeyras, M. (1990). Analyzing a critical-thinking reading lesson. *Teaching and Teacher Education, 6,* 210–214.

Corson, D. (1997). The learning and use of academic English words. *Language Learning, 47,* 671–718.

Cummins, J. (1979). Linguistic interdependence and the educational development of bilingual children. *Review of Educational Research, 49,* 222–251.

Cummins, J. (1986). Empowering minority students: A framework for intervention. *Harvard Educational Review, 56,* 18–36.

Cummins, J. (1989). *Empowering minority students.* Sacramento: California Association for Bilingual Education.

Cummins, J. (2002). Foreword. In P. Gibbons (Ed.), *Scaffolding language, scaffolding learning: Teaching second language learners in the mainstream classroom* (pp. i–ix). Portsmouth, NH: Heinemann.

Cummins, J. (2003). Reading and the bilingual student: Fact and friction. In G. G. Garcia (Ed.), *English learners reaching the highest level of English literacy* (pp. 2–33). Newark, DE: International Reading Association.

Cunningham, A., & Stanovich, K. (1998, Spring–Summer). What reading does for the mind. *American Educator,* pp. 8–17.

Cunningham, J. W. (2001). Essay book reviews: The National Reading Panel report. *Reading Research Quarterly, 36,* 326–335.

Cunningham, P. M. (2000). *Phonics they use: Words for reading and writing* (3rd ed.). New York: Longman.

Cunningham, P. M., & Allington, R. L. (1999). *Classrooms that work: They can all read and write.* New York: Longman.

Cunningham, P. M., & Hall, D. P. (1994). *Making words: Multilevel, hands-on developmentally appropriate spelling and phonics activities.* Parsippany, NJ: Good Apple.

Cunningham, P. M., Hall, D. P., & Sigmon, C. M. (2001). *The teacher's guide to the Four Blocks: A multimethod, multilevel framework for grades 1–3.* Greensboro, NC: Carson-Dellosa.

Day, J. (2001). How I became an exemplary teacher (although I'm really still learning just like anyone else). In M. Pressley, R. L. Allington, R. Wharton-McDonald, C. C. Block, & L. M. Morrow (Eds.), *Learning to read: Lessons from exemplary first-grade classrooms* (pp. 205–218). New York: Guilford Press.

Delgado-Gaitan, C. (1994). Mexican adult literacy: New directions for immigrants. In S. R. Goldman & K. Trueba (Eds.), *Becoming literate in English as a second language* (pp. 9–32). Norwood, NJ: Ablex.

Delgado-Gaitan, C. (2001). *The power of community: Mobilizing for family and schooling.* Lanham, MD: Rowman & Littlefield.

Delgado-Gaitan, C. (2002). Words in and out of print: The power of literacy in community. In D. L. Schallert, C. M. Fairbanks, J. Worthy, B. Maloch, & J. V. Hoffman (Eds.), *51st yearbook of the National Reading Conference* (pp. 16–22). Oak Creek, WI: National Reading Conference.

Dickinson, D., & Tabors, P. (Eds.). (2001). *Beginning literacy with language.* Baltimore: Brookes.

Dillon, D. (2000). *Reconsidering how to meet the literacy needs of all students.* Newark, DE: International Reading Association.

Droop, M., & Verhoeven, L. (1998). Background knowledge, linguistic complexity, and second language reading comprehension. *Journal of Literacy Research, 30,* 253–271.

Drucker, M. J. (2003). What reading teachers should know about ESL learners. *The Reading Teacher, 57,* 22–29.

Duke, N. K. (2000). 3.6 minutes per day: The scarcity of informational texts in first grade. *Reading Research Quarterly, 35,* 202–224.

Duke, N. K., Bennett-Armistead, V. S., & Roberts, E. M. (2003). Bridging the gap between learning to read and reading to learn. In D. M. Barone & L. M. Morrow (Eds.), *Literacy and young children: Research-based practices* (pp. 226–242). New York: Guilford Press.

Dykstra, R. (1968). Summary of the second-grade phase of the Cooperative Research Program in primary reading instruction. *Reading Research Quarterly, 4,* 49–70.

Dyson, A. H. (1992). Whistles for Willie, lost puppies, and cartoon dogs: The sociocultural dimensions of young children's composing. *Journal of Reading Behavior, 24,* 433–462.

Dyson, A. H. (1997). *Writing superheroes: Contemporary childhood, popular culture, and classroom literacy.* New York: Teachers College Press.

Dyson, A. H. (2003a). *The brothers and sisters learn to write: Popular literacies in childhood and school cultures.* New York: Teachers College Press.

Dyson, A. H. (2003b). Popular literacies and the "all" children: Rethinking literacy development for contemporary childhoods. *Language Arts, 81,* 100–109.

Echevarria, J., Vogt, E., & Short, D. J. (2004). *Making content comprehensible for English language learners: The SIOP model* (2nd ed.). Boston: Allyn & Bacon.

Edwards, P. A., Pleasants, H. M., & Franklin, S. H. (1999). *A path to follow: Learning to listen to parents.* Portsmouth, NH: Heinemann.

Ehri, L. (1998). Grapheme–phoneme knowledge is essential for learning to read words in English. In J. Metasala & L. Ehri (Eds.), *Word recognition in beginning literacy* (pp. 3–40). Mahwah, NJ: Erlbaum.

Faltis, C. J. (2001). *Joinfostering: Teaching and learning in multilingual classrooms* (3rd ed). Upper Saddle River, NJ: Prentice-Hall.

Farstrup, A. E. (2002). There is more to effective reading instruction than research. In A. E. Farstrup & S. J. Samuels (Eds.), *What research has to say about reading instruction* (3rd ed., pp. 1–7). Newark, DE: International Reading Association.

Fitzgerald, J. (1995). English-as-a-second-language learners' cognitive reading process: A review of research in the United States. *Review of Educational Research, 65,* 145–190.

Fitzgerald, J., & Noblit, G. (1999). About hopes, aspirations, and uncertainty: First grade English language learners' emergent reading. *Journal of Literacy Research, 31,* 133–184.

Fitzgerald, T. (2003, March 27). Meet the first Internet babies. *Media Life Magazine.* Retrieved from *www.medialifemagazine.com/news2003/mar03/mar24/4_thurs/ news1thursday.html*

Flatley, J. K., & Rutland, A. D. (1986). Using wordless picture books to teach linguistically and culturally different students. *The Reading Teacher, 39,* 276–281.

Fountas, I. C., & Pinnell, G. S. (1996). *Guided reading: Good first teaching for all children.* Portsmouth, NH: Heinemann.

Freeman, D. E., & Freeman, Y. S. (2000). *Teaching reading in multilingual classrooms.* Portsmouth, NH: Heinemann.

Freeman, D. E., & Freeman, Y. S. (2003). Teaching English learners to read: Learning or acquisition? In G. G. Garcia (Ed.), *English learners reaching the highest level of English literacy* (pp. 34–35). Newark, DE: International Reading Association.

Fry, E. (1980). The new instant word list. *The Reading Teacher, 34,* 28–89.

Ganske, K. (2000). *Word journeys: Assessment-guided phonics, spelling, and vocabulary instruction.* New York: Guilford Press.

Gee, J. P. (1996). *Social linguistics and literacies: Ideology in discourses* (2nd ed.). New York: Taylor & Francis.

Gee, J. P. (2000). Discourse and socioculural studies in reading. In M. L. Kamil, P. B. Mosenthal, P. D. Pearson, & R. Barr (Eds.), *Handbook of reading research* (Vol. 3, pp. 195–207). Mahwah, NJ: Erlbaum.

Gee, J. P. (2001). A sociocultural perspective on early literacy development. In S. B. Neuman & D. K. Dickinson (Eds.), *Handbook of early literacy research* (pp. 30–42). New York: Guilford Press.

Gee, J. P. (2003). *What video games have to teach us about learning and literacy.* New York: Palgrave Macmillan.

Gibbons, P. (2002). *Scaffolding language, scaffolding learning: Teaching second language learners in the mainstream classroom.* Portsmouth, NH: Heinemann.

Goldenberg, C. (2001). Making schools work for low-income families in the 21st century. In S. B. Neuman & D. K. Dickinson (Eds.), *Handbook of early literacy research* (pp. 211–231). New York: Guilford Press.

Good, R., Simmons, D., & Kame'enui, E. (2002). The importance and decision-making utility of a continuum of fluency-based indicators of foundational reading skills for third-grade high-stakes outcomes. In U.S. Department of Education (Ed.), *The reading leadership academy guidebook* (pp. 1–29). Washington, DC: U.S. Department of Education.

Goodman, K. S. (1993). *Phonics phacts.* Portsmouth, NH: Heinemann.

Goodman, Y. M. (1985). Kidwatching: Observing children in the classroom. In A. Jaggar &

M. Smith-Burke (Eds.), *Observing the language learners* (pp. 9–18). Urbana, IL: National Council of Teachers of English/Newark, DE: International Reading Association.

Goodman, Y. M., Watson, D., & Burke, C. (1987). *Reading miscue inventory: Alternative procedures.* Katonah, NY: Owen.

Graves, D. (1994). *A fresh look at writing.* Portsmouth, NH: Heinemann.

Graves, M. (2000). A vocabulary program to complement and bolster a middle-grade comprehension program. In B. Taylor, M. Graves, & P. Van Den Broek (Eds.), *Reading for meaning* (pp. 116–135). New York: Teachers College Press.

Gutierrez, K. D., Asato, J., Pacheco, M., Moll, L. C., Olson, K., Horng, E. L., Ruiz, R., Garcia, E., & McCarty, T. (2002). "Sounding American": The consequences of new reforms on English language learners. *Reading Research Quarterly, 37,* 328–343.

Hadaway, N. L., Vardell, S. M., & Young, T. A. (2002). *Literature-based instruction with English language learners.* Boston: Allyn & Bacon.

Hanhan, S. F. (2003). Parent–teacher communication: Who's talking? In G. Olsen & M. L. Fuller (Eds.), *Home–school relations: Working successfully with parents and families* (pp. 111–133). Boston: Allyn & Bacon.

Harris, T., & Hodges, R. (Eds.). (1995). *The literacy dictionary.* Newark, DE: International Reading Association.

Harste, J., Short, K., & Burke, C. (1989). *Creating classrooms for authors: The reading/writing connection.* Portsmouth, NH: Heinemann.

Harste, J., Woodward, V., & Burke, C. (1984). *Language stories and literacy lessons.* Portsmouth, NH: Heinemann.

Hart, B., & Risley, T. (1995). *Meaningful differences in the everyday experience of young American children.* Baltimore, MD: Brookes.

Head, M., & Readence, J. (1986). Anticipation guides: Meaning through prediction. In E. Dishner, T. Bean, J. Readence, & D. Moore (Eds.), *Reading in the content areas* (2nd ed., pp. 229–234). Dubuque, IA: Kendall/Hunt.

Heath, S. B. (1983). *Ways with words: Language, life and work in communities and classrooms.* New York: Cambridge University Press.

Henderson, E., & Templeton, S. (1986). A developmental perspective of formal spelling instruction through alphabet, pattern, and meaning. *Elementary School Journal, 86,* 305–316.

Hernandez, A. (2003). Making content instruction accessible for English language learners. In G. G. Garcia (Ed.), *English learners reaching the highest level of English literacy* (pp. 125–149). Newark, DE: International Reading Association.

Herrell, A. L. (2000). *Fifty strategies for teaching English language learners.* Upper Saddle River, NJ: Merrill.

Hixson, J., & Tinzmann, M. B. (1990). *Who are the "at-risk" students of the 1990s?* Retrieved *www.ncrel.org/sdrs/areas/rpl_esys/equity.htm*

Hoffman, J. V., Roser, N. L., Salas, R., Patterson, E., & Pennington, J. (2000). *Text leveling and little books in first grade reading* (CIERA Report No. 1–010). Ann Arbor, MI: Center for the Improvement of Early Reading Achievement.

Holdaway, D. (1979). *The foundations of literacy.* New York: Scholastic.

Hoyt, L. (2000). *Snapshots: Literacy minilessons up close.* Portsmouth, NH: Heinemann.

Hudelson, S., & Serna, I. A. (2002). Optimizing oral language learning experiences for bilingual and second language learners. In C. Vukelich, J. Christie, & B. Enz (Eds.), *Helping young children learn language and literacy* (pp. 57–66). Boston: Allyn & Bacon.

Hull, G., & Schultz, K. (Eds.). (2002). *School's out!: Bringing out-of-school literacies with classroom practices.* New York: Teachers College Press.

International Reading Association (IRA). (2000). *Making a difference means making it different: Honoring children's rights to excellent reading instruction.* Newark, DE: Author.

International Reading Association (IRA). (2001). *Second language literacy instruction: A position statement of the International Reading Association.* Newark, DE: Author.

International Reading Association (IRA) & National Association for the Education of Young Children (NAEYC). (1998). *Learning to read and write: Developmentally appropriate practices for young children: Joint position statement.* Washington, DC: NAEYC/Newark, DE: IRA.

Karchmer, R. A. (2001). The journey ahead: Thirteen teachers report how the Internet influences literacy and literacy instruction in their K–12 classrooms. *Reading Research Quarterly, 36,* 442–466.

Karchmer, R. A., Mallette, M. H., & Leu, D. J., Jr. (2003). Early literacy in a digital age: Moving from a singular book literacy to the multiple literacies of networked information and communication technologies. In D. M. Barone & L. M. Morrow (Eds.), *Literacy and young children: Research-based practices* (pp. 175–194). New York: Guilford Press.

Klemp, R. (1994). Word storm: Connecting vocabulary to the student's database. *The Reading Teacher, 48,* 282.

Krashen, S. D. (1985). *Inquiries and insights: Second language teaching, immersion and bilingual education, literacy.* Hayward, CA: Alemany Press.

Krashen, S. D. (1993). *The power of reading: Insights from the research.* Englewood, CO: Libraries Unlimited.

Krashen, S. D. (1999). *Three arguments against whole language and why they are wrong.* Portsmouth, NH: Heinemann.

Krashen, S. D., & Terrell, T. D. (1983). *The natural approach: Language acquisition in the classroom.* Hayward, CA: Alemany Press.

Kuhn, M. (2003). How can I help them pull it all together?: A guide to fluent reading instruction. In D. M. Barone & L. M. Morrow (Eds.), *Literacy and young children: Research-based practices* (pp. 210–225). New York: Guilford Press.

Labbo, L. D. (1996). A semiotic analysis of young children's symbol making in a classroom computer center. *Reading Research Quarterly, 31,* 356–385.

Labbo, L. D., & Kuhn, M. (1998). Electronic symbol making: Young children's computer-related emerging concepts about literacy. In D. Reinking, M. McKenna, L. D. Labbo, & R. Kieffer (Eds.), *Handbook of literacy and technology: Transformations in a post-typographic world* (pp. 79–92). Mahwah, NJ: Erlbaum.

Ladson-Billings, G. (1994). *The dreamkeepers: Successful teachers of African-American children.* San Francisco: Jossey-Bass.

Ladson-Billings, G. (2000). Fighting for our lives: Preparing teachers to teach African American students. *Journal of Teacher Education, 52,* 206–214.

Lebo, H. (2003). *The UCLA Internet report: Surveying the digital future. Year three.* Retrieved from ccp.ucla.edu/pdf/UCLA-Internet-Report-Year-Three.pdf

Lenhart, L., & Roskos, K. (2003). What Hannah taught Emma and why it matters. In D. M. Barone & L. M. Morrow (Eds.), *Literacy and young children: Research-based practices* (pp. 83–100). New York: Guilford Press.

Lenski, S., & Nierstheimer, S. (2004). *Becoming a teacher of reading: A developmental approach.* Upper Saddle River, NJ: Pearson.

Leu, D. J., Jr., Kinzer, C. K., Coiro, J., & Cammack, D. (2004). Toward a theory of new literacies emerging from the Internet and other ICT. In R. Ruddell & N. Unrau (Eds.), *Theoretical models and processes of reading* (5th ed., pp. 1570–1613). Newark, DE: International Reading Association.

Lewis, A. (2001). There is no "race" in the school yard: Color-blind ideology in an (almost) all-white school. *American Education Research Journal, 38*(4), 781–811.

Lieberman, E. (1985). *Name writing and the preschool child* (Doctoral dissertation, University of Arizona, 1985). *Dissertation Abstracts International, 46*(12), 3593A.

Luke, A., & Freebody, P. (1997). The social practices of reading. In S. Muspratt, A. Luke, & P. Freebody (Eds.), *Constructing critical literacies* (pp. 185–225). Cresskill, NJ: Hampton Press.

Luke, C. (2000). Cyber-schooling and technological change: Multiliteracies for new times. In B. Cope & M. Kalantzis (Eds.), *Multiliteracies: Literacy learning and the design of social futures* (pp. 69–91). London: Routledge.

Marsh, J. (1999). Batman and Batwoman go to school: Popular culture in the literacy curriculum. *International Journal of Early Year Education, 7*, 117–131.

Marsh, J., & Millard, E. (2000). *Literacy and popular culture: Using children's culture in the classroom.* London: Paul Chapman.

Martens, P. (1996). *I already know how to read: A child's view of literacy.* Portsmouth, NH: Heinemann.

Martinez, M., Roser, N., & Strecker, S. (1998–1999). "I never thought I could be a star": A Readers' Theatre ticket to fluency. *The Reading Teacher, 52*, 326–334.

Mautte, L. (1990). The effects of adult interactive behaviors within the context of repeated storybook reading upon the language development and selected prereading skills of prekindergarten at-risk students. *Florida Educational Research Council Research Bulletin, 22*, 9–32.

McCarrier, A., Pinnell, G., & Fountas, I. (2000). *Interactive writing.* Portsmouth, NH: Heinemann.

McGee, L. (2003). Book acting: Storytelling and drama in the early childhood classroom. In D. M. Barone & L. M. Morrow (Eds.), *Literacy and young children: Research-based practices* (pp. 157–172). New York: Guilford Press.

McGee, L., Lomax, R., & Head, M. (1988). Young children's written language knowledge: What environmental and functional print reading reveals. *Journal of Reading Behavior, 20*, 99–118.

McGill-Franzen, A., & Goatley, V. (2001). Title 1 and special education: Support services for children who struggle to learn to read. In S. B. Neuman & D. K. Dickinson (Eds.), *Handbook of early literacy research* (pp. 471–483). New York: Guilford Press.

Miles, P. A., Stegle, K. W., Hubbs, K. G., Henk, W. A., & Mallette, M. H. (in press). A whole class support model for early literacy: The Anna Plan. *The Reading Teacher.*

Moll, L. C. (1994). Literacy research in community and classrooms: A sociocultural approach. In R. B. Ruddell, M. R. Ruddell, & H. Singer (Eds.), *Theoretical models and processes of reading* (4th ed., pp. 179–207). Newark, DE: International Reading Association.

Moll, L. C. (1997). The creation of mediating settings. *Mind, Culture, and Activity, 4*, 192–199.

Moll, L. C. (1998). Turning to the world: Bilingual schooling, literacy, and the cultural mediation of thinking. In T. Shanahan & F. V. Rodriguez-Brown (Eds.), *47th yearbook of the National Reading Conference* (pp. 59–75). Chicago: National Reading Conference.

Moll, L. C., Amanti, C., Neff, D., & Gonzalez, N. (1992). Funds of knowledge for teaching: Using a qualitative approach to connect homes and classrooms. *Theory into Practice, 31*, 132–141.

Moll, L. C., & Gonzalez, N. (1997). Creating zones of possibilities: Combining social contexts for instruction. In L. C. Moll (Ed.), *Vygotsky and education* (pp. 319–348). Cambridge, UK: Cambridge University Press.

Morris, D. (1983). Concept of word and phoneme awareness in the beginning reader. *Research in the Teaching of English, 17,* 359–373.

Nagy, W. E., & Scott, J. A. (2000). Vocabulary processes. In M. L. Kamil, P. B. Mosenthal, P. D. Pearson, & R. Barr (Eds.), *Handbook of reading research* (Vol. 3, pp. 269–284). Mahwah, NJ: Erlbaum.

National Reading Panel (NRP). (2000a). *Report of the National Reading Panel.* Washington, DC: National Institute of Child Health and Human Development.

National Reading Panel (NRP). (2000b). *Teaching children to read: An evidence-based assessment of the scientific research literature on reading and its implications for reading instruction. Reports of the subgroups.* Washington, DC: National Institute of Child Health and Human Development.

National Telecommunications and Information Administration (NTIA). (2000, October). *Falling through the net: Toward digital inclusion. A report on Americans' access to technology tools.* Retrieved from *www.ntia.doc.gov/ntiahome/fttn00/falling.htm#1*

National Telecommunications and Information Administration (NTIA). (2002, February). A nation online: How Americans are expanding their use of the Internet. Retrieved from *www.ntia.doc.gov/ntiahome/dn/html/anationonline2.htm*

Neufeld, P., & Fitzgerald, J. (2001). Early English reading development: Latino English learners in the "low" reading group. *Research in the Teaching of English, 36,* 64–105.

Neuman, S. B. (1996). Children engaging in storybook reading: The influence of access to print resources, opportunity, and parental interaction. *Early Childhood Research Quarterly, 11,* 495–513.

Neuman, S. B., Copple, C., & Bredekamp, S. (2000). *Learn to read and write: Developmentally appropriate practices for young children.* Washington, DC: National Association for the Education of Young Children.

Neuman, S. B., & Roskos, K. (1993). Access to print for children of poverty: Differential effects of adult mediation and literacy-enriched play settings on environmental and functional print tasks. *American Educational Research Journal, 30,* 10–32.

New London Group. (1996). A pedagogy of multiliteracies: Designing social cultures. *Harvard Educational Review, 66,* 60–92.

New London Group. (2000). A pedagogy of multiliteracies: Designing social futures. In B. Cope & M. Kalantzis (Eds.), *Multiliteracies: Literacy learning and the design of social futures* (pp. 9–37). London: Routledge.

Nieto, S. (2000). Placing equity front and center. *Journal of Teacher Education, 52,* 180–187.

Nieto, S. (2002). *Language, culture, and teaching: Critical perspectives for a new century.* Mahwah, NJ: Erlbaum.

Oglan, G. R., & Elcombe, A. (2000). *Parent to parent: Our children, their literacy.* Urbana, IL: National Council of Teachers of English.

Ogle, D. (1986). K-W-L: A teaching model that develops active reading of expository text. *The Reading Teacher, 39,* 564–570.

Ogle, D. (1989). The know, what to know, learn strategy. In K. Muth (Ed.), *Children's comprehension of text: Research into practice* (pp. 205–223). Newark, DE: International Reading Association.

Olson, D. R. (1997). Talking about text and the culture of literacy. In B. Davies & D. Corson (Eds.), *Oral discourse and education* (pp. 1–9). Boston: Kluwer.

Orellana, M. E., & Hernandez, A. (1999). Talking with the walk: Children reading urban environmental print. *The Reading Teacher, 51,* 612–619.

Pailliotet, A. W. (2002). Visual literacy. In B. J. Guzzetti (Ed.), *Literacy in America: An encyclopedia of history, theory, and practice* (pp. 665–667). Santa Barbara, CA: ABC-CLIO.

Paley, V. (1990). *The boy who would be a helicopter: The uses of storytelling in the classroom.* Cambridge, MA: Harvard University Press.

Pappas, C. (1991). Fostering full access to literacy by including information books. *Language Arts, 68,* 449–462.

Paratore, J. R. (1999). *What should we expect of family literacy?: Experiences of Latino children whose parents participate in an intergenerational literacy project.* Newark, DE: International Reading Association.

Paratore, J. R. (2001). *Opening doors, opening opportunities: Family literacy in an urban community.* Boston: Allyn & Bacon.

Paratore, J. R. (2003). Building family literacies: Examining the past and planning the future. In A. DeBruin-Parecki & B. Krol-Sinclair (Eds.), *Family literacy from theory to practice* (pp. 8–27). Newark, DE: International Reading Association.

Paratore, J. R., Melzi, G., & Krol-Sinclair, B. (2003). Learning about the literate lives of Latino families. In D. M. Barone & L Morrow (Eds.), *Literacy and young children: Research-based practices* (pp. 101–118). New York: Guilford Press.

Pearson, P. D., & Gallagher, M. (1983). The instruction of reading comprehension. *Contemporary Educational Psychology, 8,* 317–344.

Pellegrini, A., & Galda, L. (1982). The effects of thematic-fantasy play training of the development of children's story comprehension. *American Educational Research Journal, 19,* 443–452.

Peregoy, S. F., & Boyle, O. F. (2001). *Reading, writing, and learning in ESL: A resource book for K–12 teachers* (3rd ed.). New York: Longman.

Peregoy, S. F., & Boyle, O. F. (2004). English learners reading English: What we know, what we need to know. In R. D. Robinson, M. C. McKenna, & J. M. Wedman (Eds.), *Issues and trends in literacy education* (3rd ed., pp. 103–118). Boston: Allyn & Bacon.

Perez, B. (Ed.). (1998). *Sociocultural contexts of language and literacy.* Mahwah, NJ: Erlbaum.

Perez, B. (2001). Communicating and collaborating with linguistically diverse communities. In V. J. Risko & K. Bromley (Eds.), *Collaboration for diverse learners: Viewpoints and practices* (pp. 231–250). Newark, DE: International Reading Association.

Perfetti, C. (1985). *Reading ability.* New York: Oxford University Press,

Pinnell, G. S., Lyons, C. A., DeFord, D. E., Bryk, A. S., & Seltzer, M. (1994). Comparing instructional models for the literacy education of high-risk first graders. *Reading Research Quarterly, 29,* 9–38.

Pressley, M. (2000). What should comprehension instruction be the instruction of? In M. Kamil, P. Mosenthal, P. D. Pearson, & R. Barr (Eds.), *Handbook of reading research* (Vol. 3, pp. 545–562). Mahwah, NJ: Erlbaum.

Pressley, M. (2001). *Effective beginning reading instruction: A paper commissioned by the National Reading Conference.* Chicago: National Reading Conference.

Pressley, M., Dolezal, S., Roehrig, A. D., & Hilden, K. (2002). Why the National Reading Panel's recommendations are not enough. In R. L. Allington (Ed.), *Big Brother and the national reading curriculum: How ideology trumped evidence* (pp. 75–89). Portsmouth, NH: Heinemann.

Pressley, M., El-Dinary, P. B., Gaskins, I., Schuder, T., Bergman, J. L., Almasi, J., & Brown, R. (1992). Beyond direct explanation: Transactional instruction of reading comprehension strategies. *Elementary School Journal, 92,* 513–555.

Purcell-Gates, V. (1996). Stories, coupons, and the *TV Guide*: Relationship between home literacy experiences and emergent literacy knowledge. *Reading Research Quarterly, 31,* 406–428.

Purcell-Gates, V. (2000). Family literacy. In M. Kamil, P. Mosenthal, P. D. Pearson, & R. Barr (Eds.), *Handbook of reading research* (Vol. 3, pp. 853–870). Mahwah, NJ: Erlbaum.

Raphael, T. (1986). Teaching question–answer relationships, revisited. *The Reading Teacher, 39*, 516–523.

Raphael, T. (2000). Balancing literature and instruction: Lessons from the book club project. In B. Taylor, M. Graves, & P. van den Broek (Eds.), *Reading for meaning: Fostering comprehension in the middle grades* (pp. 70–94). New York: Teachers College Press.

Rasinski, T. (1998). Fluency for everyone: Incorporating fluency instruction in the classroom. In R. Allington (Ed.), *Teaching struggling readers* (pp. 257–261). Newark, DE: International Reading Association.

Read, C. (1975). *Children's categorizations of speech sounds in English* (NCTE Research Report No. 17). Urbana, IL: National Council of Teachers of English.

Reese, L., Balzano, S., Gallimore, R., & Goldenberg, C. (1995). The concept of educacion: Latino family values and American schooling. *International Journal of Educational Research, 23*(1), 57–81.

Reinking, D. (1998). Synthesizing technological transformations of literacy in a post-typographic world. In D. Reinking, M. McKenna, L. D. Labbo, & R. Kieffer (Eds.), *Handbook of literacy and technology: Transformations in a post-typographic world* (pp. xi–xxx). Mahwah, NJ: Erlbaum.

Richgels, D. (1995). A kindergarten sign-in procedure: A routine in support of written language learning. In K. Hinchman, D. Leu, & C. Kinzer (Eds.), *Perspectives on literacy: Research and practice. 44th yearbook of the National Reading Conference* (pp. 243–254). Chicago: National Reading Conference.

Rodriguez-Brown, F. V. (2003). Family literacy in English language learning communities: Issues related to program development, implementation, and practice. In A. DeBruin-Parecki & B. Krol-Sinclair (Eds.), *Family literacy from theory to practice* (pp. 126–146). Newark, DE: International Reading Association.

Roskos, K., & Neuman, S. B. (2001). Environment and its influences for early literacy teaching and learning. In S. B. Neuman & D. K. Dickinson (Eds.), *Handbook of early literacy research* (pp. 281–292). New York: Guilford Press.

Rowe, D. (1994). *Preschoolers as authors: Literacy learning in the social world of the preschool*. Cresskill, NJ: Hampton Press.

Schon, D. (1987). *The reflective practitioner: How professionals think in action*. San Francisco: Jossey-Bass.

Shanahan, T., & Barr, R. (1995). Reading Recovery: An independent evolution of the effects of an early instruction intervention for at-risk learners. *Reading Research Quarterly, 30*, 958–996.

Shanahan, T., & Neuman, S. B. (1997). Literacy research the makes a difference. *Reading Research Quarterly, 32*, 202–210.

Slavin, R. E. (1991). *Every child, every school: Success for All*. Thousand Oaks, CA: Corwin.

Slavin, R. E. (1994). Preventing early school failure: Implications for policy and practice. In R. E. Slavin, N. L. Karweit, & B. A. Wasik (Eds.), *Preventing early school failure: Research, policy, and practice* (pp. 206–231) Boston: Allyn & Bacon.

Sleeter, C. E., & Grant, C. A. (2001). Race, class, gender, and disability in current textbooks. In M. W. Apple & L. K. Christian-Smith (Eds.), *The politics of the textbook* (pp. 78–110). New York: Routledge.

Snow, C. (1999). Foreword. In P. A. Edwards, H. M. Pleasants, & S. H. Franklin, *A path to follow: Learning to listen to parents* (pp. xiii–xiv). Portsmouth, NH: Heinemann.

Snow, C., Burns, M., & Griffin, P. (Eds.). (1998). *Preventing reading difficulties in young children*. Washington, DC: National Academy Press.

Spandel, V. (1996). *Seeing with new eyes* (3rd ed.). Portland, OR: Northwest Regional Educational Laboratory.

Stahl, S. A. (2001). Teaching phonic and phonological awareness. In S. B. Neuman & D. K. Dickinson (Eds.), *Handbook of early literacy research* (pp. 333–347). New York: Guilford Press.

Stahl, S. A., Duffy-Hester, A. M., & Stahl, K. A. D. (1998). Everything you wanted to know about phonics (but were afraid to ask). *Reading Research Quarterly, 33,* 338–355.

Stahl, S. A., & Murray, B. (1994). Defining phonological awareness and its relationship to early reading. *Journal of Educational Psychology, 86,* 221–234.

Stanovich, K. (1980). Toward an interactive–compensatory model of individual differences in the development of reading fluency. *Reading Research Quarterly, 21,* 360–407.

Stauffer, R. (1980). *The language experience approach to the teaching of reading* (2nd ed.). New York: Harper & Row.

Street, B. (1984). *Literacy in theory and practice*. Cambridge, UK: Cambridge University Press.

Street, B. (1995). *Social literacies: Critical approaches to literacy in development, ethnography and education*. New York: Longman.

Sulzby, E. (1985). Children's emergent reading of favorite storybooks: A developmental study. *Reading Research Quarterly, 20,* 458–481.

Taba, H. (1967). *Teacher's handbook for elementary social studies*. Reading, MA: Addison-Wesley.

Tabors, P. O. (1997). *One child, two languages*. Baltimore: Brookes.

Taylor, D. (1983). *Family literacy: Young children learning to read and write*. Portsmouth, NH: Heinemann.

Taylor, D., & Dorsey-Gaines, C. (1988). *Growing up literate: Learning from inner-city families*. Portsmouth, NH: Heinemann.

Temple, C., Nathan, R., Temple, F., & Burris, N. (1993). *The beginnings of writing* (3rd ed.). Boston: Allyn & Bacon.

Tompkins, G. E. (2002). *Language arts: Content and teaching strategies* (5th ed.). Upper Saddle River, NJ: Prentice-Hall.

Tompkins, G. E. (2003). *Literacy for the 21st century* (3rd ed.). Upper Saddle River, NJ: Prentice-Hall.

Tompkins, G. E. (2004). *Teaching writing: Balancing process and product* (4th ed.). Upper Saddle River, NJ: Merrill/Prentice-Hall.

U.S. Department of Education. (2001). *Executive summary of the No Child Left Behind Act of 2001*. Retrieved from *www.ed.gov/nclb/overview/intro/execsumm.html*

U.S. Department of Education. (2002). *Survey of the states' limited English proficient students and available education programs and service*. Washington, DC: Author.

Vacca, R. T., & Vacca, J. L. (2001). *Content area reading: Literacy and learning across the curriculum* (7th ed.). New York: Longman.

Valdez-Menchaca, M., & Whitehurst, G. (1992). Accelerating language development through picture book reading: A systematic extension to Mexican day care. *Developmental Psychology, 28,* 1106–1114.

Vellutino, F. R., & Scanlon, D. M. (2001). Emergent literacy skills, early instruction, and individual differences as determinants of difficulties in learning to read: The case for early intervention. In S. B. Neuman & D. K. Dickinson (Eds.), *Handbook of early literacy research* (pp. 295–321). New York: Guilford Press.

Venesky, R. L. (1998). An alternative perspective on Success for All. In K. K. Wong (Ed.), *Advances in educational policy: Vol. 4. Perspectives on the social functions of schools* (pp. 145–165). Greenwich, CT: JAI Press.

Vukelich, C., Christie, J., & Enz, B. (2002). *Helping young children learn language and literacy.* Boston: Allyn & Bacon.

Vukelich, C., Evans, C., & Albertson, B. (2003). Organizing expository text: A look at the possibilities. In D. M. Barone & L. M. Morrow (Eds.), *Literacy and young children: Research-based practices* (pp. 261–290). New York: Guilford Press.

Vygotsky, L. (1978). *Mind in society.* Cambridge, MA: Harvard University Press.

Warschauer, M. (2003). *Technology and social inclusion: Rethinking the digital divide.* Cambridge, MA: MIT Press.

Wasik, B. H., Dobbins, D. R., & Herrmann, S. (2001). Integenerational family literacy: Concepts, research, and practice. In S. B. Neuman & D. K. Dickson (Eds.), *Handbook of early literacy research* (pp. 444–458). New York: Guilford Press.

Wells, G. (1986). *The meaning makers: Children learning language and using language to learn.* Portsmouth, NH: Heinemann.

Whitehurst, G., & Lonigan, C. (1998). Child development and emergent literacy. *Child Development, 69,* 848–872.

Wollman-Bonilla, J. (2000). *Family message journals: Teaching writing through family involvements.* Urbana, IL: National Council of Teachers of English.

Wright Group. (1996). *The Wright way to level.* Bothell, WA: Author.

Xu, S. H. (1996). A Filipino ESL kindergartner's successful beginning literacy learning experience in a mainstream classroom. In D. J. Leu, C. K. Kinzer, & K. A. Hinchman (Eds.), *Literacies for the 21st century: Research and practice* (pp. 219–231). Chicago: The National Reading Conference.

Xu, S. H. (1999). Reexamining continuities and discontinuities: Language minority children's home and school literacy experiences. In T. Shanahan & F. Rodriguez-Brown (Eds.), *48th yearbook of the National Reading Conference* (pp. 224–237). Chicago: National Reading Conference.

Xu, S. H. (2001). Exploring diversity issues in teacher education. *Reading Online, 5*(1), 1–17. Retrieved from *www.readingonline.org/newliteracies/lit_index.asp?HREF=action/xu*

Xu, S. H., & Rutledge, A. (2003). Children starts with Ch!: Kindergartners learn through environmental print. *Young Children, 58,* 44–51.

Yatvin, J. (2000). *Report of the National Reading Panel: Teaching children to read. Reports of the subgroups: Minority view.* Washington, DC: National Institute of Child Health and Human Development.

Yopp, R. H., & Yopp, H. K. (2000). Sharing informational text with young children. *The Reading Teacher, 53,* 410–423.

INDEX

ABC, I Like Me! (Carlson), 75
Academic language, 47, 140–141
Accessibility of print, 74
Acting out stories, 21–22, 64–65
Activities
  for developing oral language, 20–22
  to develop writing, 37–38
  directed listening-thinking, 86
  for home literacy development, 183–195
  for phonological awareness, 38, 40
  related to books, 219
  for supporting print concepts, 22, 24–27
  word sort, 187
  word storm, 158, 159
Adequate yearly progress (AYP) requirements, 206, 209
All about Frogs (Arnosky), 163–164
All about Owls (Arnosky), 150–151
All about Rattlesnakes (Arnosky), 151
Alphabet books, 76, 183–184, 186
The Alphabet from Z to A with Much Confusion along the Way (Viorst), 136
Alphabetic principle, 81–82
Analytic approach to phonics instruction, 82
Anecdotal notes, asking families to take, 178, 180
Animals A to Z (McPhail), 76
Anna Plan, 199–205, 209–210
Anticipation guides, 124–125
Ask Jeeves for Kids, 110, 212
Assessment
  of book and print concepts, 29, 32–33
  of developmental spelling, 134–135
  of name writing, 19
  of oral language, 22, 23, 66, 67
  of reading focused on comprehension, 27–29
  of reading with ELLs, 70–72
  self-assessment rubric, 122
  of story retelling, 30–31

  of word study, 41, 43
  of writing, 38, 39
At-risk readers
  Anna Plan for, 199–205, 209–210
  descriptive approach to, 197–198
  ecological approach to, 199
  overview of, 197
  predictive approach to, 197
  unilateral approach to, 198
Authenticity of text, 61
Authors
  learning about, 163
  resources on, 218
  same, books written by, 59
AYP (adequate yearly progress) requirements, 206, 209

Basic interpersonal communicative skills (BICS), 47, 140
Beginning readers and writers
  comprehension and, 86–87
  description of, 7, 10, 80–81
  fluency and, 86
  reading and, 11, 81–87, 88, 89
  word knowledge and, 11–12
  word study and, 95–96
  writing and, 11, 87, 90–94
Benchmarks
  of fluency, 114
  of literacy development, 7–8
Berit's Best Sites for Children, 111
Bilingual books, 58
Book concepts, 29, 32–33
Book models, 133
Book orientation, 29
Book sets on content topics, 152–153
Books on tape, 142
Brown Bear, Brown Bear, What Do You See? (Martin), 58, 65
Bulletin board of family literacy activities, 16

Caldecott Medal Home Page, 218
Cars! Cars! Cars! (Maccarone), 60
Character maps, 71
Charts
  for rereadings: words per minute and miscues,
    115, 116
  sign-in, 16–18
Checklists
  oral reading development, 89
  writing, 91
  writing traits, 132
  See also Forms
Chicka Chicka Boom Boom (Martin &
    Archambault), 76
Children's literature resources, 217
Choral reading, 115
Class books, 26
Classroom
  first-grade, visiting, 96–100
  kindergarten, visiting, 76–79
  language- and print-rich for ELLs, 53–54
  preschool, visiting, 42, 44–45
  routine, familiarizing ELLs with, 54–56
  second-grade, visiting, 136–138
  social context of, 4
  third-grade, visiting, 164–169
  transitions into, recommendations for, 15–18
Classroom community
  inviting families to, 178, 179, 181, 183
  overview of, 14–15
  transitions into, 15–18
Classroom Connect's Teacher Contact
    Database, 110
Clusters, 125–126
Cognitive academic language proficiency
    (CALP), 47–48, 140
Comic strips, 186
Commands, simple, using, 57
Communicative language, 47, 140
Community visits, 175–176
Comprehension
  activities to support, 24–27
  assessment of, 27–29
  for beginning readers, 86–87
  definition of, 209
  for ELLs, 149–151
  for transitional readers, 119–127
Computer
  Kids Pix Deluxe, 104–106
  Microsoft Word, 101–104
Computer software
  drill and practice, 101
Concept maps, 167
Concept of word, 9
Concept sorting, 40–41, 42
Consolidation of learned literacy knowledge,
    113
Context clues, 83–84

Conversations in classroom, 4–6
Culture
  books reflecting native, 59
  concepts and, 57–58
  family involvement and, 173
  literacy learning and, 4
Culture-specific content, 149

Daily schedule, displaying, 55
Data charts, 126
Decodable text, 84–85
Deductive approach to phonics instruction, 82
Descriptive approach to at-risk readers, 197–198
Developing literacy readers and writers, 7, 9–10
Developmental model of literacy, 7–9
Developmental spelling, assessing, 134–135
Dialogical-thinking reading lesson, 123–124
Dictation, 92
Digital divide, 108
Directed listening-thinking activity, 86
Directionality of print, 29, 32
Discrete language skills, 140–141
Discussions of text, 186–187
Do Not Touch (Carrier), 136
Double-entry draft, 119–120, 121
Do You Want to Be My Friend? (Carle), 68–70

Early intervention
  Anna Plan for, 199–205, 209–210
  at-risk readers and, 197
  No Child Left Behind legislation and, 205–
    210
*Eating the Alphabet: Fruits and Vegetables from A
    to Z* (Ehlert), 76
Echo reading, 115
Ecological approach to at-risk readers, 199
The Egypt Game (Snyder), 5–6
Elementary and Secondary Education Act
    (1965), 205
Engaging families. *See* Family involvement
Engagingness of text, 61
English language learners (ELLs)
  books for, 219
  challenges for, 47–48
  coming to know, 48–51
  culture-specific content and, 149
  familiarizing with classroom routine, 54–56
  fluency and, 141–145
  kindergarten classroom, visiting, 76–79
  language- and print-rich classroom,
    developing for, 53–54
  oral language for, 56–57, 63–66
  parent survey, 50
  reading and, 66, 68–72
  selecting books for, 62
  structural differences between narrative and
    expository text and, 147–149
  structure of written text and, 145, 147

support for, 46–47
textual scaffolding, providing for, 152–154
at transitional stage, 139–141, 161–165
vocabulary development, enhancing for, 154–160
welcoming, 51, 53
word study for, 75–76
written language for, 57–62, 72–75
Environmental print, 25–26, 59, 187
Exemplary teachers, expectations of, 2–3
Exploring
genres, 113, 184, 186
letters, 40
long-vowel patterns, 135–136
prefixes and suffixes, 158–160
sentence structures, 164
Expository text structures, 147–149
Extensive reading for ELLs, 142, 144, 145

Familiarity of text, 58–60
Family books, 26
Family involvement
anecdotal notes, taking, 178, 180
classroom community, inviting families to, 178, 179, 181, 183
literary activities for, 183–195
misconceptions about, 171–173
overview of, 170
See also Parents
Family structures, 170–172
Fire! Fire! (Gibbons), 156
First-grade classroom, visiting, 96–100
First Grade Studies, 2, 81
Fluency
for beginning readers, 86
definition of, 209
for transitional-level ELLs, 141–145
for transitional readers, 113, 114–118
Fluency rubric, 118
Forms
anecdotal notes guide, 179, 180
family interview, 172
guide to document oral reading errors, 191
home visit guide, 177
learning logs, 162
literary practice, 181, 182
reading log, 144
reproducible material in book, 220–221
show-and-tell evaluation, 143
See also Charts; Checklists
Four-square strategy, 128
Froggy Goes to School (London), 18

Generative principle, 90
Genres, exploring new, 113, 184, 186
Gestures, using, 57
Get Ready for Gabi!: A Crazy Mixed-Up Spanglish Day (Montes), 139

Gifts of literacy materials, 194
Goldfish (Harper & Randall), 37
Grade levels and benchmarks of literacy development, 7
Graphic organizers
comprehension and, 70
family involvement and, 188
informational text structure and, 125–126
retelling informational concepts through, 71–72
Grapho-phonic cuing system, 83–84
Great Sites for Kids, 111
Guided reading, 87, 88

Head Start program, 197
Henny Penny (Galdone), 21
Heterogeneity, 155
Home language survey, 48
Home literacy experiences
learning about, 175–178
redefining, 174–175
rethinking, 178, 181, 182
Homemade books, 188
Home visits, 176–178
Hybrid texts, 152

Idioms, avoiding, 57
If You Give a Mouse a Cookie (Numeroff), 60
I Hate English! (Levine), 46, 56
Illustrations
as contextual clues, 60
and print, differences between, 29
Illustrators, resources on, 218
Income level and family involvement, 173
Incrementality, 155
Independent writing, 87, 90
Inductive approach to phonics instruction, 82
Informational picture books with labels, 154
Informational text strategies for comprehension, 124–127
Information and communication technology, 107–108
In My Family/En Mi Familia (Garza), 58
Input, comprehensible, providing for ELLs, 57–58
Interactive walk in community, 175–176
Interactive writing
for beginning writers, 92–94, 99
for developing literacy, 37–38
for ELLs, 78
Interdependence hypothesis, 48, 51
International Reading Association (IRA), 2, 13
Internet access, 108–109
Internet projects, 110–111
Internet resources, 188, 212–219
Interrelatedness, 155

Journals
  school-home, 181
  student, 37, 93, 168, 189
Julian's Glorious Summer (Cameron), 133
Junie B., First Grader (at Last!) (Park), 80

Keep books, 26
Kid Pix Deluxe software, 104–106
Kidwatching, 189
Kindergarten classroom, visiting, 76–79
KWL strategy, 124, 125, 150

Labeling objects
  for developing literacy, 25, 38
  for ELLs, 54
  for home literacy, 187
Language. *See* Native languages; Oral language
Language development, beginning stages of, 49
Language experience activity, 37
Language experience approach, 85–86
Language proficiency
  categories of, 47, 140
  dimensions of, 140–141
Learning logs, 126, 127, 161, 162
Learning to read, description of, 1–2
Letter name strategy, 95
Letters, exploring, 40
Library visits, 189
Lightspan Network Internet Project Registry, 110
Limited English proficiency (LEP) students, 46. *See also* English language learners (ELLs)
Linguistic patterns, 74–75
List-group-label strategy, 128, 129
Literacy organizations, 213–214
Literacy prop boxes, 26–27
Long-vowel patterns, exploring, 135–136

Making words, 83
Matilda (Dahl), 112
Media centers, 65–66
Message boards, 189
Modeling by family, 187–188
The Mouse Mess (Riley), 58
Multimedia texts related to content, 153–154
Multimensionality, 155
Multiple literacies in preschool classroom, 101–107

Name writing, 16–18, 19
Narrative text strategies for comprehension, 119–124
Narrative text structures, 147–149
National Association for the Education of Young Children, 13
National Reading Panel, 81, 82, 206–207, 210
Native languages
  assessment of reading in, 71
  learning about, 48, 51, 52

phonological system of, 76
  print concepts and, 74
Nests, Nests, Nests (Canizares & Reid), 21
Newbery Medal Home Page, 218
New literacies, instruction in, 110–111
New literacy studies field, 174
Newspapers, 190
Nick Jr. website, 108
No Child Left Behind legislation, 3, 205–210
Nursery rhymes, 26

Objects
  labeling, 25, 38, 54, 187
  referring to, 56–57
The Official Guide to Bionicle (Farshtey), 158
Oral language
  activities for developing, 20–22
  assessment of, 22, 23, 66, 67
  for ELLs, 56–57, 63–66, 141–142, 143
Oral reading
  development of, checklist for, 89
  at home, 190–191
Outlines, partially completed, 150–151

Parents
  ELL survey for, 50
  as language teachers, 22
  See also Family involvement
Partial alphabetic word knowledge, 95
Peer acceptance of English language learners, 47
Phonemic awareness, 208
Phonics, 208
Phonics instruction, 38, 81–82
Phonological awareness, 38, 40
A Picture Book of Martin Luther King, Jr. (Alder), 155, 156
Pictures, using, 56–57
Piggie Pie (Palatini), 161
A Pinky Is a Baby Mouse and Other Baby Animal Names (Ryan), 147
Play centers, 22, 65
Play events related to reading, 21–22
Poetry-, rhyme-, or sound-focused books, 217–218
Polysemy, 155
Portfolio of writing, collecting, 131
Predictability of text, 58
Predictable books, 190, 192
Predictive approach to at-risk readers, 197
Prefixes, exploring, 158–160
Preschool classroom, visiting, 42, 44–45
Primary Spelling Inventory, 95
Print concepts
  for developing literacy, 29, 32–33
  for ELLs, 74
  rethinking, 107–108, 109
Projects, involving families in, 181, 183
Puzzles related to books, 219

Question-answer relationships, 123
Quotes from text, 192

Rains (Kalan), 64
Ramona books (Cleary), 133
Readers' Theatre, 115, 117, 219
Reading
    for beginning readers, 11, 81–87, 88, 89
    benchmarks of, 8
    comprehension for transitional readers, 119–127
    computer technology and, 109–110
    developing literacy readers and writers and, 9–10
    fluency for transitional readers, 114–118
    for transitional readers, 12
    vocabulary for transitional readers, 127–129
    year-round, 194
    See also Oral reading; Reading for ELLs
Reading books aloud
    for developing literacy, 20–21, 24
    ELLs and, 63–64
    at home, 192
    resources for, 216
    responses to, 37
Reading First grants, 207
Reading for ELLs
    assessment of, 70–72
    culture-specific content, 149
    facilitating comprehension, 149–151
    overview of, 66, 68–72
    structural differences between narrative and expository text and, 147–149
    structure of written text and, 145, 147
    textual scaffolding, providing for, 152–154
    vocabulary development, enhancing, 154–160
Reading logs, 144
Reading Recovery, 198, 200
Reading-writing connections, 161
Remedial reading, historical approach to, 196
Repeated reading, 115, 116
Reproducible material in book, 220–221
Research in reading, 206–210
Research laboratories, 212–213
Resources
    Internet, 188, 212–219
    native languages, 51
Retelling stories
    for developing literacy, 27–29, 30–31
    in native languages, 71
Reversed word clusters, 155, 156
Revision of writing, 130–132

Same concept/theme, books with, 59
Scaffolding
    description of, 6
    literacy experience, 102–104
    oral language for ELLs, 63–66
    reading for ELLs, 66, 68–72

word study for ELLs, 75–76
    writing for ELLs, 72–75
School-home journals, 181, 183
Scribbling, 33–37
Search engines, 110–111, 212
Second-grade classroom, visiting, 136–138
Self-assessment rubric, 122
Semantic cuing system, 83
Sentences
    collecting different types of, 163–164
    structures, exploring, 164
Sequencing story events, 71
Series book reading, 117–118
Shapes, Shapes, Shapes (Hoban), 57, 71
The Shapes of Things (Dodds), 57
Show and tell with content focus, 141–142, 143
Sight words, 85–86
Sign-in charts, 16–18
Silent reading, uninterrupted sustained, 193
Sketch to stretch technique, 120, 123
Slowing down speech, 56
Social-constructivist theory of learning, 4–7
Spelling words, 192–193
Spot's First Walk (Hill), 28–29
The Stinky Cheese Man and Other Fairly Stupid Tales (Scieszka), 161
A Story for Bear (Haseley), 1
Story grammar, 170
Student-centered approach to teaching, 5–6
Subtlety of developmental growth in transitional phase, 113
Success for All, 198
Suffixes, exploring, 158–159
Survival, books about, 59
Swimmy (Lionni), 21
Syntactic cuing system, 83
Synthetic approach to phonics instruction, 82

Teachers
    challenges of ELLs and, 48
    "highly qualified," 206, 209
    importance of, 2–3
Teaching literacy
    challenges of, 1–2, 3
    student-centered approach to, 5–6
    word-learning strategies, 128–129
    words, 127–128
Technology
    information and communication, 107–108
    Internet access, 108–109
    multiple literacies in preschool classroom, 101–107
    overview of, 101
    rethinking instruction based on, 109–111
Tell Me a Story, Mama (Johnson), 170
Terminology of books, 33
Textual scaffolding, providing for ELLs, 152–154

Thematic exploration, 193
Think-aloud strategy, 86–87
Third-grade classroom, visiting, 164–169
The Three Little Pigs (Galdone), 70, 71
The Three Little Wolves and the Big Bad Pig (Trivizas), 161
Tomorrow's Alphabet (Shannon), 40
Total physical response, 57
Traits of writing, 130–133
Transitional readers and writers
  comprehension and, 119–127
  concerns of, 112–114
  description of, 12, 112
  ELLs as, 139–141
  fluency and, 114–118, 141–145
  reading and, 12
  vocabulary and, 127–129
  word knowledge and, 13
  word study for, 134–136
  writing and, 11–12, 129–133
Transitional-stage English language learners
  culture-specific content and, 149
  facilitating comprehension for, 149–151
  structural differences between narrative and expository text for, 147–149
  structure of written text for, 145, 147
  textual scaffolding, providing for, 152–154
  vocabulary development, enhancing for, 154–160
  writing for, 161–165
Transitions into classroom, recommendations for, 15–18
The True Story of the Three Little Pigs (Scieszka), 145, 161
TV shows and movies, books adapted from, 59, 60

Unilateral approach to at-risk readers, 198

Variations of books or multiple books on same topic, 145, 146
Venn diagrams, 125–126
The Very Hungry Caterpillar (Carle), 64–65
Visual literacy, 193–194
Vocabulary
  development of, 208
  development of, enhancing for ELLs, 154–160
  strategies to build, 20–21
  for transitional readers, 127–129
  See also Word knowledge; Words; Word study

Web resources, 188, 212–219
Welcome sign, 16
Wide reading, 127, 128

Will I Have a Friend? (Cohen), 14, 46
Word knowledge
  beginning readers and writers and, 11–12
  benchmarks of, 8
  developing literacy readers and writers and, 10
  development of for ELLs, 154–155
  transitional readers and writers and, 13
Word-learning strategies, teaching, 128–129
Wordless books, 66, 68–70
Word-processing programs, 101–104
Words
  big, collecting, 156, 157
  concepts of, 108
  family involvement in learning, 194
  interesting, collecting, 156–158
  making, 83
  sight words, 85–86
  teaching, 127–128
  See also Vocabulary; Word knowledge; Word study
Word sort activity, 187
Word storm activity, 158, 159
Word study
  assessment of, 41, 43
  beginning readers and writers and, 95–96
  concept sorting, 40–41, 42
  for ELLs, 75–76
  exploring letters, 40
  phonological awareness, 38, 40
  for transitional readers and writers, 134–136
Word walls, 54
Writing
  assessment of, 38, 39
  beginning readers and writers and, 11, 87, 90–94
  benchmarks of, 8
  developing literacy readers and writers and, 10
  for ELLs, 57–62, 72–75
  explorations in, 33–38
  name, 16–18, 19
  social context of, 33
  student-centered approach and, 5–6
  transitional readers and writers and, 11–12
  for transitional-stage ELLs, 161–165
  for transitional writers, 129–133
  year-round, 194
Written response, providing, to material read, 119–120, 121, 122

Yahooligans, 110, 212
Year-round reading and writing, 194

Zone of proximal development (ZPD), 6, 194